Tamesis Studies in Popular and Digital Cultures

Volume 4

POPULAR CULTURE, IDENTITY, AND POLITICS IN CONTEMPORARY CATALONIA

TAMESIS STUDIES IN POPULAR AND DIGITAL CULTURES

ISSN: 2752–3063 (print)
ISSN: 2752–3071 (online)

Series Editors

Thea Pitman – University of Leeds
Stephanie Dennison – University of Leeds

Editorial Board

Tori Holmes (Queen's University Belfast), Edward King (University of Bristol), Yeidy Rivero (University of Michigan), Paul Julian Smith (Graduate Center, CUNY), Nuria Triana Toribio (University of Kent), Luís Trindade (University of Coimbra), Eduardo Viñuela (University of Oviedo), Scott Weintraub (University of New Hampshire)

This new series aims to publish intellectually enriching and engaging research into the popular cultures of the Hispanic and Lusophone worlds, both analogue and digital. Topics covered in the series include visual and audio-visual art forms (photography, graphic art and comics, advertising, graffiti, animation, film, telenovelas and television more generally), literature (folklore, mass-market novels and novellas, the 'middle-brow', visual novels), embodied arts (performance art, theatre, dance, popular and traditional music, body art and fashion), as well as all the potentially 'viral' new genres of popular culture facilitated by the Internet and social media platforms (blogs, memes, YouTube videos, hashtag campaigns, video games and so on). The series encompasses studies both of these particular manifestations and of the industries and practices that accompany them; and it analyses not only 'grassroots' cultural expressions but also the ways in which Hispanic and Lusophone cultural forms have been appropriated, commodified and distributed transnationally. Providing a forum for cutting-edge studies on demotic forms of cultural production as well as the new cultural dynamics facilitated by digital technologies, the series seeks to advance scholarly understanding of how people creatively explore, debate and challenge events, attitudes, ideas and identities. The series is open to standard monographs and edited collections as well as short-form monographs.

Other books in the series may be viewed at https://boydellandbrewer.com/series/tamesis-studies-in-popular-and-digital-cultures.html

Popular Culture, Identity, and Politics in Contemporary Catalonia

Edited by Alessandro Testa and Mariann Vaczi

TAMESIS

© Contributors 2023

All Rights Reserved. Except as permitted under current legislation no part of this work may be photocopied, stored in a retrieval system, published, performed in public, adapted, broadcast, transmitted, recorded or reproduced in any form or by any means, without the prior permission of the copyright owner

First published 2023
Tamesis, Woodbridge

ISBN 978 1 85566 403 6

Tamesis is an imprint of Boydell & Brewer Ltd
PO Box 9, Woodbridge, Suffolk IP12 3DF, UK
and of Boydell & Brewer Inc.
668 Mt. Hope Avenue, Rochester, NY 14620-2731, USA
website: www.boydellandbrewer.com

The publisher has no responsibility for the continued existence or accuracy of URLs for external or third-party internet websites referred to in this book, and does not guarantee that any content on such websites is, or will remain, accurate or appropriate

A CIP record for this title is available from the British Library

Contents

List of Illustrations · vii
List of Contributors
 · viii

Introduction: Culture, Identity, and Politics in Contemporary Catalonia · 1
  Alessandro Testa and Mariann Vaczi

1. *Castells*, Myths, and Allegories of Nation-Building · 19
  Mariann Vaczi

2. The Ritual Making of Central Catalonia 1: National Identity and the Hanging of the Donkey · 35
  Alessandro Testa

3. The Ritual Making of Central Catalonia 2: *Comparses* and the Dynamics of Inclusive Nationalism · 55
  Alessandro Testa

4. Reclaiming the Cathar Past: At the Crossroads between Identity Politics and Tourist Economies in Catalonia · 77
  Camila del Mármol

5. The Heritage of the Humiliated: Popular Resistance in Defense of the "*Bous*" in the Lands of the Ebro · 93
  Manuel Delgado, Romina Martínez Algueró, Sarai Martín López

6. Communities without Festivities? Community Effects, Transformations, and Conflicts after Covid-19 in Catalonia · 109
  Xavier Roigé, Mireia Guil, Lluís Bellas

7. *Bon Profit!* Food as National Identity in Catalonia · 127
  Venetia Johannes

Afterword: Beneath the Nation: Collective Creation and Civic Need · 147
  Dorothy Noyes

Bibliography · 157
Index · 177

The Introduction to this book is published Open Access thanks to the generous support of the Faculty of Social Sciences, Charles University, Prague.

Illustrations

1. A human tower team (*colla*) making a base (*fer pinya*) for a pillar structure at the *festa major* of Vilanova i Geltrú in 2008. Source: Wikimedia Commons. Author: Núria i JC.   21
2. The Castellers de Vilafranca building a record-high ten-level tower in 2013. Source: Wikimedia Commons. Author: Diari AVUI.   23
3. The Dance of the Giants. Source: Lluís Closa.   44
4. The Hanging of the Donkey. Source: Jordi Soldevila i Corominas.   44
5. Carnival poster featuring *el Gegant Boig* as a veritable symbol of Catalan *independentisme*. Source: Author.   46
6. Members of a *comparsa* holding a banner referring to 'Law 155', which was activated after the 2017 referendum, abrogating Catalonia's autonomy for several months. Source: Author.   50
7. Solsona's town hall in 2018. Source: Author.   51
8. Two members of the same *comparsa* being wed by the mayor in Solsona's town hall in 2019. Source: Author.   61
9. A typically gigantic *sopar de comparses* (dinner of the *comparses*). Source: Vilaseca and Trilla 2011, 118–119.   62
10. *Festa dels càtars* 2018. Source: Author.   88
11. *Bous al carrer* in Horta de Sant Joan in September 2018. Source: Marc Sampé Compte.   95
12. *Bous amb corda* in Ulldecona in August 2015. Source: Eduard Solà.   103
13. *Picada*, a grainy paste of herbs, spices, and ground nuts with some liquid. Source: Author.   136
14. *Pastís de la Diada* from a Barcelona bakery on sale during the *Diada*, decorated with Catalonia's national flag, the *Senyera*. Source: Author.   142

The editors, contributors and publisher are grateful to all the institutions and persons listed for permission to reproduce the materials in which they hold copyright. Every effort has been made to trace the copyright holders; apologies are offered for any omission, and the publisher will be pleased to add any necessary acknowledgement in subsequent editions.

Contributors

Lluís Bellas is a PhD student in ICH and Museum Studies at the Universitat de Barcelona (Predoctoral Grant, Government of Catalonia). He holds a BA in Social Anthropology and an MA in Museology and has attended postgrad courses in ICH Management and Community-Based Cultural Policies in Spanish and Latin American universities. His research interests focus on the musealization and heritagization of festivals in Catalonia, the safeguarding of Intangible Cultural Heritage (ICH), social museology, and cultural policies.

Manuel Delgado is Professor of Religious Anthropology at the Universitat de Barcelona. He is a member of the research groups GRECS (Grup de Recerca en Exclusió i Control Socials) at the UB and CPC (Cultura Popular i Conflicte) at the Institut Català d'Antropologia, working especially on religious violence and social appropriations of urban spaces. He is the author of *De la muerte de un dios* (1986), *La ira sagrada* (1991), *Las palabras de otro hombre* (1992), *El animal público* (Anagrama Essay Award 1999), *Luces iconoclastas* (2001), *Sociedades movedizas* (2007), *L'espace public comme ideologie* (2016), and *Ciudadanismo* (2017).

Mireia Guil is a PhD candidate in Anthropology at the Universitat de Barcelona. She graduated in Romance Philology and in Social and Cultural Anthropology. She then obtained an MA in Medieval Cultures at the same university. Her research interests revolve around heritage processes in the Pyrenees and UNESCO's ICH policies.

Venetia Johannes completed her DPhil in Anthropology at the University of Oxford in 2015, where she also completed the MSc in Social Anthropology in 2011. The subject of her doctoral research was how Catalans use food to express their national identity. As a postdoctoral research affiliate with the Institute of Social & Cultural Anthropology, University of Oxford, she published *Nourishing the Nation: Food as National Identity in Catalonia* in 2019 (published in paperback in 2022) and co-edited *The Emergence of National Food: The Dynamics of Food and Nationalism* (2019).

Sarai Martin López is a research fellow at the Department d'Antropologia Social at the Universitat de Barcelona. She is currently developing a thesis on the African colonial legacy in the field of museums of the city of Barcelona and the processes of reparation of the colonial past. She is a member of the research groups GRECS (Grup de Recerca d'Exclusió i Controls Socials) at the Universitat de Barcelona and CPC (Cultura Popular i Conflicte) at the Institut Català d'Antropologia. In recent years, she has been involved in research projects on the heritage processes of folk festivals and the restoration of democratic memory from a gender perspective.

Camila del Mármol is Associate Professor of Social Anthropology at the Universitat de Barcelona. She has pursued ethnographic research in the Catalan Pyrenees, focusing on the development of heritage processes in its intersection with changing ruralities. Her areas of interest and publications include the transformation of rural areas, bringing together the analysis of macroeconomic change and its impact on social identities and moralities, structures of feeling, and local uses of the past.

Romina Martínez Algueró has a PhD in Anthropology from the Universitat de Barcelona. She has participated as a researcher in the R&D Affric, Transàfrica, and MOVER, in which she carried out ethnographic work in Senegal. Currently, she is working as a postdoctoral researcher in the Universitat Autònoma de Barcelona on the project "Between science and religion: an empirical study to understand the role of religious and spiritual beliefs in opposition to biomedical technologies" (ECIREL). She is also a member of the CPC (Cultura Popular i Conflicte) research group of the Institut Català d'Antropologia.

Dorothy Noyes is Arts & Sciences Distinguished Professor of English, Professor of Comparative Studies, and Director of the Mershon Center for International Security Studies at the Ohio State University. Past president of the American Folklore Society, she studies the traditional public sphere in Europe and the uses of performance in international relations. Her current book project is entitled *Exemplary Failures: Gesture and Influence in Liberal Politics*.

Xavier Roigé is a Senior Lecturer in Social Anthropology at the Universitat de Barcelona. His research focuses in particular on intangible heritage, ethnological museums, memory spaces, and cultural heritage management, fields in which he has published extensively. He has directed different research projects in relation to cultural heritage and has also participated in the realization of museological projects and curatorship of exhibitions. His latest research concerns the effects of Covid-19 on intangible heritage and the interrelationship between heritage and cultural sustainability.

Alessandro Testa is Associate Professor at the Faculty of Social Sciences, Charles University, Prague. Previously, he was Lise Meitner Postdoc at the University of Vienna. He did his BA, MA, and PhD studies in Italy and France. Among his main publications are *Politics of Religion* (with Tobias Köllner, 2021), *Rituality and Social (Dis)Order* (2020), *Re-enchantment, Ritualization, Heritage-making* (with Cyril Isnart, 2020), and *Ritualising Cultural Heritage and Re-Enchanting Rituals in Europe* (2023). So far, he has also authored nearly 70 peer-reviewed articles in journals and edited collections and delivered more than 150 talks and conference presentations in some 30 countries.

Mariann Vaczi is Assistant Professor of Basque Studies and Anthropology at the University of Nevada, Reno. As an ethnographer, she works at the intersections of sport, culture, and politics. Her main work includes *Soccer, Culture, and Society in Spain: An Ethnography of Basque Fandom* (Routledge 2015), *Sport and Secessionism* (co-edited with Alan Bairner, Routledge 2021), *Catalonia's Human Towers: Castells, Cultural Politics, and the Struggle toward the Heights* (Indiana University Press, 2023), and *Indigenous, Traditional, and Folk Sports: Contesting Modernities* (co-edited with Alan Bairner, Routledge forthcoming).

Introduction: Culture, Identity, and Politics in Contemporary Catalonia

ALESSANDRO TESTA AND MARIANN VACZI

For many, Catalonia is a conundrum. An extraordinary case of collective effort, identity assertion, and political escalation, it has been one of the greatest if not *the* greatest cause of political polarisation in Spanish society for more than a decade now and one of the many thorns in the side of the EU and its institutional bodies, continually faced with a cascade of political, ideological, and juridical quandaries. A relatively recent phenomenon as a set of mature socio-cultural claims and coherent political vision, Catalan regionalism or nationalism (*catalanisme*), and its more radical manifestation, independentism (*independentisme*), are one of the not unique but rare examples of nationalism that is upheld eminently (though not exclusively) by progressive parties, and which identifies with and seduces especially 'the left'. This leaves many, but not scholars of nationalism, rather puzzled, for as one of the most prominent among them once remarked, nationalism is a protean phenomenon formed of different concepts, representations, and practices, whose different combinations 'point them in different directions, creating the various kinds of nationalism with which we are familiar' (Smith 2013, 36). Catalan independentisme has been noted for its bottom-up civil mobilisation that aims for secession from Spain due to an accumulating set of (real or imagined) grievances over cultural, linguistic, economic, and political matters since the Transition from the Franco dictatorship and especially in the past decade. This volume will address how these developments are both constructed and reflected by/in popular culture.

Along with notions such as 'culture', 'religion', 'tradition', and others, 'nation' is one of the ontological black diamonds in the historical and social sciences: a terminological crystal of many facets, absorbing, reflecting, and deflecting definitions and semantic boundaries, and yet, in spite of its polysemy and hazy aura, inevitable, just like those other concepts, in use and thought both emically and etically. There can be no doubt that the gravitational force of nations permeates our lives, shaping the configuration of our states, their sense of the past, their vision of the future, and the public and political debates of our time as much and perhaps even more than in certain periods of the 19th and 20th centuries. Far from being relegated to the past, nations, nationhood, and nationalisms are as much alive today as they have ever been.

As one of the foundational elements of modernity and a veritable factor of progress and modernisation since the French Revolution (in which it played an eminent role), nationalism has been, apparently in contradiction with itself, one of the main forces of liberation as well as oppression for the peoples in the modern and late modern world. Indeed, since the end of the *Ancien Régime*, the most noble as well the most atrocious acts have been committed in the name of the nation. No wonder then, if among scholars as well as in the much wider political and social arenas, the concepts and practices of nation and nationalism bear a polarising force, being as they are not only conceptually problematic and politically controversial, but also morally and even emotionally charged and charging.

In this volume, we have tried to unpack some of these tightly interwoven problems looking at one of the most interesting recent examples, Catalonia, where intellectuals, political actors, and independentists often feel the potential contradictions of nation building, state formation, and related processes of mass identity construction, reproduction, and legitimation. Who belongs to the nation? Who has the right to a state? 'Does the state exist after the nation-state?', as Xavier Rubert de Ventós, a Catalan intellectual, asked himself some years ago (2000, 72). Can Catalan nation-building, 'Catalanisation', and the idea of a Catalan Republic avoid the fate of becoming a mere sub-national variant of the (much criticised) homogenising tendencies of the Spanish state? Many of these questions and dilemmas are played out through culture, as this work will show.

Indeed, Catalonia is not undeservedly known for its lavish popular culture, and popular culture has always been one of the main pastures from which ideas of the nation and practices of nationhood and nationalism have sprung, been cultivated, and harvested. From the early theorisation of Herder and Romanticism generally, all the way up until our late modern times, folkloric traditions – just like language and religion – have been widely considered – or implicitly associated with – the constitutional elements of what a nation is or how it imagines itself (or is imagined by others) to be. In this volume, we look at the ways in which different dimensions of collective action and representation such as public rituality, cultural heritage-making, and the politics of culture influence, and are in turn influenced by, patterns of national identity formation and nationalist trends in contemporary Catalonia, especially since the crucial, watershed years of 2010 (in which the reform of the Statute of Autonomy of Catalonia was rejected), 2012 (the year of the biggest and most impressive mass demonstration on the Catalan National Day, the *Diada*), and 2017 (when the last, at present, referendum for independence was held). Indeed, these years were characterised by head-spinning developments, including the rise of record-attendance demonstrations, clashes with riot police, illegal referenda, imprisonments of elected officials, an eight-second independence declaration, and Spanish governmental standby. Spaniards voted four times over four years at general elections between 2015 and 2019, in part due to the Catalan conundrum.

Post-Franco political transformations contextualise the chapters of this volume. After the Franco dictatorship (1939–1975), the moderate *catalanisme* of the centre-right Jordi Pujol government (1980–2003) successfully pursued Catalan linguistic and cultural interests but never formulated secession as a political goal. In 2003, the new centre-left, tripartite Catalan government pushed for fiscal reform and greater economic autonomy from the state, but its drafts of a reformed Statute of Autonomy were rejected in 2005 and 2010 by the Spanish Constitutional Court. From 2010 on, a quick succession of events resulted in a growing mobilisation and in a sharply polarised regional climate. As 'social discontent has been mostly channeled through the prism of identity and sovereignty, [this has led to] the largest series of popular mobilisations ever seen in modern Europe' (Dowling 2018, 5). A shortlist of such events should include: 1) The already recalled *Diada* of 2012, possibly the largest mass event in the history of Catalonia and maybe of Europe in its entirety; 2) The 2014 referendum on independence, in spite of the Spanish Constitution's ban on regional referenda; 3) The 2015 Catalan regional elections, which became a quasi-plebiscite, with pro-independence parties forming the Catalan government for the first time after the Transition; 4) Another independence referendum in 2017, this time resulting in a police crackdown on voters, and the exile or imprisonment of several high-profile Catalan politicians (among whom the President of the Generalitat himself, Carles Puigdemont), and leaders of NGOs; 5) In the year 2019, a series of demonstrations ensued across the region, including violent and mostly unprecedented night-time clashes with riot police, following the sentencing by the Spanish courts of Catalanist leaders to 9–13 years in prison.

These events or clusters of events all showed the extent of mass mobilisation, fostered by an effervescence of social movements, associationism, and other sectors of civil society. They reappropriated forms and symbols from popular culture, as this book will show in greater detail in the following chapters. In the post-2010 Catalan social landscape, 'the form adopted of political expression became that of the popular performance of mass mobilisation, with the incorporation of music and folkloric festivals' (Dowling 2018, 102). At the basis of these phenomena, there was the belief that collective action, catalysed by moral indignation and by a sense of social justice, would eventually lead to political change and social improvement (Klandermans 1997).

The Catalan 'territorial question' thus went from 'challenge' to 'crisis' and was only overshadowed by the outbreak of the Covid-19 pandemic in early 2020. In February 2021, yet another pro-independence regional government was elected in Catalonia, this time with a popular majority vote of over 50%, although with a record low turnout. At the time of writing, Catalonia's and Spain's major concern is the Covid-19 pandemic. Once that battle is over, however, the territorial question will predictably resurface in Spain.

FROM AUTONOMY TO INDEPENDENCE: CATALONIA'S ECONOMIC, POLITICAL, AND CULTURAL GRIEVANCES

Catalonia's secessionist turn consisted in a shift from less than 20% supporting independence in 2005 to about 50% by 2015 and the election of pro-independence governments in the 2015, 2017, and 2021 regional elections. What happened in the decade that turned Catalonia away from devolution to secession?

The reasons behind this shift are complex. Independentist Catalans cited that they wanted self-government, institutional modernisation, more progressive social reform, cultural and linguistic identity maintenance, financial growth, and a divorce from what they saw as a corrupt and conservative Spanish government. These desires were framed by arguments of regional sovereignty, the will of the Catalan people, and the democratic right to vote at a referendum. In turn, centralists (Constitutionalists and monarchists) argued that the Catalan nationalist revival was the result of top-down indoctrination through the educational system, the media, and the activism of intellectuals;[1] that it aggressively promoted the Catalan language and identities at the expense of Spanish ones; that it was motivated by selfish capitalist accumulation

---

[1] The idea of Catalanism being a top-down project percolating from the echelons of the high bourgeoisie, the universities, and the intellectuals into the lower classes is a very common trope in discussions about Catalonia, and a recurrent one, along with the presumed primacy of economic motivations for secessionism, in informal conversations with centrists, and in the media. In general, it has been noted that 'for most of the period since 2010, the perception of the Catalan movement from Madrid is that it is a top-down movement' (Dowling 2018, 161).

at the expense of national solidarity; and that the referendum was illegal, as the Constitution prohibits regional referenda.

Many scholars and commentators have attempted to pin down the independentist surge in one or another factor. However, the current political quest is rather a multifaceted, stratified situation where three major types of factors aligned to change popular opinion: economic, political, and cultural. This alignment happened against, and sometimes drew from, a historical background wherein Catalonia has been reclaiming local liberties more or less intensively since at least 1714. Catalonia was again on the losing side after the Spanish Civil War (1936–1939) and spearheaded the 1975 Transition from the Franco dictatorship to the *España de las Autonomías*. The first two events feed into Catalan narratives of victimhood, and the third to narratives of being 'cheated' out of the promise of the Transition. These sensations and self-perceptions resurfaced at first slowly during the 1990s and the 2000s, then erupting in the years 2010s.

With the impending economic crisis and a relative regression as an economic centre, Catalonia aimed to pursue greater financial independence from Spain. The state's rejection of a *pacto fiscal* triggered debates over sovereignty in the political realm and grievances of identity, status, and recognition in the cultural realm, as well as issues related to growing migration, or rather immigration (Dowling 2014, 2018). In 2006, the Catalan government drafted and accepted a reformed Statute of Autonomy, whose main purpose was to gain broader competences in collecting taxes and managing finances. After four years of deliberation, however, the Spanish Supreme Court rejected the reformed Statute in 2010.

Many Catalans felt that the rejection was insulting in several ways. The rejection itself, as well as the grievances that it has triggered, are regarded as a watershed in the recent history of Catalonia and Catalanism. First, the court's time frame of four years of deliberation was seen excessive and dismissive of regional priorities. Second, the Supreme Court rejected a proposal that was widely supported among Catalans and the regional government, which generated a sense of frustration. Third, the rejection showed Madrid's intransigence in a crisis situation and its expectation that Catalonia would simply go along with its directions. Fourth, the Constitutional Court not only rejected the economic proposal, but responded that Catalonia, among others, may not call itself a 'nation' but only a 'nationality', as the first designation is reserved for Spain. The 2010 Supreme Court decision led to the first significant rally that floated the prospect of secession under the banner '*Som una nació, nosaltres decidim*' ('We are a nation, we decide'). Furthermore, Catalan secessionism was branded by centralists as economically driven, adding another layer of insult to injury, as it resonated with disdained stereotypes of Catalans as stingy, money-grubbing capitalists (Brandes 1990). This view insinuated that Catalonia was acting selfishly in a situation of crisis, against the solidarity principle and redistributive system of the Constitution. It also undermined Catalan arguments that independence was necessary precisely because they wanted a more just and solidary society.

The argument that Catalan *independentisme* is mostly driven by economic considerations has been questioned by multiple studies. Research shows that the economic crisis did not appear to have played a significant a role in the political process. Some studies found the contrary: that the perception of the economic situation and increased fiscal power positively correlated with the support of a 'yes' vote, and subsequent economic recovery did not diminish a secessionist voting preference (Bel et al 2019; Boylan 2015). Cuadras-Morató and Rodon (2019) called the so-called fiscal grievances 'the dog that didn't bark': they found that unemployment, the disappearance of jobs and firms, or income loss in different municipalities did not correspond to higher support for independence. Others argued that, rather than a cause, the fiscal argument was something of a rationalisation: identity and partisanship were more important drivers of support for independence, and economic motivations tended to impact ambivalent party and identity positions (Muñoz and Tormos 2015). In sum, questions of national identity and related grievances were more relevant for the emergence of secessionist sentiments (Prat i Guilanyà 2012), while pragmatic factors of fiscal autonomy, taxes, and regional sovereignty certainly resonate (Dowling 2018; Serrano 2013). For example, the populist narrative that '*Espanya ens roba*' ('Spain is robbing us') is an oft-cited general sentiment among independentists (Barrio et al 2018).

In the political realm, the rejection of the reformed Statute of Autonomy brought issues of sovereignty to the surface. The question of where sovereignty lies in the case of a conflict of interest, in the state or in the region, has been a significant ambiguity in the Constitution itself.[2] With Joan Resina (2017), one could call it the 'ghost' in the Spanish Constitution, as ambivalent definitions of sovereignty continue to haunt today. After the end of the Franco dictatorship in 1975, the new Constitution's main priority was the speedy transition to democracy before a potential relapse into dictatorship. This resulted in hasty drafting and an ambiguous statement of state vs regional sovereignties in 1978. The new Constitution aimed to strike a compromise between the supporters of a unitary state and those of a decentralised or federal state. The main contradiction lies in Article 2, which asserts the indissoluble unity of the Spanish nation, the common and indivisible country of all Spaniards, while

---

[2] This was not unlike the theoretical *and* practical questions that the Badinter Commission, established in 1991 to arbitrate between disputing parties in Yugoslavia, was supposed to answer, with consequences that are all too familiar.

it also recognises and guarantees the right to autonomy of the nationalities and regions. Finally, it guarantees solidarity among them all through its fiscal system of redistribution (Comas 2003). The result was a sort of hybrid constitutional and administrative system that Andrew Dowling has summarised as follows: 'The territorial model adopted in Spain has been termed "an imperfect or incomplete federation", "semi-federal", "a hybrid system of federalism and regionalism", "a federalising unitary state", a "covertly federal state" and a "quasi-federal" state model' (2018, 157, where also references to those who have formulated those terms over the years can be found).

The 2010 rejection of the reformed Statute of Autonomy brought into sharp relief the competing interpretations as to where sovereignty lay. The Constitutional Court found several issues with the 2006 draft, which conjured up old complaints of asymmetry and political verticalism. The decision generated a new complex of symbolic grievances and a painful conclusion about regional sovereignty:

> Jurists held that Catalonia could not call itself a 'nation' in the legal sense; could not give the Catalan language preferential status in public administration; could not shield already-devolved policy areas from future central-government involvement; could not unilaterally put a cap on what it paid into the central treasury; could not raise its own taxes; could not impose a floor below which central-government investments in the region would not be allowed to drop; and could not run its own justice system. While constitutional courts in other federal systems might well have ruled similarly, for Spain this decision marked the end of constitutional ambiguity: For the first time, the limits of regional autonomy had been authoritatively drawn. (Mueller 2019, 147)

Similarly, when it comes to the question of a referendum, competing interpretations about sovereignty prevail. Centralists argue that a region's self-determination is unconstitutional because Spain is indivisible, while independentists point at the wording that guarantees their autonomy. For centralists, Spain's indivisibility renders Catalonia's self-determination illegal. For independentists, their right to autonomy should make it legal.

Further political phenomena behind the secessionist shift have been identified in terms of 'a series of cooperation failures' (Mueller 2019, 151): between competing and in-fighting Catalan parties, between the Catalan and Spanish governments, and between the Catalan government and other autonomous communities (Colomer 2017; Dowling 2018). *Pactisme*, Catalonia's historical consensus-seeking attitude that worked so well for and during the Transition (Desfor Edles 1999) failed now. Mueller traces political impasses to the so-called 'majoritarian democracy' (Mueller 2019). As opposed to a 'consensus democracy', decisions in a majoritarian democracy depend on simple majority.

On the one hand, this led to the cancellation of the voice of a substantial minority. On the other hand, it produced absurd outcomes: in 2017, after an illegal referendum, then president Puigdemont declared Catalonia's independence and suspended it eight seconds later. Independentists too realised that a popular vote of a simple majority was not enough for such a substantial transition and that a more generalised consensus-building was necessary.

The Constitutional Court's decision that Catalonia may not call itself a 'nation' but only a 'nationality' was seen as proof of vertical power relations where regional identities and languages were ranked lower than centralist ones in the cultural realm. This, again, evoked a series of grievances that have constituted historical memory and a Catalan 'mythscape' (Crameri 2012): the loss of autonomy to the Bourbon monarchy in 1714, the loss of the Civil War to Franco (which powerfully resurfaced in the debate around the Salamanca papers), and even losing out on the Transition, as it was now experienced. Burg summarised the independentist turn as 'reform, recognition, and resentment' (2015, 290) and argues that the fervour for independence will diminish with greater recognition of the status of Catalonia. Bel summarised the same as 'disdain, distrust and dissolution': he argues that the tendency toward schism is owing to deep-rooted negative stereotypes about and hostility to Catalans state-wide and what Catalans feel as a lack of respect.

Finally, in the cultural camp, most attention has revolved around language. As Dominic Keown has noted, 'in the case of Catalonia, language, culture and politics were inseparable and would remain so evermore' (2011c, 36). Language has in fact been a primary tool in the development, articulation, and expression of Catalanism, Catalan nationalism, and Catalan independentism; no wonder that language has always been considered a 'site of political struggle' (Dowling 2018, 48).

The above-mentioned issues often revolve around the proverbial elephant in the room already evoked in this Introduction: nationalism. The object of 'continued condemnations [...] as evil' (Llobera 1994, ix), nationalism has been often associated with – and reduced to – the extreme nationalist currents that developed especially during the first half of the 20th century, with their blatant ethnocentric and racist ideological axioms and policies. But that is only part of the story nationalism has to tell, although certainly the most tragic one. Less discussed in the scholarship is, for example, the role of nationalism in the construction of the idea of human and collective rights, in the birth and development of modern democracies and welfare states, and as the foundation of anti-colonialist and anti-imperialist movements of liberation (Majumdar 2007, 111–126; Smith 2013). Catalan nationalism has been traditionally distinguished from the Basque one, for example, for its culturalist rather than ethnicist terms (Conversi 1997) and has been broadly considered as cultural or civic (Llobera 2004) and inclusive (Testa this book), i.e., a mostly 'emancipatory' movement aimed at addressing the 'democratic deficit' experienced as a result of Spanish rule (Guibernau 2014, 2013). Lately, however, the question of whether there was an 'ethnicity bias' (Vergés-Gifra and Macià Serra 2022) in the current movement as a result of Catalan language promotion, or as centrists would say, indoctrination, has arisen. This recent view goes against the more broadly established scholarship claiming that the ethnicist component in Catalan nationalism has always been minor compared to its culturalist component.

The *resistencialisme* and *normalització* tradition in culture and language policies have had their discontents and ambiguities since the Transition (Colom-Montero 2021). Recently, studies have confirmed that in the current secessionist turn the Catalan language has been a main identity marker, but parties did not use it for 'ethnic outbidding' (Sanjaume-Calvet and Riera-Gil 2022). Rather than a sign of ethnicist authenticity, the Catalan language is increasingly serving a purpose of civil discourse and cosmopolitanism (Byrne 2020; Woolard 2016). Most independentists have realised that not only is monolingualism practically unachievable, but it would at any rate not achieve their objectives, and they have been actively seeking the involvement of Spanish-speaking immigrants in Catalonia's national debate (Argelaguet 2021).

Besides language, cultural politics and heritage have also been an important terrain of Catalanist revival. This book explores how the political emerges in Catalonia's popular culture, heritage-making process, and festival squares during the years of the recent territorial crisis, and how popular culture both reflects and constructs the political shift towards independentism. It also shows how, contrariwise, the cultural and the performative dimensions emerge from the political one, for these spheres can hardly be disentangled in contemporary Catalonia. Therefore, this book aims to provide up-to-date insights into the politics of culture in a fast-changing political environment, and therefore to fill in a lacuna in the scholarship. Indeed, until recently, in Catalan studies 'the fields of history and linguistics [have been] much over-studied when compared to, say, gastronomy, sport, and festivals' (Keown 2011b, 9). We have tried to strike a balance.

POST-TRANSITION TRANSFORMATIONS IN POPULAR AND REGIONAL CULTURE

The profound changes that have occurred since the Transition may be summarised through five major developments: the proliferation of associations; the reappropriation of 'the street', that is, the public sphere; the integration or greater participation and visibility of women; the gentrification and heritagisation of popular culture, including the impact of tourism; and the progressive politicisation of popular culture, including its pro-independence manifestations.

The Franco dictatorship (1939–1975) controlled almost all facets of life in Spain, including popular culture. Regional languages were outlawed, and customs and traditions were only tolerated as long as they did not foster regional nationalism and were compatible with Franco's ideals of national Catholicism. The evidence and literature on these aspects are abundant. Symptomatic of Francoist control of the public sphere was the reaction of Manuel Fraga, former Tourism and Information Minister, with his phrase '*La calle es mía*' ('the street is mine') in response to complaints about police repression and the banning of rallies. Towards the later years of the dictatorship, the grip of Francoist repression ultimately loosened in different social sectors, from the economy to culture and education. Catalan culture and Catalanist consciousness burst forth with new energies after the death of the Caudillo. Not only was Francoist repression a failure, but it also probably had the opposite effect of strengthening, by reaction, Catalan language and culture (Dowling 2018, 6–29; Keown 2011a, 2011b; Llobera 2004, 58–110; Sánces-Biosca 2007).

The Transition responded with calls and movements of '*sortir al carrer*' ('go out onto the streets') and the reclamation of public space for the purposes of free expression and public use (MacClancy 2014; Ofer 2017). This period was described as 'the public occupation of the street, cultural effervescence, sexual tolerance, the appearance of a series of leisure spaces, [and] the everyday practice of newfound liberty' (Carles Feixa quoted in Noyes 2011, 215). Catalonia rekindled its old traditions and penchant for associational culture or *associacionisme*, which has traditionally made space for cultural and political rearticulation 'through notions of participation, community, and self-expression' (Dowling 2018, 31). The Transition witnessed the emergence of thousands of neighbourhood associations with social, cultural, political, or leisure goals. The '*recuperació*' or 'recovery' of popular festivals was an important step towards granting popular agency to young people, who had been at the margins of politics. Over the years, popular culture has become a source of sovereignty and local empowerment (Dowling 2010, 101; Kammerer 2014; Noyes 2011; Testa in this book).

The Transition ushered in modern and, among others, feminist ideas and the revision and change of gender roles. Under Franco, women's roles had been largely reduced to domestic ones as wives and mothers who raised patriotic children for the state's National Catholic agenda (Gómez Amat 2007). Women's presence in the festival *plaça*, the paradigmatic public sphere, was largely reduced to spectatorship or auxiliary chores while men were the protagonists of cultural performances (Pink 1997).

The Transition changed traditional gender arrangements, and women became increasingly integrated, as actors, in the performances of popular culture. Traditional *colles* and *comparses*, which were eminently masculine and were formed and performed during carnivals and carnivalesque, but also religious, festivals, opened up to the active participation of women. Women's integration in popular performance genres affected wide-ranging feminist questions such as women's 'place' and public visibility, leadership roles, and conceptualisations of women's bodies and physical abilities.

Women's greater participation coincided with the general gentrification of popular culture in terms of social class, heritage-making, and tourism. The middle classes and professionals were attracted to, and spearheaded, the organisation of practices that fostered the revival of Catalan culture after Francoism. The intensification of tourism in Spain in general, its branding as sun, sand, and sea, Catalonia's *costa brava* and *costa daurada*, the wholesale transformation of Barcelona for the 1992 Olympic Games, and its thriving sport and cultural life, turned the region into a top European tourist destination. Partly as a response to the market that tourism created, heritage regimes affected the general regularisation and institutionalisation of popular culture, a process that has been profusely studied in Europe (Testa 2021). Catalonia's UNESCO Intangible Heritage titles include the *Patum* festival of Berga (granted in 2005), the ancient Pyrenees fire festival *Fallas* (2015), and the human tower-building, *Castells* (2010) (Llosa 2014; del Mármol Cartañà and Roigé Ventura 2014; Vaczi 2023). Before the UNESCO Convention for the Safeguarding of Intangible Cultural Heritage (2003) and its adoption and ratification by Spain (2006), other, national heritage denominations and cataloguing existed: up until the end of the 1970s, several Catalan festivals were on the Spanish list of *Fiestas de Interés Turístico Nacional* (in Spanish). From the early 1989s, this denomination was taken over by a corresponding Catalan scheme, recognising the *Festes tradicionals d'interès nacional* (reclassified in 2009 as *Festes patrimonials d'interès nacional*). In the last three decades, this labelling has proliferated, becoming an important part of the cultural and heritage policies of the Generalitat (del Mármol Cartañà and Roigé Ventura 2014).

Heritagisation, however, poses its own dilemmas. At the supra-national level, while these titles yield prestige and potentially help energise declining practices, they also move agency away from local practitioners to global decision-makers (Noyes 2016), as some of the case studies in this book will reveal. Within Spanish borders, it seems evident that since the 1990s 'heritage has become a source of low intensity conflict between Madrid and Barcelona' (Dowling 2018, 49).

In recent years, popular *festes* and the public sphere have become increasingly politicised as pro-independence feelings have expanded in Catalonia (Kammerer 2014; Noyes 2003, 2016; but see especially the chapters in this volume). *Catalanisme*, a feeling of local attachment and the promotion of Catalan language and culture had been proper to these spheres. But *catalanisme* is not consubstantial with *independentisme*; it is possible to be *catalanista* while wanting to remain part of Spain. The two national flags, the *senyera* and the *estelada*, also express the difference. The *estelada*, which began to be used in the 1970s, is typically flown by supporters of independence; the *senyera*, which is one of the oldest flags in Europe, may be flown by people of both pro-independence sentiments or just regional attachment without the desire to secede.

After the death of Franco and during the Transition, the Catalan national days (*Diada*) were mostly celebrated in the spirit of both *catalanisme* and unionism: '*ser y estar*' (in Spanish), that is, to be Catalan and be part of Spain (Humlebæk and Hau 2020). After 2010, regionalist *catalanisme* was substituted or complemented by *independentisme*. In 2005, only 15% of Catalans wanted the region to become independent; in 2015, the region elected its first pro-independence government with a popular vote of 48%. In 2021, the pro-independence coalition formed the government with more than 50% of the votes. This political shift was increasingly visible in the festival public sphere as pro-independence flags and messages populated the streets and town squares. The strengthening of pro-independence, mostly (but not exclusively) leftist politics appealed to many actors of popular culture, which has important roots in urban working-class sociality as well as in rural and provincial traditions. At the same time, middle-class and professional segments became attracted to Catalanist practices that, as cultural heritage, had assumed greater social and cultural prestige.

CULTURE, IDENTITY, AND POLITICS IN CONTEMPORARY CATALONIA: OVERVIEW OF THE VOLUME

The ethnographic loci of this collection include festivals such as Josa de Cadí and the Solsona carnival (among others) and other important features of Catalan culture such as gastronomy, the traditional sport and cultural performance called *castells*, and the *correbous* bull runs. Their focus runs from the Pyrenees in the north to the river Ebro in the south, two geographical borderlands that occupy an important place in the national imagination. The chapters reveal, through the lenses of culture, the idiosyncrasies of the current, distinctive era in Catalan politics. They variously address the emergence, transformation, and contestation of identities; they identify not just desires, but some dilemmas, contradictions, and fears when it comes to the politicisation of culture. This book problematises such concepts as 'nationhood', 'inclusion', 'integration', 'authenticity', 'belonging', and 'identity' in contemporary Catalonia. It highlights and interprets power relations as local actors interact with cultural policy-makers, heritage regimes, and political entities.

INTRODUCTION

Whether considered as history, ritual continuity, or tradition, the past is the quintessential symbolic matter shaped and used for identity production and reproduction. So it is in the many case studies analysed in this entire volume, and so it is in Camila del Mármol's chapter focusing on the Cathar past and/as the Catalan past in the region of the Catalan Pyrenees. The Cathar presence in the 12–13th century in the Catalan Pyrenees, and its national myths of democracy, feminism, enlightenment, and egalitarianism, became part of a project that Mármol calls the 'imagining of independence'. Intersecting and mutually reinforcing pasts are ritually reunited in the festival of Josa de Cadí, which also offers the opportunity, del Mármol observes, to express and mediate local, regional, and national identities, while at the same time allowing the local communities to imagine possible futures, in a situation of present hardships and transformations.

In this study we see at work, again, the complex interplay of the local with the general and the regional with the national. We are also given to understand the role of tourism in the adaptation, reinforcement, and reproduction of the Cathar past and the set of narratives centred on it. Hence, identity politics, the politics of culture, the tourist economy, and demographic factors (also explored in the chapter) blend together as important socio-cultural components of the Catalan *procés*, in and for which the transmission of discourses and narratives plays a role as important as the ritual practices that foster their embodiment.

Mariann Vaczi's chapter explores sensory forms of belonging and citizenship (see Manning 2007; Trnka et al 2013; Vaczi and Watson 2021) and asserts that the nation may be not only imagined, but also embodied. Human tower-building (*castells*) is a 200-year-old tradition at the intersections of folklore, rituality, and sport (Erickson 2011; Vaczi 2016, 2023; Weig 2015). Originating from the south of Catalonia, the practice has survived the Franco dictatorship, revived during the Transition, and boomed in the 21st century. Today, as a basic function of neighbourhood integration and associational culture, more than a hundred teams build 15,000 towers a year across the festival squares of Catalonia. This spectacular success is owing to various factors: the integration of women in the 1980s, the gentrification of the practice and its expansion to the middle classes, the desire to reclaim Catalan culture in the wake of the Franco regime, and the thrill and breathtaking athleticism of these human formations.

Human towers have lent the current pro-independence movement image, social base, and vocabulary. The iconic imagery of building lends itself easily to linkages with nation-building, and dozens of human tower teams participate at Catalonia's national days (*Diadas*) each year, vindicating the right to vote. 'Making a base' (*fer pinya*), a human tower base, which relies on body diversity and body count, has become a frequently used neologism for 'making a country', and rallying diverse segments of the population behind the cause of independence.

Vaczi traces the body performances of Catalan nationalism and takes performance for the somatisation of political desires, dilemmas, and risks. The salience of *castells* for the current *procés* lies in the practice's meanings as myth and allegory in what Walter Benjamin would call a 'dialectic image' (see Buck-Morss 1989). Vaczi unpacks the narratives built in the representational process of this traditional sport and the insights they yield into the Catalan independence movement.

An increasing volume of food studies has created linkages between gastronomy, commensality, and politics in Spain (Lesh 2009; MacClancy 2007) and beyond. Venetia Johannes shows that the nation may be not only imagined and embodied, but also tasted. She traces the expression of Catalanness through food across centuries through three basic channels: cookbooks, national dishes, and the gastronomic calendar. Food and commensality in Catalonia have been a means of enculturation, community-making, and political resistance.

Johannes argues that, starting with the Middle Ages and across the Catalan Renaixança, cookbooks had a 'dual role': they were not only cooking manuals, but also important records of Catalan language and culture. In the early 20th century, as *catalanisme* emerged as a distinct political identity, some cookbooks were explicitly linked with Catalan nationhood. Images of the 'native land' and the 'hearth' were symbolically connected, to the point of 'glorifying cuisine as a rallying point' of Catalan nationalism. During the Francoist repression (1936–1939) of regional languages and cultures, the re-edition of cookbooks in Catalan in the 1960s and 1970s became an unexpected source of cultural resistance and language maintenance. They became part of private Catalan language libraries people kept, sometimes secretly, at home.

In Catalan cuisine, sauces and stews may be interpreted as symbols of Catalan identity and national character. Foodstuffs and their preparation reflect an openness and adventurousness that Catalonia has claimed as its own as an open and modern nation. Basic sauces may be added to any dish to 'Catalanise' them, and stews are expressions of rural simplicity and frugality. Johannes too links cuisine to the ubiquitous 'national' character *seny*: Catalan national dishes reflect a sensible, rational, down-to-earth attitude, thriftiness, and a practical approach to life in their simplicity and frugality. In the current pro-independence context, Johannes highlights that the politicisation of cuisine is visible, but also reluctant. After all, food is so ubiquitous that it cannot be appropriated by a single ideology.

Bull sports in Spain have long been politicised due to their associations with the Spanish state as its *fiesta nacional* (Abrisketa and Abrisketa 2020;

Brandes 2009; Douglass 1984). Manuel Delgado, Romina Martínez Algueró, and Sarai Martín López discuss the Catalan bull run (*correbous*) as a site where heritage, identity, and mainstream, institutionally endorsed forms of Catalanness are contested. The *correbous* is celebrated in the south of Catalonia, in the Ebro river delta. Its various modalities may feature a calf, ox, or cow released in the street or in the sea; the animal may wear a fireball on its horns or partake in exhibition and skills competitions. Unlike in the Spanish bullfight, the animal is not killed at the end.

The southern, Ebro region of Catalonia has witnessed a conspicuous increase in *correbous* events in recent years. In 2011, 208 bull runs were celebrated, and in 2018, this number was 439. The increase is all the more conspicuous because there is a contrary trend in Catalonia: a marked withdrawal from bull sports and the Spanish *fiesta nacional*. Catalonia's banning of the Spanish bullfight in 2010 was a political move of distancing the region itself from 'backward' Spain, and the region's bullrings have been converted into malls or the home of more 'politically correct' practices such as, famously, the biannual human towers championship *Concurs*.

The resurgence of the *correbous* in the southernmost corner of Catalonia runs counter to the general tendencies of mainstream Catalan nationalism. 'Hegemonic Catalanness', as the authors name it, was consolidated under the 23-year post-Franco rule (1980–2003) of the centre-right Democratic Convergence (CDC) party and its leader Jordi Pujol and espouses a Catalanness that is civic, open to dialogue, has a moderate temperament (*seny*), and endorses language as a core marker of identity. As such, it rejects violence of any kind. The *correbous*, in turn, came to signify 'the other "Catalanness"', one that runs counter to institutionally sanctioned expressions of identity and Catalanism. The Ebro bull runs claim the recognition of cultural plurality within Catalonia and contest the homogenising tendencies of mainstream nationalist politics and heritage regimes.

Alessandro Testa's sibling chapters centre upon public rituality in the *comarca* of Solsonès in central Catalonia, outlining the sagas of its major regional festival and the actors that play a role in it. In these two chapters, Testa opens up a window onto how the socio-cultural dimensions of ritual life, group and supra-individual configurations, collective forms of participation, the local political order, and regional/national identity construction interact and interweave in the public arenas of a central Catalonian town, which is also compared with other kin or close Catalan contexts. He does so by blending theoretical speculation and empirically (i.e., ethnographically) informed, thickly-described evidence.

The two essays also explain how these dimensions have changed along with and due to the general politics of culture in Catalonia during the Transition, in particular about folklore and festive culture, and how such changes have escalated since the 2010s.

Different forms and aspects of 'Catalanness' are therein distinguished and problematised as components and vehicles of national identity, nationhood and nationality, nationalism and Catalanism, and finally Catalan independentism. How are these different attitudes and perspectives negotiated, contested, or reproduced through and during those 'denser' moments of hyper-socialisation that festivals and public rituals create? How do representations and practices of nationhood and nationalism, and other matters national identity is made of, coalesce over, and because of, such moments of hyper-socialisation? And do they struggle or collide with other ethnic, national, and religious identities, in spite of Catalanism being generally considered an inclusive and progressive kind of nationalism?

By interpreting the symbolic and ritualised stratagems and dynamics through which national identity is constructed and vehiculated, in particular through the cultural works of the *comparses* (festive semi-formal groups) and the Catalan language, Testa demonstrates how incorporated, transmitted, and 'familiarised' behavioural forms of collective action allow the local society to reproduce social and political patterns of belonging and identity assertion. Therefore, a strong case is made for how the microcosmos of Solsona's central-Catalonian popular culture becomes a veritable matrix, but also a mirror, through which the macrocosm of Catalan national identity is both manufactured and reflected.

Given this richness of public sociality, the Covid-19 pandemic hit Mediterranean cultures such as the Catalan particularly hard. Presence, body proximity, and touch lend these cultures their human warmth, and they were now a potential source of illness and death. Public sociality, festivals, commensality, and performances came to a halt for the sake of that rather foreign notion, social distancing. Mármol and Vaczi's papers briefly address how the pandemic affected festival and performance genres; Xavier Roigé, Mireia Guil, and Lluís Bellas devote their entire chapter to a more systematic analysis of how public sociality responded to the pandemic.

Xavier Roigé, Mireia Guil, and Lluís Bellas explore the timely topic of how changing festival practices under the impact of the Covid-19 pandemic affected public life and discourses in post-referendum Catalonia. The chapter mobilises a number of ethnographic examples to explore these transformations, arguing that the pandemic has added yet another layer of complexity to an already structured and stratified situation in which identity concerns, political claims, practices of heritage, and adaptations of traditions have been intersecting for years.

Adaptations, improvisations, and veritable new cultural creations have also taken place through the newly available media, fostering a 'digitalisation' of festive events and electronic forms of cultural resilience that are indeed interesting phenomena *per se*. These changes may also be considered, the authors suggest, as modes of resolution of the rising conflicts between the logic of the lockdowns and the logic of festivities – and collective phenomena in the public sphere more generally, one might add.

The authors also show how the Covid-19 situation seems to have exacerbated issues of identity and politics (at any rate typically Catalan) reflected and negotiated in the festive rituals. At the same time, the pandemic has also triggered debates about authenticity and the appropriateness of certain means for transmitting local traditions, as well as the relationship between localities and the state and the legitimacy of forms of resistance and transgression in order to guarantee the ritual reproduction of communal life in spite of adverse contingencies.

These different themes, problems, and perspectives are wrapped up in the afterword by folklorist and anthropologist Dorothy Noyes, the author of the ground-breaking ethnographic monograph about Catalonia, *Fire in the Plaça* (Noyes 2003), which is based on a long and intensive period of fieldwork the author undertook between the end of the 1980s and the early 1990s. This book is now rightly considered a classic. Noyes also turned her attention to Catalonia in several follow-up studies and has been a close observer of the development of Catalan matters for over three decades.

1

Castells, Myths, and Allegories of Nation-Building

MARIANN VACZI

On June 8, 2014 at noon, eight human tower teams (*colles*) built eight towers (*castells*) simultaneously in eight European capitals at the event called "Catalans Want to Vote: Human Towers for Democracy". The rally was organized by Òmnium Cultural, one of the two most influential Catalanist pro-independence NGOs. The deployment of this traditional sport across Europe aimed to call international attention to Catalan desires to vote about the question of independence from Spain. The *castells* action *fer pinya*, which refers to the building of the base of a human tower, became analogous with laying down the foundations of a new country. This is how the rally's promotion explained the choice of this cultural performance for the vindication of voting rights:

> Us Catalans will decide our future at a referendum. Together we build a base [*fem pinya*] for a better country. We believe in peace, effort and cooperation. We are a sovereign nation that wants to live in a normal country. Our dream is shared, our path is democracy. We want to tell the world because the world needs to know. [...] All the human tower groups share the same objective: an important protest of the country to project ourselves in the world. From the base [*pinya*] of a human tower to the *enxaneta* [the child who "crowns" the tower by waving], together we touch the sky. It is a chance to make our message reach Europe clearly: Catalans want to vote. Help us build a base! (Òmnium Cultural 2014).

The day after the Catalans Want to Vote rally in 2014, images of the event populated the media, showing human towers on the most emblematic squares and next to the most famous buildings of Europe: Berlin's Alexanderplatz,

Brussel's Grande Palace, Geneva's Place des Nations, Lisbon's Bélem Tower, London's Tower Bridge, Rome's Gianicolo, Paris's Eiffel Tower, and Barcelona's Sagrada Família towers.

"Building castells is building nation", I heard repeatedly from castellers at similar rallies during my two-year-long fieldwork in Catalonia, where I performed with the Castellers de Barcelona "gang". As expressions of desire and ideology, buildings have their particular mythic effects; architecture, Roland Barthes writes, is "always a dream and a function" (1979, 6). Buildings are "the will of the age conceived in spatial terms" (Mies van der Rohe in Harvey 1992, 21), as the built environment including its shape, color, and materiality has reflected philosophical and political concerns (see Fehérváry 2013). For example, the buildings of world expositions aimed to convey national greatness and social progress through industry and architecture. The phallocentric masculinity of American city skylines fulfils its "symbolic duty" (D'Eramo cited in Graham 2016, 757) of conveying status and power. By placing flesh and blood human towers by the most iconic buildings of Europe, pro-independence actors drew from their mythical functions and presented their particular dream: the building of a new national edifice in the heart of Europe.

Castells is a 200-year-old cultural performance originating in the south of Catalonia. At the crossroads of folklore, ritual, popular culture, and sport, the performance consists of a hundred plus, sometimes a thousand plus, amateur performers – men, women, and children – first organizing themselves into a compact, round base, on which then lighter and lighter performers climb and create subsequent levels by interlocking arms, holding bodies, and balancing on shoulders. The top levels consist of children, including the *enxaneta* who crowns the tower by raising her hand. They then dismantle the tower as they built it, level by level. Human tower-building is a great spectacle of communal effort, organization, defiance of gravity, and facing the risk of collapse. Since the transition to democracy from Franco's dictatorship, *castells* have undergone a spectacular boom. From seven traditional teams in 1975, the world of *castells* went to more than a hundred in 2020, which is an extraordinary trajectory for traditional sports that usually struggle for existence. Moreover, human towers became a lead symbol for the current secessionist politics by lending it image, vocabulary, and social base.

In town squares populated with secessionist messages, the physical order of tower-building bodies expressed a desired cultural order: they became what Walter Benjamin called a "wish image" (in Buck-Morss 1989, 56) for a political utopia. This chapter addresses how *castell* building, a cultural performance and traditional sport, rose to serve as the mythical and allegorical function of the current independence movement, which needed a positive symbol of rootedness, solidarity, and collective effort. The ethos and body technique of *castell* building was striking as an apparently "natural" fit for the transmission

CASTELLS, MYTHS, AND ALLEGORIES OF NATION-BUILDING

1. A human tower team (*colla*) is making a base (*fer pinya*) for a pillar structure at the *festa major* of Vilanova i Geltrú in 2008. *Fer pinya* requires organization and cooperation. The *castells* term "make a base" became a political idea for drawing disparate political parties into the same objective of independence from Spain. Source: Wikimedia Commons. Author: Núria i JC.

of pro-independence messages for nation-building. At the rallies and *plaças*, the building action of a tower would conjure up thoughts and sentiments about nation-building towards an ambitious edifice in the political realm. But the politics of culture has its own contradictions and precarities, suggested by *castells* themselves. It is precisely a shaking and wobbling human tower that flashes the allegorical reverse of construction projects: that ideas, just like human towers, may collapse and end in ruins.

CATALONIA'S HUMAN TOWERS

Human tower-building goes back to the late 18th century, to the south of Catalonia, and evolved from a Valencian street dance. *Castells* started out as a rivalry between two gangs in the small town of Valls, whose town square is considered the 'km 0', or center of *castells*. The rivalry between the two foundational teams, now called Colla Vella Xiquets de Valls and Colla Joves dels Xiquets de Valls, has spanned more than two centuries and continues to energize this world. Human tower teams, *colles*, are neighborhood associations whose basic objective is to provide low-cost sociality to its members through communal participation. They maintain a bar, restaurant, and workout facility called *local* and have workout sessions (*assaig*) three times a week. Unlike other performative elements of popular culture that are concentrated in week-long *festes*, belonging to a human tower team is very much like doing sport. It is an intensive lifestyle, as it requires about ten hours of practice during the week, and teams perform almost every other weekend between March and October.

Below and beyond their recent political undertones, the purpose of *castells* is neighborhood integration as part of Catalonia's associational culture (*associacionisme*). Teams offer individuals and families cheap leisure-time sociality and the pleasure of belonging to a community that attracts widespread admiration for its spectacular body practice. Furthermore, associationism empowers individuals and groups in their civic, leisure, educational, and political pursuits. The two most robust NGOs, Òmnium Cultural and the Catalan National Assembly (ANC), have grown into influential political actors that, quite unprecedentedly in Europe, pushed formal politics toward the idea of independence.

As neighborhood associations, *castells* teams fulfil a host of solidarity functions. They organize low-cost or free summer camps for children and offer free textbooks, tutoring, and movie nights, for example. For adults, belonging to a *colla* means a network of friends, travel opportunities, and social capital that may help when seeking a job. Teams maintain themselves from regional governmental subsidies, sponsorship, and the performance fees they collect from the municipalities or private businesses that invite them to perform.

With the post-Franco Transition, the practice started to boom across Catalonia and spread from its southern, "traditional zone" small towns and Barcelona northward. Today, more than a hundred teams build more than 15,000 human towers a year on weekend performances (*diadas*), and *colles* are established even abroad. The biannual human tower championship *Concurs* in Tarragona attracts mainstream European media, which is increasingly fascinated by these photogenic human formations. This is remarkable growth for a folkloric performance and traditional sport, as old performative genres are often endangered in contexts of urban modernity (Noyes 2016).

Castells' post-Franco success owes itself to several social, cultural, economic, and political factors. First, the Transition to democracy achieved a feeling of liberation and the desire to reclaim the street, which fostered the establishment of neighborhood associations. Second, the ideological liberation that marked the end of national Catholicism opened up the way for the integration of women in the 1980s. Women's presence "tamed", as it were, and gentrified the practice that had previously had a rough, boisterous, male, working-class reputation. *Castells* now also attracted middle-class professionals who were vocal about popular sovereignty in a general atmosphere of post-Franco awakening. The 1990s witnessed a further boom as the newly emergent, Catalanist regional media featured local folklore like human towers generously. The 2008 economic crisis made many people seek cheap forms of sociality such as *castells*, and the current independence fervor attracts those who want to promote Catalan culture through a Catalan-speaking cultural activity.

As a currently thriving and evolving practice, human towers are in a liminal state of transformation, which allows it to occupy different identities non-exclusively. It displays features Testa calls the "-ations" of heritage

2. The Castellers de Vilafranca are building a record-high ten-level tower in 2013. The social purpose of *castells* is neighborhood integration. Castellers (performers) claim the sport relies on strength, courage, balance, and common sense (*força, valor, equilibri i seny*). Source: Wikimedia Commons. Author: Diari AVUI.

transformations (Testa 2020b, 84). Castells is undergoing heritagization like the acquisition of the UNESCO Intangible Heritage (2010) title or the establishment of a museum. At the same time, the practice is clearly a high-skilled athletic feat, and signs of sportification are distinctly recognizable as the practice is moving "from ritual to record" (Guttman 1978): the quantification of results, the ranking system, and the *Concurs* championship are salient features of this sportification process. Commercialization happens in a controlled fashion, as teams accept sponsors but resist the display of commercial entities on their performance shirts. Professionalization has been staunchly resisted in the name of equality and by the mandate of the UNESCO heritage title to remain amateur, despite sportification tendencies including the fact that some performance positions require high skill and constant training.

Human towers have built *castells* at secessionist rallies and town squares under pro-independence flags and banners. The politicization of culture, however, may have problematic consequences: the naturalization of *castells* as a pro-independence Catalanist arena and the resulting threat of exclusion or intimidation of people who are pro-Spain centralist. Where the body is a shifter between experience and essence, subtle mechanisms of essentialization may happen imperceptibly.

THE SPECTACULARIZATION OF POLITICAL DESIRES

In its bottom-up constructions manifest in pro-independence or pro-right-to-vote rallies, Catalan *independentisme* has shown a great penchant for design, image, and symbolization. Catalonia's September 11 national day (*Diada*) celebrations are noteworthy not just for their shift from Catalanism to independentism and the massive crowds they have attracted (Humlebæk and Hau 2020), but also for their concern with visual and symbolic meaning production. It is apparent that a great deal of thinking and planning goes into the visualization of political messages. Human towers, themselves a highly visual genre, fitted into these broader purposes of nation-building through their iconic imagery, and became staples at national day *Diadas*. These rallies demonstrated, and in great part owed their success to, the communication power of Catalan cultural elites, including the deployment of cultural elements and symbolism (see Crameri 2015, 110).

Since 2010, when great masses first demonstrated against the Spanish Constitutional Court and under the banner "We are a Nation, We Decide", *Diadas* have closely resonated with and responded to political processes. The year 2012 was one of the turning points in the secessionist politics of Catalonia. Emboldened by the successful mobilization of the civil sphere, the regional government, the *Generalitat*, openly declared its independentist political stance. That year, the Catalan National Assembly (ANC) organized a March Towards Independence (*Marxa cap a la Independència*), which culminated in the September 11 national day celebration under the banner "Catalonia, New State of Europe" (*Catalunya, Nou Estat d'Europa*). The banner was carried by representatives of the main Catalan parties in an unprecedented disclosure of the official turn towards independence. The crowd, which was estimated to number between 600,000 and 1.5 million, held up green cards in response to the questions about independence announced by the ANC. The symbolism suggested that Catalan society gave free rein to independentist politics through a massive sea of green cards.

A year later, in 2013, Catalanist NGOs organized the Free Way Towards Independence (*Vía Catalana cap a la Independència*), which was a 400-kilometer human chain, starting in the French region of the Països Catalans, the historic Catalonia that stretches from across the Pyrenees all the way down south to Valencia. The idea of the human chain was borrowed from the Baltic Way of 1989, linking Lithuania, Latvia, and Estonia. Human chains and their related genres (such as relay runs like the Basque *korrika*) are a ritual of reterritorialization as bodies create new physical borders.

The 2014 Catalan national day was called *Ara és l'Hora* (Now is the Time) and featured in the capital, Barcelona, a letter V for *Vía Catalana* (Catalan Way) or Victory. The crowd, now estimated at 1.8 million by the organizers, stretched along the two greatest avenues of the city, the Diagonal and the Gran Vía. Participants carried red and yellow cards, and Barcelona displayed an 11-kilometer giant V in the Catalan colors as its two main avenues met, suggestively, at the Plaça de les Glòries Catalanes.

In 2015, the Free Way to the Catalan Republic rally (*Vía Lliure*) featured a yellow cardboard arrow carried by runners in a relay. The arrow cut its way through the crowd energetically as it moved forward and aimed to make a Free Way to the Catalan Republic at the upcoming regional parliamentary elections two weeks later, where Catalonia voted for its first pro-independence government in the post-Franco era. The 2016 national day was called *A Punt, Endavant República Catalan* (Ready, Next Comes Catalan Republic). It was a multi-sited event, where each city involved symbolized a distinct goal for the new republic: Salt stood for solidarity and diversity, Berga for culture, Tarragona for progress, Lleida for territorial equilibrium, and Barcelona for liberty.

The 2017 *Diada del Sí* took place only a couple of weeks before the illegal independence referendum on October 1, which was followed by clashes between voters and the police, injuring more than 800. The 2018 *Fem la República Catalana* (We Make the Catalan Republic) *Diada* responded to these events: a sonorous wave yelling Independència across six kilometers of the Diagonal avenue. The act aimed to vindicate politicians who were exiled or imprisoned because of the 2017 referendum. In 2019, the *Diada* was organized at the Plaza España of Barcelona, an enormous roundabout whose eye condensed the rally's name "Objective: Independence". This rally took place only a few weeks before the Spanish Supreme Court would announce its decision to imprison the organizers of the 2017 referendum for 9–13 years in prison, which unleashed a months' long wave of protests and nighttime clashes with riot police, which would be halted by the global pandemic.

Human towers have been part of this landscape, and about 50–60 teams participated at the *Diadas*. *Castells* lent these rallies a social base and became the attention-grabbing feature of the panorama, as they stuck out physically and visually from the multitude. "*Estelades* [pro-independence flags], castells, and yellow ribbons", the Basque regional television channel Eitb summarized the main symbolic tool kit of Catalan pro-independence politics at these rallies.

The *Diadas*' imagery and symbolism are planned so that they become a memorable "image encounter" (Sonnevend 2012) for global viewers. Their spectacular imagery is meant to be photographed from helicopters or tall buildings. They usually align the vast expanse of the crowd into color combinations and a sign. The next day, the images of the rally awe the world for their expressiveness and organization. The imagery of independentisme is to a great degree directed at global flaneurs of the Internet, these post-modern deciphers of urban signs who encounter the *Diadas*' images on mainstream television or the pages of the *New York Times*. Through visual lavishness, the careful design and symbology communicate to the international viewer that this movement is planned and controlled and that it is festive, socially transversal and peaceful, as opposed to the chaos and radicalism of violent forms of secessionism.

Castells performance creates a constellation with its environment, and they constitute a unique aura of time and space (see Benjamin 1969). Each new tower is a gamble with the body, and performance draws its surroundings into a sense of mutual destiny in terms of glorious crowning, or catastrophic collapse. In the context of visual meaning production, the iconic outcome of tower-building gains paramount importance: a tower that collapses at a pro-independence rally could be interpreted as greatly ominous for the political project. Only 3–5% of human towers collapse on average, but performers feel the special stakes involved in these towers. In 2015, at the Free Way *Diada* rally, we gathered to build a human tower so that aerial photography could capture the moment our *enxaneta* gloriously crowned the tower as the arrow passed by. We chose a well-rehearsed, low-risk but still spectacular eight-level tower. Even so, fear of collapse had a special meaning at that moment. As we took our positions to make the base (*fer pinya*), we heard the murmur of the crowd expecting the arrow to pass and our building to start. As the ascent started, someone next to me whispered, "Oh no. Let it not collapse *now*!" A ruinous heap of human bodies would have sent the message that political ambitions, like buildings, might collapse.

THE CHANGING BODY POLITIC OF *CATALANISME*

The relationship between movement, the body, and political expression has been noted in general (Brownell 1995; Manning 2007), and in the context of Spain in particular (Vaczi 2023; Vaczi and Watson 2021; Weig 2015). Manning (2007) shows the inventive and generative aspects of body movement for space, time, subjectivity, and sovereignty, which fits with the fluid and always-becoming character of "the urban", the public space *per se* as discussed by Delgado (1999). Human towers, which are a particularly urban genre performed on the *plaça*, have been called a "bodily commentary" on social and political matters (Weig 2015, 435), or "sensory politics" (Erickson 2011) for integration.

Reading the body allegorically may reveal broader narratives and political processes. For example, Elias and Jephcott's seminal study of body proximity captures the history of social class markers and their "civilizing process" (Elias and Jephcott 1994). For Bourdieu (1978), the body was an expression of *habitus*, a system of dispositions that differs according to social class. A social class's disposition toward a sport or body performance is based on its particular relationship to the body, or certain ethical and aesthetic affinities.

When political movements choose a body performance through which to express themselves, they articulate the legitimate body and the legitimate uses of the body from their ideological perspective. The changing dispositions of Catalanism are traceable through their flagship cultural performances. Catalonia's national dance, the *sardana*, was a great example for the intersectionality of political ideology, class *habitus*, and the body. The *sardana* became the Catalan national dance in the second half of the 19th century and reflected the democratic values of the emergent, Catalanist-nationalist bourgeoisie. A circle dance that anyone may join by holding hands, it expressed the ideal bourgeois uses of the body: corporeal control, respectable distance, rules, and measure. The dance's democratizing quality rested in women's ability to join the dance safely, and the agency to enter the circle and leave it at any time. The fact that one had to count was even linked to Catalans' stereotypes as money-grubbing capitalists (Brandes 1990). The *sardana* dance was the body technique that *gent d'ordre*, bourgeois, and petit bourgeois social classes associated with that other Catalan character stereotype, *seny* or common sense.

In the 20th century, Catalonia's increasing confrontations with Spanish politics, the Civil War, and the ensuing Franco dictatorship aligned with another body technique that expressed a confrontative, outward-oriented, antagonistic relationship: soccer. The newly imported sport of soccer, which in its modern home Great Britain was in great part associated with the "vulgar" working classes, possessed the necessary *agôn* (Caillois 1961) for the expression of an antagonistic political relationship. FC Barcelona became a Catalanist symbol where, due to the binary logic of the game, Catalans could challenge Franco's favorite team, Real Madrid, on a level playing field that was in all other social fields denied to the losers of the Civil War (1936–1939). The *Clásico* between FC Barcelona and Real Madrid is arguably the most paradigmatic sports rivalry in the world, watched by 600 million people. Besides the agonic structure of the game, FC Barcelona's civil society, membership management, and voting practices also fostered meanings of resistance in a dictatorship where voting and self-government were out of the question in the political terrain.

Fire festivals are another cultural performance genre that has assumed Catalanist meanings. They too imply a gamble with the body, given the dangers that playing with fire entails. On the night of Sant Joan, the streets turn into a burning, smoking, exploding field of fire. Residents throw old objects on the bonfires in an act of ritual purification and teach children how to safely throw firecrackers. Catalonia's most well-known fire festival, the *Patum* of Berga, is a throbbing Dionysian mass of bodies that dance to the rhythm of drums and a repetitive tune, with fire devils spouting sparkles from a contraption attached to their head (Noyes 2003). Fire also resonates with the working-class, anarchist traditions of the region, whose iconic culmination was the 1909 Tragic Week (*la Setmana Tràgica*) of Barcelona, when more than a hundred buildings were set on fire as part of the anti-militarist revolt.

Human towers are suited to present secessionism as an old Catalan tradition that has redeemed itself as a modern, progressive, inclusive practice, and it continues to belong with the common people of the *barri* (neighborhood). For the current political movement, the *castells* action of "making a base" (*fer pinya*) has become equivalent to rallying towards the same political objective. The equivalence between building a tower and building a nation is based on a sign relationship called iconicity, or "meaning something by resembling it" (Herzfeld 1997, 58). The resemblance itself, however, is not necessarily automatic. Iconicity does not exist; it becomes, it is "called into existence" (Herzfeld 1997, 57), as are the nation-building meanings of performance at the secessionist town square, or the social media site of a politician. As pro-independence flags and banners create an ideological surround, the building action and the concept of making a base (*fer pinya*) also become infected by their political message, calling into existence a sign relationship between body and ideology. In 2017, the regional government president Carles Puigdemont fled from the country following the illegal October referendum. On the day of his departure, he posted an image of a human tower base *pinya* to say goodbye with the caption "the strength of the people". The image of a *castell* base *pinya*, with hundreds of arms and thousands of fingers reaching up and pointing from their myriad vantage towards the same imaginary center, visualized what pro-independence politics needed to achieve: to cooperate rather than compete for the same objective. The term *fer pinya* became a political neologism that envisioned a solution to a political challenge by projecting inclusiveness and cooperation.

Of these cultural performances, human towers are the most fitting for the needs and purposes of the current movement. The *sardana* dance has lost much of its popularity as it has been associated with elderly people; the young find it slow and insipid. Soccer continues to be synonymous with Barcelona and Catalonia; however, FC Barcelona is also embedded in a global framework of sports business, including controversial endorsements and a high degree of commercialization. Furthermore, due to its global fandom, Barça expresses its political positions sparingly. Fire festivals might be too explosive for a movement that aims to consciously brand itself as peaceful, diverse, and festive. *Castells* fit, among others, for temperamental reasons: they best optimize *seny* and *rauxa*, "common sense," but also a "mad impulse" and willingness to take risks. Performance requires the organizational precision of an architect, but also the "mad" ambition of a visionary. Giddens argues that risk-taking is a hallmark of modern entrepreneurship and individualization, "the mobilizing dynamic of a society bent on change, that wants to determine its own future" (2003, 24), as opposed to trusting it to the vagaries of nature, tradition, or, in this case for example, the state. Through the risks that shaky human towers at secessionist rallies take, the pro-independence movement communicates that it is bent on change.

FORÇA, EQUILIBRI, VALOR I SENY: THE MYTHICAL CONTENTS OF PERFORMANCE FOR POLITICS

Castell-building consists of mythical movements: holding, ascending, reaching the top, descending, verticality, and repetition have meanings and order cultural value systems. What our *enxanetes* (child climbers) traverse is the archetypal dramatic arc itself. *Castell*-building is suspenseful in its rising action; it reaches a cathartic climax with the child's wave, and it ends in either a reassuring dénouement or a painful fall.

The particular body technique of *castells* resonates with the Sisyphean ascent. In Camus' description, Sisyphus' endless repetition of vertical movement and physical effort bears an uncanny resemblance to human tower-building, where children are our rock:

One sees merely the whole effort of a body straining to raise the huge stone to roll it and push it up a slope a hundred times over; one sees the face screwed up, the cheek tight against the stone, the shoulder bracing the clay-covered mass, the foot wedging in, the fresh start with arms outstretched, the wholly human security of two earth-clotted hands. At the very end of his long effort measured by skyless space and time without depth, the purpose is achieved. Then Sisyphus watches the stone rush down in a few moments toward that lower world whence he will have to push it up again toward the summit. (Camus 1955, 120–121)

The verticality of movement; the glory of touching the sky; the ominous possibility of fall; the dramatic arc of ascent and descent; and the collective work of bodies that complement each other, like so many clogs in a machine, conjure up cultural narratives. *Castell*-building resonates with mythical efforts and overcoming. To hold evokes Atlas; to push weight upward and repeat is the fate of Sisyphus, and the compulsive repetition of *castell* performance creates a sensation of timeless punishment. Following Nietzsche's famous concept, Kundera (1984) too elaborated on eternal return, which alone has the weight to anchor one in their community. Weight being a major experience of tower-building, performance anchors meaning and people as opposed to the "unbearable lightness of being" (Kundera 1984). The rising action, climax, and denouement of the tower-building follow the dramatic arc unless they result in the most archetypal movement of all: the Fall. Repetition, climbing back up after a collapse, a certain futility of labor that achieves nothing after all (as castellers say, a human tower does not exist but for a second of crowning), evoke the fallen and punished heroes of mythical underworlds.

A particular myth that performance evokes for Catalans in the public sphere is that of *seny* or common sense. The four catchwords of performance are strength, courage, balance, and measure/common sense (*força, equilibri, valor i seny*). These features are immediately salient in a physical as well as a social sense. *Castell*-building requires strength, as some positions have to hold as much as 400 kilograms (about 1,000 pounds). Performers need to find an equilibrium of forces from every side to keep the tower from collapsing. Courage is necessary for climbing up 12–14 meters (40–45 feet) high, or standing in a tight base where one can hardly breathe and may be buried under dozens of bodies in case of a collapse. Measure and common sense achieve the exact planning and assemblage of a tower with the vision of an architect. In a social sense, performance communicates that the strength of a group rests in its diversity and bodily complementarity, which constitute a harmonious whole.

The mythology of common sense is what Herzfeld would call an "iconizing logic" (1997, 59) behind Catalan identity construction. *Seny* is a stereotypical national trait attributed to Catalans, whose binary opposition is *rauxa* or impulsive madness. Catalan *seny* was historically presented as a distinguishing feature in opposition to impulsive Castilians as the "mirror image of quixotism" (Hughes 1992, 25). *Seny* has been associated with Catalan national virility and work ethic (Fernàndez 2020), as part of a complex of "competitive imperial manhoods" in Spanish–Catalan relations (Miguélez-Carballeira 2017, 24). *Seny* was the singular class virtue of bourgeois conservative *gent d'ordre* and governed Catalonia's centuries-long political culture, *pactisme*, which sought consensus with the Spanish monarchy rather than confrontation (Desfor Edles 1999). *Seny* features abundantly in everyday and political life: one must drink with measure at *festes* (Noyes 2003) and fall with a cool head when a human tower collapses (Vaczi 2023).

Centrist politics frequently pointed at Catalan nationalists' abandonment of their national trait *seny* in their shift towards the *rauxa* of secessionist madness. In 2015, the leading daily *El País* praised the sober, level-headed *seny* of post-troubles Basque politics and mused over the irony that "this Catalan word" should abandon its "natural habitat", Catalonia, and settle, of all places, in the Basque Country. By implying a shift to *rauxa* and pointing out an incongruence in cultural temperament, the opinion piece essentialized and hystericized both Catalans and Basques.

Indeed, while myth may bring familiarity and a sensation of roots, it also may freeze processes into essences. Barthes takes issue with "common sense" as *the* bourgeois class virtue, due to its naturalizing, essentializing, and homogenizing effects. Common sense, he writes, is "the watchdog of petit bourgeois equations: it blocks any dialectical outlets, defines a homogenous world in which we are home, sheltered from the disturbances and the leaks of 'dreams'" (Barthes 2012, 94). Barthes considered common sense an "obscurantist myth" that claimed that everything noble had to be governed by it; it was an "aggressive form" of bourgeois class consciousness (2012, 30, 112). Common sense, Barthes argued, is the ultimate evidence of the upper classes' "impotence to imagine the Other" and face alterity (2012, 40).

But there is a sense in which human towers put a dent in the reign of *seny* as a naturalized Catalan trait. The planning and execution of a human tower needs precision, calculation, and a cool head that controls panic. However, many performers will point out the relevance of *rauxa*: the very fact of engaging in this activity, and saving a difficult tower presumes a certain madness. Barthes captured the same ambiguity through "form" and "leap" for cycling the Tour de France:

> The strength the racer possesses in order to confront Earth-as-Man may assume two aspects: *form*, a state more than an impulse, a privileged equilibrium between quality of muscles, acuity of intelligence, and force of character; and *leap*, a veritable electric influx which erratically possesses certain racers beloved of the gods and causes them to accomplish superhuman

feats. Leap implies a supernatural order in which man succeeds insofar as a god assists him. (2012, 126)

Therefore, below and beyond its mythical catchwords and movements, *castells* reveal an ambiguous ethics between *seny* and *rauxa* for building projects, including national construction.

THE ALLEGORICAL WAY OF SEEING PERFORMANCE

The national cause, Žižek writes, "is ultimately nothing but the way subjects of a given ethnic community organize their enjoyment through national myths" (1993, 202). The mythologizing tendencies of nationalist movements are not new: 19th-century nationalisms used folklore for their objectives in their quest for eternal rootedness and identity (Smith 2009). But a generation's quest for myth may be a symptom not of revolutionary transformation, but of crisis. In the words of Marx:

> And just when they see themselves revolutionizing themselves and things, in creating something that has never existed, precisely in such periods of revolutionary crisis they anxiously conjure up in the spirits of the past to their service and borrow from them names, battle cries and costumes in order to present the new scene of world history in this time-honoured disguise and this borrowed language. (1969, 398)

At their best, national myths are a source of enjoyment, as Žižek describes; at their worst, they collude in the worst of historical catastrophes, as the 20th century showed us. Myths are appealing because they stabilize history and anchor the subject – but they also freeze processes into signs and habits into essence.

Benjamin believed that it was possible to condense complex conceptual understanding into imagery. In the myriad particular moments, metal pieces and rivets of the Eiffel Tower, he saw the construction of history and capitalist modernity. For Barthes, the Eiffel Tower attracted meaning as a pure signifier and nourished the fantasies of citizens and visitors. Besides its mythical contents of national and economic greatness, the heights of the Eiffel Tower had a less acknowledged feature, he argued: it provided a new perspective, that of panoramic vision. Altitude, and the ability of the bird's eye view to decipher, added the "incomparable power of intellection" to perception (1979, 9). If Barcelona was presented as an architectural sign, it would be through its Sagrada Família towers, known for their innovative modernist style and incompletion. Antony Gaudí's famous towers have been under construction since 1883, and their partial status has become an allegory for Catalan modernity itself: fragmentariness and transiency, which stand for a progressive, ever-growing, open society.

But how to see the flesh and blood counterparts of these towers as a total event, a story? In a volume that became transformative for anthropology, James Clifford promoted the "allegorical way of seeing" as a quest for "the *narrative* character of cultural representations" (Clifford 1986, 100). In Coleridge's definition, allegory happens when "the difference is everywhere presented to the eye or imagination, while the likeness is suggested to the mind" (in Clifford 1986, 101). The first-time observer of human tower-building feels that something is happening here, but does not know what it is. The performance strikes us as different and yet familiar. Human towers are not traditional buildings, in the sense that they come in and out of being, and sometimes they collapse. It is only apparent that they stand for completion, stability, and constancy. As performance, they constantly move and become, which is yet another layer of meaning for a movement that has targeted radical transformation.

It is only apparent that a human tower stands; crowning is but one fleeting moment of many movements that never halt but ascend and descend, wobble and shake constantly. One sure sign of imminent collapse is if movement stops for whatever reason, which might be *castells*' greatest lesson for life and politics. What redeems human towers from becoming an essentializing, mythologizing image is precisely their constant movement and the possibility of collapse. The *sardana* dance, various authors remark, was effectively "frozen" into a national icon; its "stylistic ossification" (Brandes 1990, 28) prevented its growth and affected its demise (Martí i Pérez 1994; Weig 2015). However, *castells*' ruins, the constant threat of ruins, and the rebuilding on top of them, turn performance into an allegory with moral content. Ruins for Benjamin were emblematic of the fragility and destructiveness of capitalism and warned of the "transitory splendor" of civilization and the myth of progress (in Buck-Morss 1989, 161). Performance, therefore, flashes history not only in its triumphs but also in its precarities and ruins. As an allegory, performance may banish the illusion of given orders; the painful collapses intimate the transitory splendor of performance and politics.

CONCLUSIONS: PUBLIC SOCIALITY AND THE GLOBAL PANDEMIC

The world of human towers reminds us of the body's special truth: personal presence. The sensory intensity of *castells*, their touch, and body proximity enabled a more immediate being in the world. Against the sweeping technological tendency of mediatization, distancing, and alienation on every turn, performance redeemed and rearticulated touch and body for four glaring minutes of tower-building. Touch was warmth, support, cooperation, and social thriving. With Covid-19, however, it became a source of sickness and death.

After a spring of lockdown and a temporary summer release in 2020, the fall contagion numbers of the second wave spiked again. Most walks of life had to turn virtual and find their safe, socially distanced versions, and we learned that indeed even more could be done virtually than we had previously thought. There, for a while, *colles* attempted measures like wearing masks while performing; doing only one-base (*net*) towers to reduce the number of people involved; performing before no audience on the *plaça*; washing hands and feet after each tower; frequent testing. Human tower teams, magazines, researchers, and the *colles'* governing body, Coordinadora, constantly exchanged ideas about how to keep performing. But they always returned to the same conclusion: there is no virtual substitute for touch and presence. The global pandemic made the body-centrism of performance and of public sociality even more salient.

What, it was frequently asked, would be the fate of public sociality and *cultura popular* after Covid-19? In the thick of lockdowns, the world was yearning for that simple, taken-for-granted ability to show up and be present. For some time post-pandemic, people will surely revel in it. But in its most cynical way, Covid-19 taught us too well how to function remotely and live in isolation. When I first made a base with the Castellers de Barcelona in 2014, I saw *castells* as a quixotic effort that, among other things, resists new tendencies towards alienation and social withdrawal. Post-pandemic, that effort will appear even more relevant, as *colles* will have to work harder for that most paradigmatic political act: bodies showing up on the *plaça*.

2

The Ritual Making of Central Catalonia 1: National Identity and the Hanging of the Donkey

ALESSANDRO TESTA

Preliminary Note

'The Ritual Making of Central Catalonia' is a two-part essay, subdivided into two independent chapters, Chapter 2: 'National Identity and the Hanging of the Donkey', and Chapter 3: '*Comparses* and the Dynamics of Inclusive Nationalism'. They are very closely related. The division has been made for editorial reasons. I strongly recommend reading them both as one sole study.

INTRODUCTION: SOLSONA AND THE SOLSONÈS

The town of Solsona (population 9,000) lies at the core of its *comarca*,[1] Solsonès (population 13,000), which in turns lies at the geographical core of Catalunya. If, on the one hand, the *comarca* is located on the margin of the historical region of '*Catalunya Vella*' ('Old Catalonia'), on the other the general feeling in the area is that of being part of '*Catalunya Profunda*' ('Deep Catalonia'). For example, the village of Pinós, in Solsonès, some 25 kilometres (16 miles) from Solsona, is considered the geographical navel of Catalonia and

---

[1] A comarca is a county or province in the Spanish and Catalan administrative division.

is proudly thought of as that by many locals. Pinós is also, as is stated on its website, 'a remarkable geographical reference of the most profound and traditional Catalonia' ('*un referent geogràfic remarcable de la Catalunya més profunda i tradicional*': Turisme Solsonès 2019).

This geographical centrality and its rurality are widely translated by both the locals and the distant urban dwellers into symbolic centrality, its perceived cultural representativity associated with genuine rustic life. Catalonia is a country particularly proud of its economic and historical connection with '*la terra*' (the 'earth', 'land', 'soil')[2] and of its capacity to keep culinary and folkloric traditions alive. While Barcelona is usually described as populated by 'heterogeneous and hybrid identities' (Dowling 2018, 76), central Catalonia in general is widely associated by its own inhabitants and by other Catalans with tropes of authenticity, typicity, traditionality, and greater cultural homogeneity:[3] the veritable cradle of Catalan nation and identity (Llobera 1997).[4] Hence, it comes as no surprise that the *comarca* of Solsonès is commonly considered

---

[2] The economy of the Solsonès is still driven by agricultural activities, as it has always been (Aldomà i Buixadé and Pujadas i Rúbies 1987), with industry and the tertiary sector having an ancillary role and being mostly concentrated in the main town, Solsona. 'Terra' is also a political metonymy for Catalonia, especially among leftist Catalanists, who often greet one another with the exclamation '*Visca la Terra!*' ('Long live the Land!'). An important evocation of *la terra* is also in the Catalan national anthem ('Els Segadors', 'The Reapers'), which celebrates both the proud character and the agricultural roots of the nation, and whose chorus goes, '*Bon cop de falç, defensors de la terra!*' ('Hit with your sickle, defenders of the land!').

[3] According to Andrew Dowling, after Franco's death 'three broad spaces existed: an interior of countryside and small towns where the Catalan language retained overwhelming presence and dominance [this is the case of Solsona and the Solsonès]. [...] In this sector of society, regional and local identification remained strongly rooted even during Francoism. A second zone is found in a wider industrial core from greater Barcelona to Tarragona where vast international migration of Spanish speakers occurred. In this area, the primary means of communication was Spanish. [...] The final zone within Catalonia comprised around a third of the city of Barcelona, where mostly middle-class identification with the Catalan language remained' (2018, 25).

[4] The symbolic geographies of Catalonia are discussed, from an anthropological perspective, in Collett 2012; Noyes 2006; Delgado et al this book. A convincing political history of the city of Solsona and its comarca is in A.a.V.v. 1994.

as one of the true bastions, together with the nearby towns of Cardona and Berga,[5] of *catalanisme* and *independentisme*.[6]

Solsona is a charming town characterised by a walled historical centre of medieval origins and structure, and a rank of smallish, outer districts encircling it. In spite of its central position, Solsona has been historically difficult to reach and poorly served by the regional transport networks (Llorens i Solé 1987, 399), as I have myself unpleasantly experienced many a time.[7] No wonder that the town can be considered as genuinely *provincial* in the common sense of the word as well as in the sense theorised by Dorothy Noyes (Noyes 2003, 9–12 and *passim*).[8] As such, it features in the typically Catalonian cultural, economic, and political interplay between the small settlements in the inner,

---

5   The towns of Solsona and Berga resemble each other in many respects (geographically, historically, socially, and economically), whence a certain rivalry between the two. Cardona is smaller, but it is also associated with a strong Catalanist identity, for its castle was the very last one to capitulate towards the end of the War of the Spanish Succession, hence becoming a symbol of the resistance for the (mostly Catalan) supporters of the Archduke Carles against the (mostly Spanish) defenders of Philip of Anjou. The territorial triangle between Berga, Solsona, and Cardona is considered the very heart of Catalonia.

6   *Catalanisme* ('Catalanism') is a form of strong attachment, appreciation, and sense of protection towards Catalan culture and all things Catalan, and can exist in purely attitudinal, poetical, or aesthetic variants as well as be shaped as a more or less structured and coherent form of regionalism or nationalism: 'Catalanism under the conditions of the Franco regime was a movement concerned with the protection and survival of a threatened cultural identity. […] Catalanism and nationalism are not interchangeable terms. Catalanism has been protean. Its extension has provided the key glue to Catalan political culture' (Dowling 2018, 60). Whereas *independentisme* ('independentism') is an eminently political movement (or political characterisation within different political movements and parties) that seeks secession from Spain and the transformation of Catalonia into an independent nation-state. The former can exist without the latter, but the latter cannot exist without the former.

7   I have been undertaking research on Catalonia in general and Solsona in particular since 2015; extensive and intensive ethnographic fieldwork in Solsona and in the immediately surrounding areas of central Catalonia was carried out over different stays, for a timespan of about 12 months in total, between September 2016 and February 2021. The first insights on my then ongoing research were published immediately after the momentous referendum of 2017 (Testa 2017a); more recent papers have focused on issues of heritage and religiosity in central Catalonia (Testa 2019, 2020b, 2021).

8   Caught between other bigger and better-known central Catalans (Berguedans, Manresans, Vigatans) and the imposing prominence of Barcelona, the Solsonians

rural areas (*pagès*), and the cities (quintessentially Barcelona). All regions and countries have centres, peripheries, towns, villages, and hamlets; but not all nations show such a hiatus between the central role that rurality plays in the historical and mythical past of the nation and the futuristic ambitions and industrial nature of the capital city. Nor do all regions exhibit such an imbalance between a huge metropolis (Barcelona is the fifth most populous urban area in the European Union) and the mostly depopulated hinterland at the core of a relatively small territory that makes this discrepancy even more striking.

EL CARNAVAL: BRIEF HISTORY AND DESCRIPTION

Solsona hosts a famous carnival celebration, one of the biggest and most popular in Catalonia. *El Carnaval* lasts for seven days and, until 2020 (in 2021 it was not celebrated due to the Covid-19 pandemic), it had been celebrated uninterruptedly since Franco's death (Vilaseca and Trilla 2011), becoming the veritable local cultural thermometer, one might say, of the process of transition from Francoism to a regime of liberal democracy first, and then from the latter to independentist ambitions.

Rooted in the carnival celebrations common in the distant past and scarcely documented before the Spanish Civil War (Bellmunt i Figueras 1994), the *Carnaval* was prohibited during the dictatorship of the Caudillo, during which, instead, the older *Festa Major* (Major Festival) flourished (Vilaseca and Trilla 2007). Just like in other Catalan centres, the general historical pattern at work at the time was the following: 'Traditional religious festivals were inflected with the heavy ceremonial of national-Catholicism [...]. Carnival was banned outright or made unrecognisable' (Noyes 2011, 217).

From 1971 onwards, it was re-enacted and given a new life, gradually emerging as a transgressive reaction to the austerity of Franco's national-Catholicism, but especially as a veritable symbol of political and cultural liberation and a free expression of Catalan (and Catalanist) sentiments – much in the same vein as the more famous festival of the *Patum*, a Corpus Christi celebration, in the nearby city of Berga. This, again, follows the clear pan-Catalan pattern already discussed in the Introduction to this book. Not only did Catalan culture remain active, albeit mostly hidden, during the central period of Francoism, re-emerging slowly in the late years of dictatorship and blooming after the death of the Caudillo; it was actually strengthened by the repression (Dowling 2018, 6–29; Keown 2011a, 2011b; Llobera 2004, 58–110; Sánces-Biosca 2007). As a token of early recognition and as yet another proof

---

live in a condition of perennial rumination over their geographical centrality but socio-economic periphery.

of the failure of cultural repression during Francoism, in 1979 Solsona's carnival was declared by the Spanish government, despite its then emerging (and today solid) anti-Spanish stance, '*Fiesta de Interés Turístico Nacional*' ('Festival of National Touristic Interest'), an official denomination that was copied a few years later by the Catalan Parliament, the Generalitat.

Initially a rather loosely organised event, *el Carnaval* gained traction and structure between the end of the 1970s and the mid-1980s, which was the period during which both the Generalitat and civic sectors of Catalan society established a coherent set of cultural policies aimed at restoring and ref(o)unding Catalan language and culture throughout the *comunitat autònoma* (Bel 2013; Costa Solé and Folch Monclús 2014; Crameri 2008; Delgado et al this book; Kammerer 2014; Noyes 2003, 2011; Roigé 2016, Villarroy 2012, Wittlin 1994).[9] By the end of the 1980s, the festival had already claimed primacy among all other events in the comarca, hegemonising the public sphere during its taking place, and gaining prominent visibility in the media.

In the last three decades, the festival has grown exponentially, becoming a mass event participated in by most of the townsfolk and visitors from surrounding areas and *comarques*, but also from Barcelona, other Catalan cities, and even Andorra. Since the 2010s, with the growing independentist mobilisation, *el Carnaval* has, in concert with what has been happening in the rest of the region, assumed an even more explicit political verve, becoming, along with the *Patum* of Berga, one of the most Catalanist festivals in central Catalonia. Presently, it is not only the main public event of the entire *comarca*, but also one of its main identity ma(r)kers, a piece of local heritage, a tourist attraction and, therefore, also a considerable source of income for many.

EL CARNAVAL: FIRST ETHNOGRAPHIC INSIGHTS AND ANTHROPOLOGICAL ANALYSES

'*Bon Carnaval!*' ('Happy Carnival!'), said the lady with an enigmatic smile at the *Botiga del Carnaval*, while handing me the receipt for my purchase. At the time (end of February 2017), I had been living in Solsona for several months

---

9 Costa Solé and Folch Monclús 2014 demonstrates how these cultural policies and politics of culture influenced, and were in turn influenced by, the juridical framework. Particularly significant is the case of the Decret 413/1983, updated ten years later as Llei 2/1993 and 9/1993, two laws aimed at the promotion of 'popular and traditional culture and cultural associationism' ('*foment de la cultura popular i tradicional i de l'associacionisme cultural*', Costa Solé and Folch Monclús 2014, 59). These decrees and laws establish, between the 1980s and 1990s, the entire juridical and administrative architecture concerning what would later, from 2003 onwards, come to be known as Patrimoni Cultural Immaterial (ICH).

already, but I could not yet know that this cheerful, apparently innocent wish would mark my entry into one of the wildest sorts of pandemonium I have ever had the fortune to witness and participate in.

Lasting for seven days, *el Carnaval* takes place mostly, but not exclusively, in the historical centre, whose streets and squares are constantly and noisily packed with people throughout the week. The festival bears the greatest significance for the local community and is participated in on a massive scale, with extreme enthusiasm and even rapture, crossing transversally economic classes, political affiliations, genders, and ages. The youth, however, are particularly, vividly, and more loudly and visibly involved in the performances. The festival reaches a climax during the crucial '*cap de setmana*', from Friday to Shrove Sunday, and especially over the Friday and Saturday nights and the following early mornings, when to a casual observer it might indeed seem that the entire town collapses into a nightmarish gush of drunkenness, frenzy, dances, never-ending noise, fatigue, and sleep deprivation.

Nevertheless, in spite of the apparent chaos, the festival is actually centred on relatively few ritualised or ritualesque acts, which are well-circumscribed public performances within the ritual week. Some of the most important of these ritualoid acts (locally called '*actes*'), among others that could be mentioned, but which will not for reasons of brevity and salience, are: '*el Sermó*' ('the Sermon'), during which one of the carnival characters addresses the local and national politicians sarcastically and critically; '*el Nomenament del Mataruc d'Honor*' ('the Appointment of the Honourable Donkey-Slaughter'), the appointment of a figure chosen from among the most prominent Catalan (and possibly Catalanist) intellectuals and artists; '*la Pujada dels Gegants*' ('the Arrival of the Giants'), when the local giants, which are very popular and common figures in Catalan folklore (Grau i Martí 1996; Kammerer 2014; Noyes 2003),[10] parade through the medieval district; '*la Penjada i la Despenjada del Ruc*' ('the Hanging and the "Unhanging" of the Donkey [or rather a simulacrum of a jackass]'), the veritable climax of the entire Carnival, during which a mass of local people gather to sing the Carnival anthem; and finally, '*la Processó i la Cremada del Carnestoltes*' ('the Funeral Procession and the Burning of Carnival at the Stake'), the act that closes the festivity.

Other, less important *actes* involving giants and fireworks also deserve to be mentioned. The '*correfocs*' (an untranslatable word etymologically associated with fire and the act of running), for instance, are very popular: on the last day of Carnival, devilish figures and a fire-spitting giant – the '*Colla de Diables La Xera*' with their '*Fènix*' – turn the main square and the surrounding

---

[10] Home of two respected giant-makers famed for their craft throughout Catalonia, the culture of *Gegants* is very deep-rooted in Solsona, which prides itself on being 'the Catalan town with more giants per square meter' (Solsona Turisme 2018).

streets into a mayhem of fire. This *acte* strongly evokes the traditional '*fuets*', '*pleins*', and other '*coses de foc*' of Berga's *Patum*, a similarity verging on plagiarism – unspeakable in Solsona, of course, given the tacit and sometimes open rivalry between the two cities. But then again, the history of the astonishingly rich folklore in Catalonia demonstrates that 'economic and political rivalry between local communities has been an important spur to collective creativity' (Noyes 2006, 37).

Without a shadow of a doubt, *el Carnaval* is the single most important annual public event in Solsona and its entire *comarca*. A sizeable portion of its civic life and economic activities gravitates around it. Highlighted yearly by the local and regional press, but also by periodicals and grey literature, it is constantly boosted before, during, and after its occurrence by documentaries, films, songs, merchandise, preliminary events, school activities, promotional material, and much more.

El Carnaval is, truly, a 'total social fact', as Marcel Mauss famously called this type of event (Mauss 1923–1924). As such, it is also, in accordance with the generally accepted historical-anthropological wisdom on festivals and public rituals, a highly codified occurrence.[11] Along evident Maussian (but also Malinowskian) lines, Vittorio Lanternari wrote that 'the communal banquet, the waste of food, the binging [...] and carnival: all of these form the context of social practices which have effects that are at the same time socialising and cathartic' (Lanternari 1981, 138). This seems to be the case especially with 'costly rituals', as cognitivists and behaviouralists would call them, i.e., those ritual events involving exaggerated/extreme behaviour and/or significant material waste – and Carnival in the history of Europe in general and in Solsona in particular falls into both categories.

Requiring not only both investment and waste, but also a noticeable collective effort of coordination and organisation, the festival mobilises different social forces and segments of the local civic society, just like many other public rituals, gatherings, and collective forms of engagement for which Catalonia is famous, like the human towers ('*els Castells*'), the colossal human chains stretching for hundreds of kilometres, or the massive street gatherings of millions for the famous *Diades* of 11 September (Johannes 2019; Kammerer 2014; Little 2019; Vaczi 2016). In this sense, *el Carnaval* is yet more robust proof of

---

[11] 'Festive events are characterised by ritual or highly formalised performances that are usually based on either a hierarchical organisation of the event or traditional features. The homeostatic calendar dimension of festivities is linked to the ritual one, and is assured by means of reiteration, tradition, and hierarchy. [...] They are also characterised by exuberance, exteriorisation of sentiments, the expenditure or waste of goods or other anti-economic attitudes, amusement, grotesque or excessive acts, or the systematic inversion of social norms' (Testa 2014a, 45–46).

how deeply and mightily *incorporated* Catalan associational culture is in the social fabric of rural and urban groups alike.

The importance of Catalan *associacionisme* could never be stressed enough, especially as a force in the catalysation, dynamisation, and structuring of collective actions for folkloric and ritual purposes (Testa 2020b; Johannes 2019; Noyes 2003), recreational and sportive aims (Kammerer 2014; Vaczi 2016), as a modality of genuine political action (Dowling 2018; Clua i Fainé 2014; Vaczi 2016), and finally as a form of interplay and linking between these different spheres. Solsona and its festival are no exception to this pattern.

The historically determined Catalan penchant for *associacionisme* expresses itself in the festive dimension of the Carnival in two distinctive ways, one institutional, the other one (apparently) informal. These are: 1) the '*Associació de Festes del Carnaval de Solsona*', a juridical entity entitled to negotiate officially with the local bodies of government, and especially with the municipality (the '*Ajuntament*'), and endowed with the right and power, which are regularly exercised, to demand public subventions for its activities, and 2) the informal local groups of '*colles*' and '*comparses*', two types of network-based socialising groups that function within, during, and for the festival – and which in our case show both typically Catalan and characteristically Solsonian features. We shall return to these declensions of *associacionisme* in the second part of this study.

THE TOWN HYMN AND THE HANGING OF THE DONKEY

The Saturday of *el Carnaval* is by far the most important and heavily participated-in day of the week. A carefully planned and coordinated, but nevertheless apparently chaotic, ritualesque progression of *actes* unfolds during the afternoon and the evening, filling the streets of the historical centre: most of the crowds of thousands are separated into *colles* and *comparses* by their colourful uniforms ('*bates*'). Some of the oldest and most respected *colles* take charge of and animate the dangerously heavy giants. They are called '*colles gengateres*', and it is they who move the giants in procession, along with the playing '*banda*', from the Passeig de Sant Antoni Maria Claret down the Portal del Castell, then all the way through the long and narrow Carrer del Castell and down to the Plaça Major. This is '*la Pujada dels Gegants*' ('the Arrival of the Giants'), followed by the equally beloved and passionately participated in '*el Nomenament del Mata-ruc d'Honor*' ('the Appointment of the Honourable Donkey-Slaughter'). Immediately afterwards, another traditional *acte*, '*la Bramada*' ('the Bray'), is performed. Later on, for the joy of children, young people, and adults alike, the puppet of the Donkey is brought from the square to the belltower, where it is solemnly hanged amid the screams and chants of a thousand voices: it is '*la Penjada del Ruc*', the apex of the Carnival, during which the Carnival hymn (and the *de facto* town hymn) is sung:

A Solsona bona gent,	*In Solsona there are good people,*
a Solsona, bona gent,	*In Solsona there are good people,*
si no haguessin mort el ruc,	*If they didn't kill the donkey,*
si no haguessin mort el ruc.	*If they didn't kill the donkey.*
Fa molts anys a dalt del campanar,	*A long time ago from the belltower,*
aquí a Solsona, aquí a Solsona	*Here in Solsona, here in Solsona,*
fa molts anys a dalt del campanar	*A long time ago from the belltower,*
aquí a Solsona el vam penjar, el vam penjar!	*Here in Solsona we hanged it!*
Adéu-siau, ens en anem	*Farewell, we part ways*
i no sabem quan tornarem.	*And we know not when we shall return.*
Som governats per quatre rucs mal educats, mal educats!	*We are governed by four ill-mannered donkeys, four ill-mannered donkeys!*

The song is an interesting folk anthem: a declaration of attachment to the city and its good people ('*a Solsona, bona gent*'), who, however, are far from being perfect, since they, just like anybody else, also have their sins to confess ('*si no haguessin mort el ruc*').

Being a relatively recent 'invented tradition', thus not deeply rooted in the past, the Carnival of Solsona does not sit on a strictly normative and ossifying conception of tradition. It does not, therefore, express the rather widespread popular idea of immutability and immanence of the traditional ritual facts (Testa 2020b), being by contrast rather creative and partly open to changes. In spite of this, continuity is emphasised in the song: '*fa molts anys* [...] *aquí a Solsona*'. Even though the act itself was introduced in the year 1985, and the song even later, evoking the time depth of the tradition is paramount to condensing symbolic significance. After all, a tradition remains a tradition, no matter how young.

In European rural and provincial contexts, parochialism is as inevitable as, at times, the need to emigrate to find a better fortune elsewhere. But those who leave might sometimes get caught by the need or will to return, whether they actually do return or not. The will or need to return (albeit perhaps only briefly in order to participate in the carnival celebrations) makes it possible for the migrating *Solsonins* (the Catalan name for people from Solsona) to remain part of the social body of the town, ideally continuing to embody 'fidelity to the community and its traditions beyond any particular political or religious

3 and 4. Two crucial *acte*s of the Carnival: The Dance of the Giants and the Hanging of the Donkey. Source: Lluís Closa (image 3), Jordi Soldevila i Corominas (image 4).

loyalty and any cultural seduction of the outside world' (Noyes 2003, 175). Fidelity means that, although they do not know when, in the end, they shall return: '*Adéu-siau, ens en anem, i no sabem quan tornarem*'.

Just like the carnival Sermon and plenty of other *actes* and features of the Carnival, the underlying social and political critique is manifest in the hymn, too: '*Som governats per quatre rucs mal educats*'. This comes as no surprise, corruption and misrule being widely considered physiological evils of both the Catalan and Spanish polity. And, in fact, it has always been impossible to politically co-opt the Carnival: if *catalanisme* in Solsona is unquestionable, and *independentisme* strong,[12] all the remaining segments of the political and ideological spectrum are very much put into question during the festival.

The donkey, which is a sort of totemic animal of all of Catalonia (Brandes 2009, 785–786), and the animal of '*la terra*' par excellence, is not the only emblem of the Carnival: the Crazy Giant ('*el Gegant Boig*') plays a prominent symbolic role, too. The craziness of the giant, which also represents the praxiological and existential mode of the carnival week, along with the proverbially slow judgment of the jackass, represent respectively the negation of two of the most quintessential Catalan virtues: '*respecte*' ('respect', 'respectability', 'deference') and '*seny*' ('judiciousness', 'good sense', 'moderation', and 'pragmatism' – as Vaczi has written, a veritable 'Catalonian Volkgeist'; Vaczi 2016, 361). The temporary negation of *seny* is nothing but a ritual ruse to actually reaffirm it after the carnival period is closed. And even at the peak of the outmost carnival exaltation of lack of *respecte* and *seny*, the last words of the hymn sung while the donkey is being hanged, it is precisely *respecte* and *seny* that are exalted, through the condemnation of the ill-mannered asses that govern us – and, in a democracy, also represent/reflect us.

If *el Carnaval* is both the distorted representation and, to a certain extent, as we shall see, one of the matrices of Solsona's social body, then the climax of the collective action to which the entire community is summoned during those few days, the hymn, is the climax within the climax. The '*Penjada*' and the anthem are, to again use Noyes' terminology about the *Patum* for our own purposes, the 'orgasmic' moment of communion with/in the community, the 'oceaning' feeling of merging with the mass of fellow participants in the collective ritual, or else, in Victor Turner's terms, the instant wherein 'communitas' (Turner 1977) is created (and, inevitably, immediately dissolved). It is a

---

[12] The scholarly literature on Catalan independence has boomed since the 2010s and, as the number of scholars interested in the subject has been growing constantly in this time span, it has become practically impossible to digest it in its entirety. Among the latest studies, I have benefitted much from reading Andrew Dowling's *The Rise of Catalan Independence* (2018); but the issue is, of course, raised and discussed in many other studies hereby cited.

5. Carnival poster featuring *el Gegant Boig* as a veritable symbol of Catalan *independentisme*. Source: Author.

very special declension of 'carnivalesque communitas' (Testa 2020a, 150–167), like elsewhere in Europe. Even the ethnographic gaze and thick description are at odds with transmitting in words the electric atmosphere and the paroxysm, a veritable social telluric discharge one can witness and, if integrated in the local community, participate in, over those crucial minutes at the peak of the hanging ceremony.

THE POLITICS OF PUBLIC RITUALITY IN SOLSONA AS (CENTRAL) CATALONIA

The politics of Solsona's main public ritual is expressed through two closely intertwined, but also clearly distinguished, dimensions: critique and Catalanism.

As already hinted, most of the 'ritualesque' (Santino 2009) *actes* of the Carnaval express in a rather vivid manner political and social critique (this character of Solsona's Carnival is also stressed elsewhere: Vilaseca and Trilla

2011: *passim*). This comes as no surprise, for the entanglements and intersections between public rituality, collective identity, nationalism, and politics in Catalonia is a very well-known and researched fact. Likewise well-known is the astonishing richness of Catalan folklore and festive traditions and the equally astonishing level of popular involvement and participation in those, something that I have, in all honesty, hardly ever witnessed in any other European land.

For sure, Catalonia's political history during Francoism, then over the Transition, and up to nowadays is complex and tormented. Certain wounds are still open: the pain they caused and cause is still recalled in squares and bars and whispered in families. Bitterness and resentment slither through the veins of the social body in Solsona, just like in many other Catalan cities. *El Carnaval* is a means to recompose a social body otherwise disarticulated by conflicting social memories, diverging political views, migration patterns, unfulfilled promises of the Transition, and other messy stuff late modernity has brought about, in a region where Catalan independentism, or *independentisme*, is no less divisive than elsewhere, but in which the consensus on it is also much greater than elsewhere. The local critical mass of independentists and Catalanists as a whole determine that most of the socially visible and active people in the public arena are ostensibly Catalanist (both within and without the Carnival), with few exceptions. It is hard to say how much this is due to the more recent resurgence of activist forms of Catalanism and greater proclivity towards independentism, which had both been brewing since the 1990s and early 2000s, and erupted during the 2010s – as has been related in detail in the Introduction. Most of my informants would swear that they have been Catalanist and/or independentists '*tota la vida*'; and the polls of legitimate elections as well as illegal referenda in the past three decades seem to confirm this. And yet the explicit or implicit critique exercised through the festival also has a conciliatory power: one might be for or against *independència*, but the status quo, corruption, misrule, and Madrid's greed remain common enemies for everybody regardless of their political affiliation.

At times, local or even national politicians are scapegoated, especially during some of the most politically charged moments of the Carnival, such as the speech of the Honourable Donkey-Slaughter and the Sermon. Frequent rants *contra personam* have over the years been met with mixed feelings.[13] In an interview held in 2017, the *alcalde* (mayor) of Solsona, member of the

---

13　The 'Sermons' are particularly vivid pieces of popular epic. They are rarely improvised and most commonly read aloud in the square in front of the crowd. Social and political critique always abounds in them – apart from attending two of them personally in 2017 and 2019, I have consulted several of the older ones, since those written and recited between 1971 and 1995 have been published: A.a.V.v. 1995.

Esquerra Republicana de Catalunya (the Republican Left of Catalonia – a historically independentist party), confessed that indeed the Carnival was a 'difficult' period for the local politicians. He told me about an episode that taught him a lesson he would never forget: in 2007, when he was still *regidor* (a member of the municipal council) and not yet mayor, he went to attend *el Sermó*. Towards the end of the speech (which is normally read and also kept in the local archive), he himself was made the object of overt criticism and scorn. While this was being exercised *contra* him, hundreds of locals turned towards him and stared and snickered at him. He felt so excruciatingly humiliated he decided never to attend another Sermon again. Now (2017), he continued during the interview, he enjoys the Carnival as a private citizen with his children and friends: he even wears the '*bata*' ('uniform') of his *comparsa*; however, he keeps his public role out of the Carnival and never attends any *acte* in his capacity of mayor; and, above all, no more Sermons.

Following a well-established pattern in European festive culture, *el Carnaval* sanctions misrule and voices the popular discontent with the status quo, the powers that be, and anything else that deserves stigmatisation and/or derision. As I was told more than once, '*durant el Carnaval les coses surten*' ('during the Carnival things get to be known'). For this reason, too, the mayor admitted that over the years the council has sometimes delayed the undertaking of a certain initiative, or a vote on a certain resolution, for fear of running up against the carnivalesque sanction. Through the ritualised social critique and the convergence of collective concern-voicing, Solsona's Carnival has not only the power to affect the perception of certain social issues, but even to influence the decision-making processes of the institutional government. The politics of the public ritual are such not only in the anthropological meaning of the word 'politics', but also literally: it is the folklorisation of politics and the politicisation of folklore (Testa 2014b).

As for the Catalanist dimension of the festival, it is a well-perceived and partly contested (though also rather evident) feature that needs further analysis – here I distinguish the Catalanist (i.e., regionalist/nationalist) trait of *el Carnaval* from its 'Catalanness' (i.e., regional/national characterisation and representativity), which will be discussed in the following section.

When, during our interview in 2017, I asked the mayor about the evident Catalanist stance of the festival, he, an attentive observer of the Carnival for many years, remarked that the Carnival is not Catalanist: the context is. After all, he continued, the majority of the population of Solsona is strongly Catalanist and mostly independentist. Hence, the fact that Carnival assumes Catalanist traits is, in his words, '*inevitable*'. And inevitable it seems to have been in the wider context, too: in central Catalonia or Calunya profunda at large. In recent years, festivals in the region have been dotted with episodes of manifest and defiant public displays of *catalanisme*: in 2014, the iconic '*Àliga*', the giant eagle of the *Patum* of Berga, wore the *Estelada*, the Catalan independentist flag. Subsequently, emulations occurred in many other localities, and the *gegants* began to be seen wrapped in *Esteladas* throughout the territory. The following year, Solsona's Carnival ended up in the pages of the entire Spanish press for staging and broadcasting the mockery of the Spanish army: that time, the common ridiculing of Spanish figures and symbols during the festival went farther than usual. The tribunal of Lleida opened a case and investigated. All these episodes, among the dozens that could be mentioned, also received media (and sometimes even judiciary) attention for their explicit independentist and/or anti-Spanish connotations.

As can be imagined, these already explicit connotations erupted even more vehemently during the Carnival of 2018, the first after *el Referèndum* and the failed attempt of Catalonia at becoming an independent state in October 2017. As my friend and informant Alba wrote to me in a WhatsApp message during those agitated days, '*realment hi haurà un abans i un després en la història de Catalunya. Res tornarà a ser igual*' ('there will truly be a "before" and an "after" in the history of Catalonia. Nothing will be the same as before'). Carnival in 2018 was indeed utterly hegemonised by references to the referendum, to Spanish political parties, politicians, judges, and other public figures, but also to Article 155 of the Spanish Constitution, which was activated shortly after the ephemeral declaration of independence and which abrogated the autonomy of Catalonia. Oftentimes, references were also made to the '*presos politics*', the political and public figures who were incarcerated and were then attending trial.

The escalation of the visual war (which has also been fought on the internet and through other media) of support for the referendum, considered as the final and inevitable step in the *procés independentista català*, was tangible and manifest everywhere, which also resulted, in Solsona, in the temporary silencing of opposing voices. This escalation had another visible side-effect in the public sphere: it also accelerated the already ongoing process of replacement of the historical national Catalan flag, *la Senyera*, considered more politically neutral, with the overtly Catalanist *Estelada* (Clua i Fainé 2014; Dowling 2018; Kammerer 2014) – as I have documented with photos, never before were there as many *Estelades* hanging from windows and balconies; entire palaces in Solsona's historical centre were covered with them.

In June 2018, I also participated in the *Patum* in Berga, and the same process was very visible there as well, but also in Girona. Days before the Carnival in Solsona in 2019, an emblematic episode of sabotage occurred that clearly showed the heightened level of polarisation in Catalan society in that period: for weeks the bridge that connects the town to the main provincial road and leads to the main portal had been covered with *llaçets grogs* ('yellow ribbons'), a popular sign of support for the political prisoners and, by metonymy, one of

6. Members of a *comparsa* hold a banner referring to 'Law 155', which was activated after the 2017 referendum, abrogating Catalonia's autonomy for several months. The law is metaphorically 'hanged' from the belltower, whence the carnival donkey is also hanged. Catalonia is indeed a context in which 'symbolism is often as important as real political change' (Dowling 2018, 163). Source: Author.

the most recent icons of *independentisme*. Hundreds of them hung from the bridge fences. The night before the first day of Carnival, they were all cut off, and the morning after the news spread quickly, causing outrage throughout the town. While I walked across the bridge and witnessed the aftermath, I bumped into a group of friends belonging to my *comparsa*, who were promptly tying new ribbons to the fences, so that the bridge could be decorated again for the imminent start of the celebrations. The passion they put into the task was remarkable, just like the remarkable effort of, hours before, cutting them all off in the dead of the night and in the middle of a busy road.

The 'war of the ribbons' betrays a deeper, unresolved tension in a situation of disrupted and unachieved transformation, a state of 'pseudo-transition', which, embedded and ethnographically observable at the micro-level, actually reflects the current situation of Catalonia as a whole and shows clearly how 'today the public arena and the contested concept of *convivència* have become

7. Solsona's town hall in 2018. The regional flag, the *Senyera*, is hanging, whereas the Spanish flag is, as always, missing, and conspicuous by its absence – it is always being 'washed in the washing machine', as the office workers in the town hall often say, therefore unable to be hung. Conversely, a banner in support of the 'political prisoners' adorns the balcony, along with a yellow ribbon and the usual *Estelad*a. Source: Author.

increasingly polarised around the issue of Catalan sovereignty and independence' (quoted from the abstract for SIEF 2019).

Cohesion and motivation characterise the work of people on both poles, but they are separated by more distance than a bridge can bridge. Johannes has written that 'one of the most visible results of the events of October 2017 has been the presence of yellow ribbons in public places' (Johannes 2019, 20), but in fact that word 'presence' does not do justice to the magnitude of the shift that occurred in the period 2018–2020, for which 'ubiquity' or 'omnipresence' are more accurate terms.

CATALANNESS, CATALANISM, AND THE FESTIVAL

The relationship between folklore or popular culture and national identity is as old as national identities themselves. Catalonia is no exception (Wittlin 1994). Folklore revival, a much more recent phenomenon than folklore itself, and also cultural heritage-making (Isnart and Testa 2020) have largely contributed, symbolically, politically, and also economically to the transitional process, as a now rich body of scholarship has abundantly and convincingly shown. This idea underlines several of the chapters in this volume, and was at the centre of the conference panel from which it stems (I quote again from the SIEF 2019 abstract): 'Catalonia's participation in the Spanish transition to democracy in the 1970s found a potent resource in traditional festival: conceptual, gestural, and tactile'; it is therefore not surprising if 'since the Transition, public gatherings and rituals have proliferated in Catalonia'.[14]

The myriad of gestures, words, images, *actes*, and micro-acts that swarm and flow during and through the Carnival contribute to the emergence of a shared narrative about being in or from Solsona and about being in or from central Catalonia. The political landscape and discourses of the last few decades have partly succeeded in converging these sentiments in a common direction, in central Catalonia: *catalanisme* – albeit not without dissidences, inconsistencies, and ruptures. Far from being an inner essence of the festival, as some want it, its Catalanism is, as the mayor rightly suggested, a by-product of the historical, geographical, and social context wherein the festival occurs and for which it is functional.

In Solsona, the typical festive and 'seasonal nature of Catalanist sentiment and activism' (Johannes 2018, 63) along with the symbolic and historical geography of the socially constructed locality, create and provide 'a concrete model for Catalanism. Berga [here read: Solsona] – Pyrenean, medieval, Catalan-speaking – was easily identified with Catalonia as a whole, particularly by Barcelonans with little experience of the hinterland' (Noyes 2003, 204), thus fostering the idea of 'a kind of primordial Catalanism' (ibid). These considerations apply, *verbatim*, to Solsona as well. Hence, *el Carnaval* falls eminently within the solid pattern of other festivals from Catalonia *profunda* that have been considered as 'culminating moments for the expression of national identity' (Daniele Conversi quoted in Johannes 2019, 25; see also Kammerer 2014; del Mármol this book; Noyes 2003, 2011; Vaczi this book). In this sense, Solsona becomes a micro-model of central and 'deep' Catalan culture as a whole, a microcosm reflecting but also modelling the macrocosm of which it is part.

Indeed, the majority of the ethnological studies on Catalan festivals have inevitably focused on Catalanism, and that for the simple fact that there is hardly a festival in that context that is not Catalanist. The *conditio sine qua non*

---

[14] 'Performing transformation, claiming transition: Public gatherings and rituals in Catalonia from the 1970s to the present' can be read at the following link: https://nomadit.co.uk/conference/sief2019/p/7113 (accessed in October 2020). Reflections on the role of this or that cultural manifestation or specific cultural trends in the development of Catalanism and Catalan independentism are present in practically all the studies cited in this chapter, whereas more general overviews of the topic of cultural transformations and initiatives during the final years of Franco's regime and during the Transition are in Crameri 2008; Dowling 2018; Keown 2011b (and in Keown 2011a more generally); Llobera 2004.

for the establishment of an implicit (and sometimes, as we have seen, explicit) equation between popular festival and Catalanism is, however, the deeper idea of 'Catalanness' ('*Catalanitat*'), that is to say, the ensemble of socio-cultural elements that are considered as specifically, exclusively, or quintessentially Catalan, for a more or less structured and aware sense of Catalanness is at the basis of *catalanisme* – and therefore of *independentisme*.[15] Catalanness is not only an academic elucubration in the shape of an ugly word, but also a notion that has turned at least partly emic as well, of late (Kammerer 2014, 67–68), and that has been explicitly appropriated also by the institutions:

> *la Festa entesa com una de les principals manifestacions cíviques de la població [és] una manifestació que constitueix el marc idoni per expressar la catalanitat a l'espai públic. [...] Avui, la festa popular és un dels pocs moviments de masses de caràcter inequívocament català del qual disposa la societat per manifestar la dimensió cívica dels seus membres*. (Ajuntament de Berga 2014)

> [the Festival conceived as one of the main civic manifestations of the population [is] a manifestation that constitutes the adequate element to express Catalanness in the public space. [...] Today, the popular festival is one of the few mass movements whose character is unequivocally Catalan, and that is available to society in order to manifest the civic dimension of its members'.]

Or else: '*el Carnaval de Solsona és un dels més genuïns i populars de la Catalunya central i el conjunt del país*. (Ajuntament de Solsona 2018 – 'the Carnival of Solsona is one of the most genuine and popular of central Catalonia and of the country as a whole').

The essentialisation of general Catalanness through festive Catalanness as well as its collapse into Catalanism is manifest in such a discourse, which emerged in the 1980s and the 1990s, accelerated in the 2000s, and precipitated after 2010, the crucial year in which the reform of the Statute of Autonomy of Catalonia was halted by the Spanish Constitutional Court – a veritable *terminus post quem* in the *procés de indipèndencia*.[16] Carnival becomes thus one of those '*fêtes qui « font pays », selon une formule lancée par les acteurs catalanistes depuis la transition démocratique, pour désigner toute action volontaire visant à la dynamisation, économique et identitaire, du territoire*' (Guiu 2013, 77–78). No wonder, then, that a glimpse of the cartography of Catalan traditional festivities confirms the arguments made in this section, which also evokes

---

[15] For a definition of *catalanisme* and *independentisme*, see note n. 6 in this chapter.
[16] This tentative periodisation could be integrated with a reference to the Covid-19 pandemic and its impact in Catalan festive culture (see Roigé et al this book). For sure, 2020–2021 will be remembered as another period of great change in Catalonia, which was harshly hit by the pandemic and the consequent health crisis.

those by other scholars who have worked on such festivities: 'une cartographie des fêtes labellisées en tant que « *fêtes d'intérêt national* » par le gouvernement de la Catalogne montre des écarts importants: [...] la majorité des fêtes reconnues comme ayant un intérêt patrimonial « national » sont situées dans la Catalogne dite « ancienne », en opposition avec la Catalogne dite « nouvelle »' (Guiu 2013, 79–80).

Catalan festivals are territorialised in 'essence' but also emanate a territorialising power. This power is intercepted and used by another very specific Catalan organisational, associational, and in-group-shaping matrix, the *comparses*, to which the following, second part of this study ('The Ritual Making of Central Catalonia 2: *Comparses* and the Dynamics of Inclusive Nationalism') is devoted.

3

The Ritual Making of Central Catalonia 2: *Comparses* and the Dynamics of Inclusive Nationalism

ALESSANDRO TESTA

The previous chapter, 'The Ritual Making of Central Catalonia 1: National Identity and the Hanging of the Donkey', demonstrates the social relevance of Solsona's main public ritual, *el Carnaval*, within the borders of the city, of its *comarca*, and of central Catalonia as a whole, describing and analysing the main characteristics of both municipality and festivity. Among these, little attention has been devoted to a feature that, however, bears a primary importance in the economy of the festival as well as in the entire local society: the *colles* and *comparses*.[1]

COLLES AND COMPARSES: DESCRIPTION AND ANALYSIS

A *comparsa* is essentially a group of people (both *colla* and *comparsa* are roughly translatable as 'group', 'gang', or 'team'). What distinguishes at first sight a normal group of people from a *comparsa* is the fact that the members of the

[1] In much of central Catalonia, *colla* and *comparsa* are, when referring to festive or folkloric groups, closely related words, almost synonyms, although each retains a certain contextual specificity. In 2013, in an interview for the 30th anniversary since the foundation of their *comparsa*, some members affirmed the following: '*en el moment de creació els 50 membres van debatre en diverses ocasions sobre quin qualificatiu era millor: colla?, grup?, comparsa?, penya?, etc. Finalment, varem decidir anomenarnos comparsa*' (Nació Solsona 2013). For simplicity and brevity, though, from now on I will refer mostly to *comparsa* (which is also far more commonly used in Solsona), mentioning the other term only if a clarification is needed.

latter each wear the same '*bata*', which is a colourful uniform used mandatorily during the carnival and exclusively (or almost so) during festive occasions. The fact of appearing associated by a uniform is reflected in the etymology of the name, which comes from '*comparèixer*' ('to appear', cfr. Latin *comparere*, Italian *comparire*). Solsona's Carnival is the realm of some 60 *comparses* populated by some 10,000 people '*portant bata*' ('wearing a *bata*').[2] The *comparses* reign supreme and undisputed over every aspect of the festival, and probably represent one of the most striking post-Francoist developments in the history of the Carnival, and in fact in the recent history of the social configuration of Solsona altogether. Many informants have often insisted that the *comparses* are the '*essència*' ('essence') of Solsona's Carnival; the author Noemí Vilaseca, in her illustrated book about the Carnival of Solsona, calls them the '*ànima viva del Carnaval*', 'the living soul of the Carnival' (Vilaseca and Trilla 2011, 116). This folk ontology of Carnival is of paramount importance, as we shall see, whereby locals and strangers alike build that sense of typicity and authenticity that is then reflected on the local communities themselves, becoming symbolic material for the construction of social meaning and collective belonging.

The association organising the festival is called the Associació de Festes del Carnaval de Solsona, which in 2021 had some 900 '*socis*' ('members'). The Associació has a ruling body called '*la Junta*', which is itself a *comparsa*. Unlike in Berga, where its *colles* are (or at least were) 'overwhelmingly male' (Noyes 2003, 49), such separation does not exist in Solsona: there are *comparses* of many types containing people of many sorts, although such sorts tend to be patterned (*comparses* can be more feminine or more masculine, more youthful or more grown-up, more undisciplined or calmer, more or less dynamic, more or less open and inclusive, etc.).

Colles and *comparses* characterise most of the folkloric and performative traditions in Catalonia. Notable examples are those of the *Patum* in Berga and the '*colles castelleres*' performing the human towers. Being based on the spirit of free association and on the practice of 'getting together' ('*fer pinya*' in Catalan; see Vaczi this book), the *comparsa* also represents, *sui generis*, the ethos that Mariann Vaczi has aptly described as 'Catalonia's thriving associational culture or *associacionisme*, which empowers individuals and groups in their civic, leisure, educational, or political pursuits' (Vaczi this book).

A *comparsa* can be formed of just a handful of people (in certain very rare cases of two or three people or, exceptionally, even one person only) or, more often, tens or dozens. Apart from colouring, dynamising, and segmenting the collective landscapes of the festival, the *comparses* bear several practical functions: they organise the *actes*, the dances, the carts, and several other

---

[2] These figures come from the organisers and represent the rough numbers of *comparses* and their members in the late 2010s and early 2020s.

performances, prepare and apply the decorations in the streets and the squares, try to prevent utter disorder and violence (which still occur regularly), and take care of every aspect of the festival that needs a minimum of supervision and coordination. They do so joyfully, willingly, and apparently 'horizontally' through self-coordination (although hierarchies and competitions do exist among as well as within *comparses*, as is about to be discussed).

Some of the activities in which the *comparses* are involved require considerable effort, time, energy, and financial resources to be carried out. Many use their days off from work to engage in the necessary preparation for these activities; others offer a hand differently. Money is normally raised by the members taxing themselves through a membership fee. The *colles geganteres*, among the oldest *comparses* of the festival, function slightly differently. They take care of and govern, as already said, the very important *gegants*, the giants, the veritable, iconic, and idolatrised *numina* of the Carnival (Testa 2020b). In the case of the *gengaters*, a rather long, hard, even dangerous learning process is required to animate the giants. Being part of a *colla gegantera* is somewhat more prestigious than being part of a common *comparsa*, and it is therefore normally more difficult to be accepted into one, but the *colles* are ultimately also considered *comparses* themselves.[3]

The totality or vast majority of native Solsonins are part of a *comparsa* (with virtually no exception in the age range 10–40), but so too are many people from all over the *comarca*, from some of the surrounding *comarques*, also, and even from Andorra (in my own *comparsa* there are several Andorrans). Notable exceptions are: 1) a few natives – it is difficult to quantify what percentage, since there is no registry of the *comparses* and their members; 2) people with a recent background of immigration, for instance some of the more recently arrived South Americans or Europeans from EU countries or also non-EU countries, who tend not to be a part of a *comparsa* during the first few years of their stay. However, if they stay for longer than that (the level of successful integration of Europeans being very high), these individuals are usually invited into a *comparsa* – or form one themselves – after one or

---

3 '*A principis dels anys 80 apareixen les comparses al Carnaval solsoní. Actualment sobrepassen de llarg la seixantena i ajuden, participen i organitzen actes, aportant una coloració molt especial a la Festa. Les comparses han donat un fort impuls a una indumentària popular per a fer costat al Carnaval. Les tradicionals bruses dels antics tractants de bestiar de primers del segle XX, que van aparèixer en els primers carnavals d'una manera lleugera i anàrquica van passar a ser, també, els uniformes multicolors de les comparses. Cada una d'aquestes té els seus colors i el seu nom; la brusa se la posen el primer dia de Carnaval i se la treuen la nit del dimecres de cendra quan es crema el Carnestoltes*' (https://carnavalsolsona.com/la-festa/comparses/, accessed October 2020).

two years; 3) many in the local minority community of Maghrebis (especially Moroccans), who have been migrating to Solsona since the 1980s and who today constitute about 8–9% of the total population (they formed less than 2% in the 1990s), out of the 14% of people of different nationalities living in Solsona (source: census IDESCAT 2019); in this case, an important exception is those who were born in Solsona in the last two decades, many of whom are now in a *comparsa* (although almost exclusively boys or young men). Until a few years ago, there were no more than a handful of young Moroccans in *comparses*, and, even today, according to several informants I have interviewed, and on the basis of my own observation, there are no more than a couple dozen members of *comparses* (predominantly boys between the age of 12 and 18), out of a total population of about 700–800, in a town of 9,000.[4] Even more strikingly, of the 899 members (as of 2021) of the Associació de Festes del Carnaval de Solsona, only one is Moroccan (according to the president of the Association).

In short, only '*pixapins*' and '*camacos*' (popular mocking hinterland nicknames for Barcelonans), tourists, and less well-integrated people living in Solsona, with very few exceptions, do not wear a *bata* and are not part of a *comparsa*. Worse, even, some '*forasters*' ('foreigners' or 'strangers') dare to wear masks and carnival costumes when visiting Solsona during the Carnival. This is regularly met with scorn and derision, and some unfortunates are occasionally ridiculed publicly for doing so. *El Carnaval* is the reign of the *bates*, and, such is the general feeling, the trivial carnival masks have no place in it. Thus, the *comparses* fulfil yet another important function with aggregative and internally cohesive powers: they signal empirically and immediately who is an insider and who is an outsider, for no Solsonin would ever dare to show up in public during the entire week of Carnival without his/her *bata* – let alone wearing a mask or a disguise.

Above all, however, the *comparses* are about having fun, eating, drinking, dancing, and jesting together. Commensality is as important for Catalonia as a whole as it is for these quintessentially Catalan groups. Commensality and its relevance will be discussed further on in this chapter.

---

4   An exact figure is difficult to gather today because of several factors. According to the official register, Moroccan citizens living in Solsona numbered around 1,000 between 2008 and 2010. This number has been declining in the past ten years, in spite of a higher birth rate among the community. This decline, I was told by the official at the immigration office of the Solsonès, is due only partly to emigration towards other Spanish areas or a return to Morocco, and it is actually mostly due to individuals from the first and second waves acquiring Spanish citizenship. This means that, while the number of Moroccans declines, the number of people of Moroccan origin is actually increasing.

The *comparses* are semi-formal groups, for although they do not exist as juridical entities, they do have their own rules, hierarchies, obligations, and rites of passage.[5] One normally gets into a *comparsa* by invitation from one or more of its senior members. Solicitations and candidacies are also a possibility. More structured *comparses* put new entries to a vote. One can leave a *comparsa* (which happens rather infrequently and usually because of *force majeure*) or even be chased away (which is very rare). An individual can belong to two *comparses*, although, given the rivalry between *comparses* for an array of available symbolic and even human capital, it is an unusual occurrence, often met with jealousy and disappointment by the other members and sometimes even with accusations of betrayal. Even though in the last couple of decades the *comparses* have both grown in number and in number of members, cases of disintegration or disappearance of a *comparsa* also exist.

The creation, reproduction, and maintenance of a *comparsa* help structure and give shape to a wide array of interpersonal and intergroup relationships, and although the *comparses* function eminently, though not exclusively, within, during, and for the Carnival, they also exist outside the carnival framework.

Hierarchy within each *comparsa* is established through a variety of complex micro-dynamics and is coded accordingly. Seniority is by far one of the most important criteria, and, as such, is exposed and made manifest though a system of 'grades' in the form of '*parxes*' ('patches') that are sewed to the *bata* to mark certain achievements and, especially, the number of years one has participated in the Carnival. Correspondence and constant contact are today maintained throughout the year by means of WhatsApp groups (every *comparsa* has its own).

As is commonly said and felt by Solsonians, 'la *comparsa* és com una família' ('a *comparsa* is like a family').[6] This strong sense of belonging among the members of *colles* and *comparses* is certified by all the ethnographers that

---

5 I partly disagree with Nina Kammerer when she writes that, in a *colla*, 'there are no official "members" or "partners" (*socis*) in any formal sense' (Kammerer 2014, 64). In Solsona at least, one cannot freely join a *colla* or *comparsa* and must go through certain steps in order to become a member. There are obligations to fulfil, among which are to always wear the uniform during the carnival week and to participate in the most important activities – and for most *comparses* to also pay the annual membership fee. A new affiliation can even be formalised through rites of passage, which vary from semi-serious oaths to nothing else than a prank or bad joke made in public at the expense of the poor newcomer. *Comparses* are neither completely formal nor informal, hence I prefer qualifying them as semi-formal.

6 The local writer and researcher Noemí Vilaseca (also a proud member of a *comparsa*) has written that '*entrar a formar part d'una comparsa és tot un ritu d'agregació i fa evident allò que el folklorista Joan Amades definia com a "esperit de confraternització" que regna aquests dies. Les comparses són una manifestació de la força de la communitas,*

have worked on the matter (Grau i Martí 1996; Kammerer 2014; Noyes 2003, 2011; Vaczi 2016), and is a rather well-established aspect. Since Catalans love *excursionisme*, nature, and the mountains, it is not uncommon to come across pictures of Solsonins by peaks and sight-seeing spots wearing their *bates* – and very often holding an *Estelada* as well. Sometimes they take and wear them when they go abroad for tourism, in order, of course, to take pictures and share them with the other fellow members. Couples belonging to the same *comparsa* may get married wearing their *bates* as wedding costumes, and their children will *ipso facto* and inevitably become new members. Children that are not born into a *comparsa* tend to be introduced into one early, for having been in a *comparsa* for a long time is a matter of great pride.

The association of the *comparsa* with a family, or even with *the* family, is not casual. Just like family bonds, those with a *comparsa* and loyalty to its members are considered strong and almost unbreakable. Since *comparses* are usually formed of individuals who already have established bonds (of family, love, friendship, work, etc.), they normally serve as a bond-catalyser. However, the admittance of new members from outside the pre-existing networks of established members is a very common phenomenon. Thus the *comparsa* can also be a bond-creator.

Being part of a *comparsa* 'as if' it were *família* and going through the years in the *comparsa/família* and transmitting this to offspring are dynamics that bear a particular historical and social significance in Catalonia. During the dictatorship, as is well-known, the Catalan language and traditions were prohibited, and 'it was in the family that Catalan lore, attitudes and customs were passed down' (Josep Llobera cited in Johannes 2019, 15). The *'casa pairal'* (the 'paternal house') was the place in which such continuity would be established, and where the self, the land, the past, and the destiny of the *família* merged together and embedded into one another (as has been said, *'pairalisme*, which could be called rural familism, conjures up a number of institutions, including the centrality of the ancestral house and of primogeniture': Llobera 1997, 300).[7] Aggregative, strong, and long-lasting like the *família* and its *casa*, the *comparsa* itself becomes a model for association and actually for more than association: a model for belonging, togetherness, and, as we shall see in the next section, also inclusion.[8]

---

amb l'abolició de deferències entre els membres, que s'indentifiquen sota uns mateixos colors' (Vilaseca and Trilla 2011, 127).

[7] Regarding this feature, see the still unmatched description and analysis in Noyes 2003, 159–164.

[8] *Comparses* dynamise the Carnival dramatically, but they can also easily become sectarian – not only metaphorically, but also literally: a place of encounter and

8. Two members of the same *comparsa* being wed by the mayor in Solsona's town hall in 2019. The best man and the maid of honour also belong to the same *comparsa*.
Source: Author.

Within the mostly small communities of central Catalonia, Solsona is subdivided not only into the more traditional 'classes' or macro-categories of people bearing their own identities (political, familial, professional, vernacular, cantonal, etc.), or rather building and 'nesting' (Herb and Kaplan 1999) their own identities into one another; they also construct and express their sense of belonging through *colles* and *comparses*, these semi-formal 'small[er] groups' (Noyes 2011, 2016a), with their specific customs and costumes, micro-ritualities, and in-group habits and regulations. A *matryoshka* that at times proves a real challenge for the ethnographer to un-nest and decipher, but which is evidently highly influential in matters of group perception, production, and reproduction.

The entering into and interacting with a *comparsa* embodies and mobilises the view and attitude (a 'grid' in Mary Douglas' words: Douglas 1970) of the individual about the functioning of the group and about his/her place in

---

socialisation open only to the veterans of Carnival, and located in a club in the second major square in the historical centre, is called '*la Secta*'.

9. A typically gigantic *sopar de comparses* (dinner of the *comparses*), where, in the spirit of the quintessential Catalan virtue, conviviality, hundreds of people from different *comparses* gather to wine and dine together, imbibing copiously. Note the different *bates* worn by the members of a same *comparsa*, sitting close to one another, thus patterning the scene. Source: Vilaseca and Trilla 2011, 118–119.

it. These views and attitudes ultimately percolate outside the *comparsa* itself, having an impact on the wider social body: once Carnival is over, everybody takes back his or her place in ordinary life, but he or she 'here and now' also remains bound to who he or she is 'there and then'. During Carnival, however, the established behavioural norms (no matter how paradoxically transgressive such norms appear) of the *comparsa* are learned through time and with time deeply incorporated (Csordas 1990), in spite of them being, often literally, toxic for the body – alcoholic intoxication is one such norm. Wearing the carnival habit, the *bata*, means ultimately wearing the carnivalesque *habitus* (Bourdieu 1994). Just like one of the many unwritten norms of the Carnival stipulates that the week-worn *bata* is undressed and washed only at the end of Carnival, so the carnivalesque *habitus* is itself temporalised and ritually reworn the following year, thus ensuring the reproduction of both the ritual and the world within and without the ritual. This generative (or regenerative) modality vis-à-vis the social order is ultimately a form of interplay that makes possible individual agency through/against/with-in the wider social structures

(Sahlins 2000), whereby both the individual and the structure are impacted and mutually influenced by said interplay.

Public visibility, capacity of aggregation, success in the carnival competitions, manufacturing skills, bravery, drinking capacity, and many other features are all currencies of the social capital that each *comparsa* desires and tries to obtain in order to succeed and *appear* (*'comparèixer'* in Catalan) even more. This also requires a constant struggle to acquire new valid and active members, maintain inner coherence, and reproduce year after year.

In spite of those few, ephemeral 'oceaning' moments of communitas (Turner 1977), and *pace* Bakhtin (1984a, 1984b), the utopian horizontality of *el Carnaval* is (sometimes verbally invoked but) factually denied by those who should instead represent it. Ultimately, the *comparses* and their individual members' agencies structure by differentiation, dynamise thorough action, but also hierarchise through rivalry the festive arena. They compete for the 'carnivalesque capital' at stake in the social *champ* (Bourdieu 1994) that they themselves contribute to establish.

COMPARSES, CATALAN LANGUAGE, AND INCLUSIVE NATIONALISM

Just like the city Solsona is clearly bounded (walled, in fact), so bounded are most of its core-communities of autochthonous and long-term inhabitants. Likewise, networks like the *comparses* 'perform themselves as bounded groups to serve collective goals, including the stabilisation of their own fluid life; and this auto-telic work is increasingly the work of community in modernity' (Noyes 2006, 32).

Comparses bear inwards socially conservative power and potentially outwards transformative force, because the festival, being a time of hyper-socialisation, also allows for the integration of non-locals and non-Catalans into the locality, thus transforming it from within. At the same time, such a socio-cultural device has its downside in the (logical) exclusion of those who do not meet the expectation of participating in the Carnival from within (i.e., being a member of a *comparsa*); this can be the case of the 'inner outsider', such as a local refusing to take part in the Carnival as a member of a *comparsa*, or an external outsider unaware of the unwritten rules of the local public rituality, like a tourist (eminently, a *pixapí*, a Barcelonian). *Comparses* make work of differentiation between themselves, but as a whole they also constitute an aggregate, bordered ensemble that inevitably establishes a dichotomous 'us/them' logic ('us' intended as those who live in or are from Solsona and take part in the carnival, 'them' intended as the *forasters* ['strangers'] and those who live in or are from Solsona but do not take part in the Carnival).

There is, however, a case wherein these two logically complementary attitudes, one inclusive towards the within and the other exclusive towards the outside, remodulate and hybridise into one sole attitude that becomes inclusive towards the outside: this happens when a new member is welcomed into a *comparsa*. And here the best ethnographic example I can offer is my own.

After being invited to join a *comparsa* in December 2016 (I will not mention its name here, but every *comparsa* has its own name), which I accepted warmly and gratefully, and once the *bata* had been sewn by one of the local tailors, I was ready to be inducted into my new group – not before, though, being publicly shamed and mocked, on the morning of the first day of Carnival 2017, for having been spotted walking through one of the town streets without my new *bata*, as I did not yet know that this was a blatant transgression of Solsona Carnival's unwritten rules. That same evening, I went through the micro-rite of passage of the '*imposiciò de la bata*' (the 'bestowal and clothing of the *bata*'), which was also duly recorded on a video by one fellow member, and after being the object of a rather gross '*broma*' ('prank') a few hours later, I officially became a member.

I did whatever was expected or asked of me during the entire week – and that was at times quite trying. After the close of the festival, and for the following months and years and up to the present day, the attitude of the locals towards me has changed radically: I was no longer the nosy stranger who had moved to Solsona a few months before (September 2016) and learned Catalan surprisingly fast (and that probably because of my previous knowledge of Latin, Italian, French, and Spanish), which was a matter of great amazement and pride for the locals. I had been (warmly) socialised into the local community and become one of its members, albeit bearing a special status: I became a '*solsoní d'adopciò*' (a 'Solsonian by adoption'), as I was called by some, or alternatively a '*català d'adopciò*', as I was also called by others. An example of 'the incorporative power of sport, music, and festivals' (Noyes 2003, 208), and perhaps also an example of how the model of/for Catalan nationalism in general may work, as I am about to argue.

Becoming a *Solsoní d'adopciò* so quickly and by synecdoche a *Català d'adopciò* was due mostly to my becoming a member of a rather popular *comparsa*, and, of course, to my manifest curiosity and respect for their culture, as well as to a genuine will to integrate (although I was always, of course, upfront with everybody about the research motive behind my fixed-term stay in Solsona). It quickly became a matter of pride for myself and for those who had 'believed in me' from the beginning. After all, Solsonins like to perceive and qualify themselves as '*gent tancada*' ('closed people') – which could in fact perhaps also be a sort of meta-perception, that is, a perception, sometimes somewhat embarrassed, of what they think is the perception of others of them. In other words, a form of 'cultural intimacy' (Herzfeld 1997). Integrating so fast was considered a rather exceptional achievement, to the extent that one or two of my friends congratulated me on managing to be accepted into such a tight community.[9]

However, becoming a member of a popular *comparsa* also had its conditions: I was invited to join not only because by then I had been socially active and visible for months in Solsona, but also because I had not confined myself to speaking Castilian (which is understandably the standard and expected linguistic behaviour for a foreigner), but had rather learnt Catalan, and in time participated in the first carnival after my arrival. As many pointed out in those months, I was the object of a certain curiosity and admiration, and one of the main arguments that I was often confronted with was that there were 'Spaniards' who had been living in Solsona for decades without learning Catalan, and look at this Italian who arrives and speaks it fluently after a handful of months.[10] (Note: obviously not all *comparses* are Catalanist, nor may all members of a *comparsa* be Catalanist; likewise, not all Catalan-speakers are Catalanist, obviously. Tensions, inconsistencies, and open disagreements concerning matters of identity and politics do exist in the microcosm of a *comparsa* just as in the wider social body of the local Catalan society; however, my own *comparsa* is one of those with a rather upfront Catalanist, and actually independentist, stance, which is by far the most common one.)

The Catalan language is widely considered, among Catalans as well as scholars, as *the* one true differential marker of the Catalan nation (Bel 2013; Clua i Fainé 2014; Dowling 2018; Johannes 2019; McRoberts 2001; Noyes 2003; Villarroya 2012; and many others). As Johannes (2019) recently remarked: 'Catalans will not consider another person to be truly Catalan unless they can speak the language, and are comfortable using it regularly'. Catalan politician and architect of modern Catalanism Jordi Pujol took the view that those who speak Catalan, and who live and work in Catalonia, are Catalan. Language has also been key to the claim of Catalonia as an open nationalism, willing to accept those who make the effort to learn the language and integrate'

---

9   One of my informants in Solsona told me – and several people in Berga confirmed – that in Berga *el Carnaval Solsoní* is considered '*tancat*' ('closed', 'inaccessible') and this especially because of the *comparses* and the difficulty for strangers to become part of one of them.

10 It should also be noted that 'the Catalan interior tends far more [than Barcelona and the coast] to monolingualism in Catalan' (Noyes 2003, 62). Catalan is the quotidian language and by far the most used idiom in Solsona and in Solsonès in general. Castilian is the language of the less integrated sectors in town. Among the large majority of the autochthons, it is confined to speaking with outsiders and little else.

(Johannes 2019, 23);[11] in other words: '*la lengua catalana ha tomado un carácter central, tanto para definir quién es catalán como para marcar el nivel de integración de los extranjeros*' (Clua i Fainé 2014, 80; same argument in Villarroya 2012, 37–38).[12] I can very much confirm this attitude, which, as I have just narrated, functioned in my case as well. (The history of my assimilation or naturalisation was surprisingly similar, methodologically, epistemologically, and perhaps above all psychologically and morally, to the integration of Dorothy Noyes in Berga as described in Noyes 2003, 31–36, 93–95.)

Strictly connected with the problem of language in the formation, maintenance, and transmission of Catalan national identity is that of its 'differential' nature, that it is in a constant dialectic of differentiation and confrontation with Spanish identity (Bel 2013; Clua i Fainé 2014; Dowling 2018; Johannes 2019; Llobera 1997, 2004; Noyes 2003, 2011; and many others).[13] Of course, the positional or relational or differential dimension is at the very basis of whatever form of social differentiation (national among others) and cannot but be grounded on an 'us ≠ them' logic (Delanty 1999): 'we' can only exist in so far as there is a 'you' or a 'they'. This logic, however, does acquire, in our Catalan case, a very specific connotation, especially given the size of the territory and the perpetual negotiation/confrontation with the 'other' *par excellence*, the Spaniards, much in the same vein as other examples of small and close nations and groups (Blok 1998; Noyes 2016; Smith 2013), which often engenders the proverbial phenomenon of the 'narcissism of minor differences', i.e.,

---

[11] This pattern has also been associated with the 'success' of Catalonia in modern times: 'the success story of Catalonia is that it has not only managed to preserve the identity of the original Catalans, but that it has largely managed to integrate the majority of immigrants into the Catalan imagined community' (Llobera 1997, 307).

[12] The question of the inclusive nature of Catalan nationalism is discussed in many works cited in this chapter, although differently. My own take on nationalism stems from years of reading the historical, philosophical, and anthropological literature tackling this thorny issue, although such a take is consciously limited to (mostly) European history and societies (past and present). I must admit, however, to have been especially influenced by Anthony Smith's approach as developed in Smith 2001 and then distilled and defended in Smith 2013, as well as by ethnosymbolism more in general (Leoussi and Grosby 2007).

[13] What complicates things is that there have been heated debates for years about the standardisation of Catalan and the adoption of this standardized version throughout the region. If the main binary opposition remains Catalan vs Castilian, the issue of linguistic regional variations in different areas of Catalonia, as well as within the macro-area of the Països Catalans, remains a *vexata quaestio* (see Strubell 2011; also Delgado et al this book).

'the idea that identity lies in difference, and difference is asserted, reinforced, and defended against what is closest and represents the greatest threat' (Blok 1998, 39).[14]

Affirming the importance of the Catalan language in the making of Catalan national identity might seem a tautology, but here I would like to stress especially the importance of *comparses*, which are no joke, either (especially if in connection with language, as in my case): they put into force and oil up the symbolic and ritual machinery on the basis of which a sense of local *as* national (and national *as* local) belonging emerges within the micro-society of Solsona. Together with numerous other factors, among which are education, state institutions, local cultural patterns, popular mythology, and political influences, this same machinery contributes to the telluric movement that makes the nation emerge, amalgamating ideas, claims, and dreams of unity and continuity into the imagination of a common past, future, and destiny. This is how the 'smaller identity' of Solsona, its being a community made of 'small groups' (Noyes 2016a), often in competition with each other, flows into the stream of a greater, 'imagined' community (Anderson 1983) of millions of individuals not knowing each other personally but nevertheless feeling associated by that collective sense of belonging, deeply rooted in the individual but aggregated in and expressed though the masses, that we call a nation. As Noyes wrote several years ago:

> all communities are imagined, but some are more imagined than others. [...] Catalonia was a linguistic, cultural, social and economic unity with clear boundaries and reasonable internal homogeneity; it was a territorial

---

14 If on the one hand social constructivism has taught us many a valuable lesson about how to de-essentialise social formations and representations, on the other it risks leaving us without interpretative tools: constructivism and its close kin, deconstructionism, are only the beginning of the analysis, not at all its end. It is, for instance, not sufficient to weaponise deconstructionism against cultural essentialisation and naturalisation, these universal and most human dynamics, nor should it be desirable to fall into the gravitational force at the opposite pole of reification: utter relativism and cultural denialism and cognitive nihilism. If all identities are socially constructed, as they indeed are, then the fact of an identity being constructed and emically naturalised is, *per se*, nothing particular or specific, and loses much of its explanatory power. What is at stake here (as it should be in any similar interpretative endeavour) is not to ascertain that these or those identities are constructed, for this is an unproblematic assumption – and a banal one at that – but rather to understand how and why certain identity configurations are produced and reproduced the way they are. And – *soit dit en passant* – the fact of national identity being, just like anything else, socially constructed, does not make it any less *real*.

political unit sufficiently inscribed in various forms of memory and practice to suggest an identity among its empirical inhabitants. Performance provided a different basis for lived experience to lend reality to imaginings. (Noyes 2003, 204)[15]

The central-Catalan phenomenon of the Solsonian *comparsa* is, ultimately, a symbolic sublimation of Catalanism and a praxiological substantiation of both its intrinsic limits and its potentially inclusive force. Its strengths and weaknesses, or more neutrally speaking its mode of existence, shape the way it embodies, emanates, and enforces 'groupness' (Brubaker and Cooper 2000) or 'togetherness' (Scruton 2014), but also affinity and familiarity, rootedness, or any other term one prefers in order to conceptualise and define the experiential, emotional, and representational kernel a nation is made of.

BOTIFFARADES, BOOZE, AND BLASPHEMY: THE INNER AND OUTER LIMITS OF INCLUSIVE NATIONALISM

The inclusive and assimilating force of becoming part of a *comparsa* and of learning Catalan was in my case fully at work. After participating in the first carnival '*a tope*' ('to the fullest'), as the locals liked to say, I began to be offered support, in whatever issue, regularly. Suddenly, all doors were open to me. A few months before I had set off to study Catalan popular culture; in the process, I had myself become popular. As will become clear in this section, however, all that glitters is not gold, and I have not indulged in this exercise of ethnographic introspection to congratulate myself for my own success in the city of Solsona. Rather more simply, I dwelled upon this case because I cannot possibly know any other any better. But my case was far from being isolated. In fact, my observations and interpretations in this chapter are based on a synthesis of the patterns associating my case and similar ones I observed and studied (or was told about) during my stay. The conclusion is that all the better-integrated immigrants in Solsona were/are part of a *comparsa* (here again with a few exceptions, which confirm the rule). But as said, all that glitters is not gold.

---

[15] Even though Noyes does not endorse or reject (or mention) Anthony Smith's idea of ethnosymbolism (Smith 2001), i.e., the *longue durée* cultural complex that is one of the sources and engines of the idea (and the factual historical reality) of nation and nationalism, these words and the conclusions of her research seem to point in this direction. In any case, Catalonian national identity and nationalism fit quite naturally into Smith's interpretative framework and lend themselves to be considered, in my opinion, a rather paradigmatic case of ethnosymbolic nation(alism).

In the first pages of this chapter, I argued that the inclusive force of the *comparses* has its boundaries and limits, as do all dynamics established and stemming from networks and grouped forms of engagement. Once a person has been socially visible and shown a will to integrate, possibly learned Catalan, and subsequentially been invited to join a *comparsa*, all that it takes to stay there and build up a strong relationship with the local community is that certain behavioural and moral codes are respected, the spirit of associationism is embraced, and a sense of reciprocity and fairness is cultivated. (I hereby note fleetingly that it is not casual that some of these virtues are normally associated with what is considered yet one other quintessential Catalan virtue: '*pactisme*', i.e., 'pragmatism' and the 'art of compromise'.) The most visible exception to this otherwise well-established pattern is the case of the Islamic minority composed of, as said, mostly Moroccans. This chapter is no place to board the complex, thorny issue of migration to Catalonia from Maghreb countries and the integration of these migrants into Catalan societies. I will content myself with a few observations that can help highlight and calibrate the main arguments I have been developing so far.

The general feeling in Solsona concerning immigration and integration today is that whereas problems do not subsist with Europeans and other nationalities, things stand quite differently with the '*moros*' (the fairly derogatory term with which Muslim Maghrebis, who make up about 8–9% of the current residents, but also other Arabs of Islamic faith, are often referred to). Cohabitation is broadly considered possible but dysfunctional, and integration poor. As I have argued elsewhere (Testa 2020b, 28–29), this might be partly explained by the decision of Muslim Solsonians not to participate in the Carnival, although, of course, abstaining from the Carnival can be considered as both a cause and a consequence of poor integration.[16]

There seems to be a rather sharp generational divide, some of the youngest male descendants of the second wave of immigration from North Africa (from around the first decade of the 21st century), not more than a few dozen though, being more participative, although still with a very visible gender gap.

---

[16] This argument can rightly recall one of the concepts of (and long-lasting debate about) '*Leitkultur*', a concept theorised by political scientist Bassam Tibi, with which he intended to highlight the fact that the failures of multiculturalism in efforts of integration in Europe in the past few decades could be mitigated by establishing policies that would lead migrant communities to embrace a set of common values and views relevant – or even essential – to the receiving country. The sharing of this ensemble of relevant ideas and practices representing the 'core' of the receiving culture (the *Leitkultur*, precisely) would lead, so the theory goes, to a better integration of migrants, or at least a better coexistence between migrants and locals (Tibi 2001).

The refusal of the adults is, however, absolute and unanimous, and is motivated by four major representational, symbolic, and behavioural aspects: 1) the widespread immoderate consumption of alcohol and consequent intoxication; states of drunkenness and hangover characterising the existential landscape of Solsona during the entire carnival week; 2) the likewise ubiquitous cooking and consumption of pork meat in streets and public squares, especially in the form of one of the all-time symbols of Carnival: the *botifarres* ('sausages'); 3) the mockery of the clergy and of religious symbolism, sometimes verging into veritable forms of carnivalesque blasphemy; 4) transgressions and excesses of all sorts and the presence of lascivious representations.

These practices are carried out, today, by men and women alike, teenage boys and girls alike, and are extremely common throughout the festival, just like sexualised and often obscene *bromes* and *actes*. These elements of the ethos of the Carnival are not specific features of Solsona's festival, though: they are solidly established *longue durée* features in the history of carnival in Europe (Testa 2020a). In Solsona, they exist as they have existed in thousands of other European cities, towns, and villages for several centuries. They are not going to disappear any time soon. But they are deemed as outrageous and utterly unacceptable by the local Islamic minority (especially the grown-ups).

Every person acquainted with southern Europe and with Catalonia in particular knows the cultural prominence of eating and drinking in company and in public. This cultural trait can hardly ever be stressed enough. Unsurprisingly, it has been the object of systematic cultural analysis, for its being a specific modality of national identity construction and maintenance in Catalonia: years ago, Alexander Robertson described food as 'the essence of conviviality in Catalonia', stressing the 'binding power' of commensality (Robertson, 2010, 72); more recently, Venetia Johannes devoted a book to this aspect (2019); in her chapter in this book, she stresses that 'through consuming festive foods and shared dishes, yet also being aware of territorial variations, Catalans are involved in creating an imagined community through food'.[17]

Solsonins love to eat out. Just like most other Catalans, they indulge in commensality willingly, passionately, and very frequently. During my ethnographic fieldwork, I counted more than 40 snack bars, restaurants, and places to eat out in a town of 9,000, which is a rather impressive ratio. During the Carnival week, at least one main meal is consumed out every day, very often both main meals, if extreme hangover does not prevent that from happening – hangover or the typical state of prostrated stupor that hits many locals after the third or fourth day of binging and not sleeping enough.

---

[17] This importance has been emphasised to the extent of subsuming commensality and community into nationalism: 'gastronationalism', as it has been called (a concept by Michaela DeSoucey discussed by Johannes in 2019, 5–11).

Drinking alcoholic beverages in company and in public has a very important, actually an essential, social function in Solsona. Abstaining from alcohol consumption and from the social practices associated with it, particularly during Carnival, is usually met with puzzlement, disappointment, and sometimes even open reprobation and contempt, no matter the social, ethnic, or religious background of the abstinent. Abstinence is a practice that, if not directly impacting coexistence, can factually and seriously impair efforts of integration.

Such excesses are obviously condemned (but ultimately tacitly tolerated) by the Catholic clergy and the most fervent believers, with even some timid, occasional, and helpless forms of condemnation. Again, Carnival and the Church have not been at odds with one another in Solsona only over the last 50 years, for they have for centuries all over Europe (Testa 2020a). This is made all the more dissonant for Solsona, as it has been proud of its episcopate, in spite of being a very small city, for centuries. Popular devotion was very strong until not so long ago (A.a.V.v. 1994; Llorens i Solé 1987), with a particular emphasis, just like the rest of central Catalonia, on Marian cults. However, Christianity and traditional forms of devotion have been losing ground of late in Solsona, no less than in other parts of the Western industrialised world.

For decades, *el Carnaval de Solsona* has incorporated elements of parody of the local '*Festa Major*' (Vilaseca and Trilla 2007).[18] The four main carnival giants themselves are a parody of those of the *Festa Major*. If the latter is historical, religious, solemn, aristocratic, and associated with Franco's *Nacionalcatolicismo*, the former is recent, desecrating, joyful, popular, and associated with post-Francoism and *catalanisme*. The resulting mocking of Christian symbolism is ostensibly displayed during the week-long celebrations, not only in parodic but at times actually overtly blasphemous ways. In fact, the ridicule or even vilification of the Catholic Church in general overflows into an interesting kind of 'carnivalesque blasphemy'. Frequently, during past carnivals, the clerical hierarchies have been the object of scorn; in particular, Solsona being an old episcopate, it is the bishop who has often been made the object of mockery. Even the most important historical statue of the city, the Romanesque *Mare de Deu*, a revered Madonna hosted in the cathedral, which is present in the local prayers and folklore, has not escaped carnivalisation: for example, in a poster adorning one of the streets during the carnival of 2010, the baby Jesus in her arms was substituted with an image of the *Xut*, the giant

---

[18] 'During the year there are two very different festivals: Carnival, at the end of winter, with continuous partying, and the solemn Festa Major (town festival), from the 7th to the 11th of September' (Solsona Turisme 2018).

owl of the local folklore. Other episodes could be mentioned.[19] No wonder the Catholic hierarchies, interpreting a role that has been theirs for centuries, have been condemning the Carnival and its excesses.

Through an array of forms of syncretism, invention, reinvention, and symbolic manipulation, the locals reflect metaphorically, metonymically, or simply creatively and playfully, on their own relationship with the Catholic Church, and on the paradoxes of this long relationship. And this is what has also happened vis-à-vis the former political order: 'overwhelmingly reclaimed in the democratic period, Carnival now forces Catalans to question themselves instead of challenging the regime' (Noyes 2011, 218). As in all complicated relationships, extremes and roles are played alternatively, and, in fact, in an only apparently funny manner, the Solsonians interpret and display their being 'good Christians' during the pious and solemn *Festa Major*, and not quite so during the transgressive Carnival. There is no contradiction in this, but rather contrast and complementarity, just like there has never been a contradiction, but rather contrast and complementarity, between Carnival and Lent: Catholic Europe has been experiencing this for some 900 years now (Testa 2020a). Ultimately, however, Carnival lacking the sympathies of the most-fervent local Catholics is not the same as being unpopular among the local Muslim Moroccans, because the abstinence of the former is excused as an exception and an eccentricity (they are born and bred Catalans, after all, and it is older people anyway, the argument goes), whereas for the latter it is a painful sign or reminder of lack of mutual understanding and shared beliefs (or shared *Leitkultur*).

Alcohol consumption and intoxication, pork meat and *botifarrades* ('sausage-centred feasts'), youth and women's transgressive and licentious behaviour, blasphemy and desecration (no matter if done in jest and not seriously) are directly and starkly at odds with Islamic religious and behavioural prescriptions, and also at odds with the values and worldview upheld by most of the Muslims of Maghrebi provenance living in Solsona. They could even be considered veritable taboos.[20] This incompatibility becomes a factual impediment not only for further integration, but also for successful coexistence, sometimes fuelling on the contrary distrust and antipathy that are also rooted

---

[19] I am in possession of a secret video, absolutely not meant for circulation, in which a carnivalesque caricature of the Mass, adorned moreover with satanic symbols, is performed by a renowned *comparsa* in a local rural chapel. Other sacrilegious acts are very common during Carnival; e.g., in 2018, a gigantic 666 was painted in red by anonymous vandals on the portal of the Episcopal palace across from the cathedral, and washed away by the sacristan the day after.

[20] These aspects are discussed also in Testa 2020b; in the same study an analysis is offered about Solsona's Carnival and the religious sphere more generally.

in reciprocally established patterns of mutual otherisation and suspicion. Although things are visibly changing through the growing participation of the youth of North African descent, who are also locally schooled and able to speak Catalan (which is one of the driving factors of this change), this concerns almost exclusively the boys and young men, who are given more freedom by their families; for the participation of girls and young women is still extremely rare, and that of adults and older people practically non-existent.

The refusal to take part in the Carnival and comply with its norms of solicited intoxication, exaggerated commensality, segmented togetherness, transgression, and ritual negation of *respecte* and *seny* is one of the reasons why, in Solsona, only rarely are the adult Moroccans considered full members of the local community, *ergo* part of the Catalan nation as a whole, for, among other reasons, as has been intelligently written, 'festival is a labour and participation is obligatory' (Noyes 2011, 208). Many Solsonians lament this lack of interest and participation from the community of Muslims; others hardly notice, or at any rate ignore or are not interested in its causes; others, on the other hand, are aware of some of the implications of this refusal, and consider it as a proof of the impossibility of true co-existence. On the one hand, the inability of Carnival to change its *longue durée* and crystallised cultural features in order to try to include the recent migrants in the cultural dynamics of the local ritual life and its networks is an inner limit (old traditions and habits are not so easily changed). On the other hand, the unwillingness of the Islamic minority to change their beliefs and attitudes towards Carnival is an outer limit. Through a ritually activated cultural osmosis, the inner and outer boundaries of Carnival inclusiveness overlap and interpenetrate with the boundaries of Catalan inclusive nationalism.

CONCLUSIONS

Solsona's Carnival can be considered a '*fête de transition*': a 'festival of transition' is a category of festive events that were invented and/or recodified, acquiring most of their forms and meanings and their utmost social relevance, during a period of political rupture, radical transformations (both influenced by and influencing the festival), and consequential transition into a new social order.[21] More than 45 years after the beginning of that transition, another

---

[21] The case of the *Masopust* of Hlinsko in the Czech Republic, which was the object of my previous ethnographic research, is, in this sense, comparable to that of Solsona. Of course, the post-socialist transition was very different from the post-Francoist, given the major ideological and political differences between those different regimes (communist and atheist the former, conservative and Catholic the latter). Nevertheless, in both cases the festival offered a symbolic capital to be

eventful rupture, the 2017 referendum, shook Catalonia, disrupting decades of *pactisme* and more or less peaceful *convivència*, determining a situation of 'pseudo-transition', and precipitating the region into a new social and political crisis. Issues of nation (what is Catalonia?), Catalanness and national identity (who is Catalan?), nationality (how can one belong to the Catalan nation?), and nationalism and Catalanism (how and why does one adhere to the Catalan nation and strive for its assertion and recognition?) have become more urgent than ever.

Like other collective forms of action powered by, among other things, the traditional Catalan proclivity for associationism, *el Carnaval*, veined and animated by its *comparses* and *colles*, reveals itself as a cultural device that connects the lived experience of the empirical small group to the imagined community of the nation, through the mediation of the meso-level of 'central Catalanness', with Solsona being the centre of this imagined centre, in the (typically Catalan) 'nesting' interplay between local, regional, and national identity (Guiu 2013; Kammerer 2014; Noyes 2003; Testa 2019).

What is particularly interesting as a consideration in the political anthropology of this case study is that the assertion and expression of national identity – whether or not we agree on calling this 'nationalism' – that are made through such a device are framed, *pace* Anderson, against (or at least in open and strong criticism against) the state and its institutions. The state is not only in the background of the nation-binding ritual device and of its complex symbolic machinery: it actually becomes its main antagonist (if not the utopian Catalan state, certainly the very real Spanish state …).

For those living it as an explicitly Catalanist festival – and they are the vast majority – *el Carnaval* stands as a model or a miniature of 'deep Catalanism' itself, based as it is on a set of solid experiential or representational pillars: 1) its being born as a form of reaction to and in defiance of the moribund Francoism of the mid-1970 – which allows the locals to symbolically capitalise on the idea of resistance to Francoism; 2) associationism and the civic spirit, embodied in the *comparses*, of doing things outside of the institutional framework (*'los catalanes hacen cosas'*, said former Prime Minister Mariano Rajoy in 2015 in an interview that immediately went viral through social media, probably thereby conveying more meaning than he himself intended); 3) the *comparses* being '*com una família*', thus naturalising membership in a rather artificial network of people into a type of family-like group to which one

---

mobilised, during the transition, in order to model a discourse of non-complicity or even open resistance vis-à-vis the regime. Other 'festivals of transition', according to my definition, are those analysed in Bertolotti 1990; Creed 2011; Noyes 2003; Testa 2017b, 2017c, just to name a few examples.

'belongs' – the simile of the family is a strong one, the importance of family being a 'charter myth' of central Catalan identity (Llobera 1997).

El Carnaval, in its complexity and articulations, tells much about Solsona. For some, it actually tells everything one needs to know about Solsona.[22] Its '*essència*', as the *comparses* have been qualified, make it possible for locals to weave the threads of the social fabric as well as to articulate and express their 'being Catalans' in central Catalonia.[23] And in fact, the preceding and complementary chapter focusses on the aspects of identity and national construction, social cohesion, and community-binding though investment of energy and time, material and financial waste, and the resulting creation of symbolic value. In this chapter, I have tried to highlight the dynamics through which these aims are achieved, and especially the role of the semi-formal network of the *comparses* in establishing and reproducing not only the behavioural and attitudinal patterns that characterise the ritual week, but actually a model of how Catalan inclusive nationalism can or could work.

We should beware, however, of a risk of reductionism and determinism. Since at least the age of Durkheim, stating that a public ritual in the form of a major popular festival is 'prosocial' is at best a tautology, at worst just a

---

[22] Solsona's Carnival has already for some time been perceived as one of its most important – if not its most important – piece of 'cultural heritage'. In this bipartite study I have not, however, tackled the issue of heritage-making and its cluster of related socio-cultural processes (such as marketisation, touristification, musealisation, and other '-ations'), as I have done elsewhere (Testa 2019, 2020b, 2021). There is now a rich body of scholarship about heritagisation in other areas of Catalonia or in the region as a whole, which has been growing after the ratification of the UNESCO ICH in 2003. The first ground-breaking study about the impact of the UNESCO policies and imaginers, which was devoted to Catalonia's first UNESCO's item, the *Patum*, is Noyes 2006 (which in many respects complements Noyes 2003). Afterwards, other scholars, especially but not exclusively Catalan, have shown a great curiosity and eagerness for the study of cultural heritage dynamics in Catalonia: an excellent introduction to this scholarship is Del Mármol Cartañà and Roigé Ventura 2014, but many other authors have been working on these topics, among whom, apart from those present in this book, at least Ferran Estrada Bonell, Claire Guiu, and Eliseu Carbonell Camós should be remembered.

[23] What I have attempted to do here had already been done, differently and about a different case study, by Dorothy Noyes in her *Fire in the Plaça* (Noyes 2003), although the situation of Catalonia has changed quite dramatically since she published her book, and even more since she did her fieldwork in Berga; see, for instance, the still exemplary analysis of the dynamics through which festivity, social memory, collective identity, community imagination, past construction, and nationalism interact and converge during the circumscribed time–space of the most important public event and ritual in Berga: Noyes 2003, 202–206.

banal statement. Prosociality should not overshadow other components that actually seem to contradict the general trend: as I explain in greater detail in another publication, 'it is important to stress this aspect here, in order not to fall into the trap of an implicit and uncritical neo-functionalism. Identity is not a monolithic social configuration, nor are its processual dynamics linear and predictive' (Testa 2019, 89).

The present chapter has tried to demonstrate, among other things, how inclusiveness and cohesion also come at a cost, and that even the architecture of the apparently 'consistent' carnivalesque infrastructure of the *comparse*s is far from being straightforward, homogeneous, or free of ruptures and tensions. And, again at odds with the traditional functionalistic interpretation of festivals, especially in rural or provincial areas, *el Carnaval* seems to represent one of the driving forces in the political polarisation that has followed the failed Catalan attempt to gain independence in 2017. Even more importantly, Solsona's main public ritual has the power to integrate and socialise individuals within its local community, within its microcosm of central and 'deep Catalanness', but also, alas, to prevent that, thus proving, by metonymy, that Catalan national(istic) inclusiveness also has its limitations, inner and outer. After all, ritually fostered cultural or civic nationalism is a form of, precisely, nationalism.[24] But then again nobody can be blamed for that, for utter inclusiveness cannot exist: it would be *ipso facto* a contradiction in terms.

---

[24] My conclusions are therefore in line, generally speaking, with the idea of contemporary Catalan nationalism being a form of 'civic' or 'cultural' nationalism (as claimed in the past by Llobera 2004; for definitions of civic and cultural nationalism, see Smith 2013 and Hutchinson 2013), although throughout the development of Catalan nationalism things have stood differently at different times (for a more recent assessment of the idea of Catalanism as a civic nationalism, see Dowling 2018, 34–36).

4

Reclaiming the Cathar Past: At the Crossroads between Identity Politics and Tourist Economies in Catalonia

CAMILA DEL MÁRMOL

In 2018, the Cathar festival of Josa de Cadí, celebrated since 1996, turned into a moving tribute to the recently-imprisoned political leaders of the Catalan government.[1] This small Pyrenean hamlet, perched at the top of a hill on the southern slopes of the Cadí mountain, was festooned with yellow ribbons – the symbol of solidarity with the Catalan detainees – interspersed among the traditional medieval coats of arms that are typically used to decorate the wooden and masonry balconies for the occasion. A large banner demanding freedom was hanging on a stone façade presiding over the village square (*plaça*). Every first weekend in August, the Cathar festival brings hundreds of people to this particular spot, inhabited by just a handful of permanent residents but a site of personal attachment for a regular community of temporary residents with second homes. This was the case of Jordi Turull, the former counselor and spokesperson for the Presidency, who was accused of sedition and rebellion in March 2018 and has been incarcerated since then. Originally from Parets del Vallès, one of the industrial areas near Barcelona, Turull is part

---

[1] This study was carried out as part of a project entitled: "Patrimonio inmaterial y politicas culturales: desafios sociales, politicos y museológicos", which was funded by the Spanish Ministry of Science, Innovation and Universities and the FEDER Program. PGC2018–096190-B-I00. I want to thank the support of Carles Gascón and Isidre Domenjó (Consell Comarcal de l'Alt Urgell), as well as the warm welcoming of the inhabitants of Josa de Cadí.

of this particular residential community that has developed strong ties to the hamlet, which had neared total depopulation during the 1980s.

Turull was granted in absentia the designation of *Bon home* (Good man), the popular name given to Cathar heretics back in the 12th and 13th centuries, considered to be pious and compassionate as opposed to the fatuous degeneracy of the Catholic Church. It was a newly created appointment made up by heritage experts working in a local administration, the Consell Comarcal de l'Alt Urgell, with the aim of honoring and advocating Jordi Turull. The President of Catalonia, Quim Torra, recently barred from public office by the Supreme Court of Spain,[2] attended the event, which turned into a massive demonstration of support for the political prisoners and a celebration of Catalan independence. During the various speeches and ceremonies held throughout this day in 2018, many comparisons were drawn between the current situation of exile and political imprisonment in Catalonia and that of the Cathars throughout the 12th and 13th centuries. A medieval religious sect of southern France that challenged the authority of the Catholic Church, the Cathars were massacred during the Albigensian Crusade (1209–1229), which forced many of its member to seek refugee across the Pyrenees. The novels and plays that reinterpreted the Cathar past in the Catalan Pyrenees since the 1980s, building on several interpretations coming mainly from France (see Biget 1979; Soula 2005), feature the Cathars as pioneers of democratic and egalitarian values, supporters of religious tolerance, precursors of feminist ideas, and victims of the absolutism and ignorance of the Middle Ages (see Del Mármol 2010). In this same vein, the 2018 celebration was filled with symbolic parallelisms. Torra himself referred to the detainees as *bons homes i bones dones* (good men and women) on several occasions, and Turull sent a statement from prison in which he declared: "We will continue through thick and thin to defend the same goals, alongside the *bons homes*, those whose aim is to peacefully support justice, democracy, and freedom, never on the side of those who want to overshadow these values."[3]

Traditional popular activities are historically linked to expressions of national identity in Catalonia (Contreras 1978; Wittlin 1994). The flowering of national feelings arising during the late 19th century and articulated through political and artistic movements (Prats 1988) was followed by the repression suffered during the Franco dictatorship and led to a marked revitalization afterwards (Contreras 1978); that, in turn, was to continue during the first years of democracy (Crespi-Vallbona and Richards 2007; Wittlin 1994). This development continued until the present, and has been intimately related to

---

[2] Torra was barred from public office for refusing to withdraw symbols of support for the political prisoners from public buildings during the electoral period in 2019.
[3] All the translations are mine.

the Catalan process (*procés*) (Clua 2014; Kammerer 2014). Referring to the Cathar history of Josa de Cadí, and specifically to the Cathar Trail that ran through the Pyrenees and was created as part of the effort to stimulate tourism in the area 15 years ago (see Roigé and Frigolé 2010; Vaccaro and Beltran 2010), the heritage expert who nominated Turull for the award stated in his speech that day in 2018: "From history we have built a road, and from that road we are building the country."[4]

This example must be understood in the context of the many uses of the past that have arisen in recent years in Catalonia in relation to the Catalan *procés*. Many narratives and imaginaries harking back to the past are currently unfolding in this autonomous region, which has reinforced its endeavors to break free from Spain in recent years (see Bel 2013; Clua 2014; Dowling 2018; Frigolé 2021; Muñoz and Guijoan 2013). My aim here is to discuss the uses of the Cathar past in the Catalan Pyrenees, specifically in relation with the festival of Josa de Cadí, viewing them as a particular way to express and mediate local, regional, and national identities, affording people the opportunity of reflecting on new futures, while also actively engaging with their changing presents (Khalvashi 2018). By connecting local narratives with national processes, these discourses about the past offer alternative grounds for the production of local identities, while relating regional experiences and understandings to national political developments. The idea is to think of these processes focusing mostly on the futurities involved – how the past is being mobilized within specific expectations, potentialities, and hopes for a changing future.

BUILDING THE COUNTRY

The ongoing conflict unfolding in Catalan society over the past decade set the context of my research, in which a broader national struggle is interacting with local narratives and dynamics. In other works, I have focused on the power of imagination in the projection of new spaces of governance in contemporary Catalonia – the way in which imaginaries work as technologies of power within governmentality regimes (Del Mármol 2019). Here I would like to pursue a wider analysis of how the Cathar past is being mobilized to enable alternative forms of producing regional subjectivity and identity. By engaging imaginatively with the local past, this example offers new ways of reflecting on Pyrenean identities more broadly and relating them to the current political situation.

---

4   All quotations from the Cathar festival are from my field notes and supported by official versions of the speeches in the case of public statements.

Imagination works as a powerful device for shaping territories, pasts, people, and their relationships with the wider world (Appadurai 1996; Ricoeur 1994). The last decade in Catalonia has been marked by the advent of an independence movement that was hardly conceivable at the beginning of the 21st century. The aspiration of independence among a sector of the political class and of civil society arose from a convoluted muddle combining experiences of repression and dispossession, mythical grievances, historical narratives, economic wrongs and discontents, as well as a longing for social justice and new models of participatory democracy in reaction to the existing Spanish political framework in the wake of the Transition from Francoism (Clua 2014; Frigolé 2021; Llobera 2004).[5] As Frigolé (2021) argues, aspirations of independence and democracy in Catalonia emerged conjointly with the experience of the 2008 economic crisis and an ongoing narrative of dispossession by the central Spanish government underpinned by political and economic arguments. Whereas in the early 2000s independence was not part of a collective claim, with fewer than 13% of the inhabitants of Catalonia considering themselves as part of the independence movement (Dowling 2018), things changed to the extent that in 2018 this number had risen to 48% in several official surveys (e.g. CEO 2018). For many, independence became a goal to achieve, a mythical future in which to project social utopias and a new relationship to politics and government. From the convoluted range of radical left to fairly right-wing political positions, a heterogeneous spectrum of social and political movements came together with a clear craving for independence, defying the conservative aura projected upon nationalist politics in 21st-century neoliberal Europe.

Social imagination has played a crucial role in this growing movement in Catalonia, a process to which we can refer as the *imagining of independence*. It was fostered alike by official channels, political parties, and civil society, building broadly on the strong tradition of community associations in Catalan society (Crespi-Vallbona and Richards 2007), and was also fostered by some sectors of the Catalan media. Perhaps one of the most relevant examples of this was the *White Paper: The National Transition of Catalonia* (Generalitat de Catalunya 2014) drafted by the Advisory Council on the National Transition created in 2013 by the Catalan Government. A compilation of reports on the complex process leading to independence, this future-oriented guide explores a variety of topics, from the reasons to break free from Spain to the various aspects of the future state. Other evidence of this imagination set in motion

---

[5] It is not the aim of this chapter to focus on the history of Catalan nationalism, nor is there enough space for venturing deeper into this topic. For further reading there is an extensive corpus of works: Barrera 1985; Clua 2008; De Riquer i Permanyer 1996; Dowling 2018; Guibernau 2004; Llobera 1990, 2004, among many others.

for the construction of the Catalan state is available, such as the 2012 supplement of a well-known newspaper (*El Punt Avui*) entirely devoted to map the characteristics of the future government,[6] covering issues that range from the future of national finances to the territorial organization and, of course, the distressing fate of a soccer league deprived of the Barça vs. Madrid games.

Endless initiatives of this kind helped in shaping the possibilities of a future independent Catalonia. Among these examples, a relevant case was the inauguration of a Center of Memory and Culture in Barcelona, in relation to the mythical date of 1714 (Breen et al 2016).[7] Shifting representations of the past have long been considered a crucial dimension in the construction of national identities (see Anderson 1983). In this vein, history has often been mobilized in recent years in Catalonia alongside the changing debates and controversies that emerged from the *procés*. This was clearly expressed in 2017, when the whole country was in suspense waiting to see if the President of the Generalitat proclaimed independence, following the mandate of the popular referendum held on October 1 and later declared unconstitutional by the Spanish Constitutional Court. Finally, a few days later, the Catalan Parliament declared the Catalan Republic. During those days, previous declarations of Catalan independence, and primarily the last one at the inception of the Spanish Civil War, were recalled in various editorials.[8] Several historic events and narratives helped to contextualize the ongoing events as part of a continuous effort of the Catalan institutions to break away from Spain. Recently, many narratives and imaginaries harking back to the past are currently emerging. The advent of the Cathar past as a pool of symbolic resources to be discussed in this current situation is just a local variation of these expressions, which first developed in the specific context of the drastic depopulation of the Pyrenees in the 1970s and 1980s, and is currently being reinforced in the changing scenario of Catalan politics.

---

[6] Supplement "La Catalunya independent, a debat", November 2012 (https://www.elpuntavui.cat/politica/article/17-politica/589328-la-catalunya-independent-a-debat.html).

[7] *La Diada*, the national day of Catalonia, commemorates every September 11 the defeat of Barcelona during the War of Succession that brough about the disintegration of Catalan institutions and laws in 1714.

[8] E.g. *Ara Cat*, "De Felip V a Mariano Rajoy", September 23, 2017; *El Nacional* "La imagen de Carlos III (con porra) detrás de Felipe VI enciende las redes", October 3, 2017; *ABC* "La mitificada independencia de Cataluña durante la Edad Media", September 17, 2017. The examples of this kind were endless during those days in 2017 and continue today.

THE CATHARS IN THE CATALAN PYRENEES

This chapter is based on long-term ethnographic fieldwork in the Catalan Pyrenees performed over the course of 16 months between 2006 and 2012, specifically in the Alt Urgell district, as well as subsequent periods of research leading up to the 2018 celebration analyzed here. Part of my work focuses on the different uses of the Cathar past in the region, following the thread of an anthropology of history and of the uses of the past (Appadurai 1981; Berliner 2005; Brow 1990; Herzfeld 1991; Sahlins 1994; Trouillot 1995) that foreground the analysis of the wide array of "practices of inquiry into the past, as well as the forms and modes in which the past is represented to others" (Palmié and Stewart 2016, 210).

The history of Catharism has been a matter of much debate and further representations at the other side of the border, across the French Midi. A symbolic niche for the forging of several images that dialogue with the subsequent presents in which they were created, the Cathars were repeatedly instrumentalized in the context of ideological and political struggles (Biget 1979; Soula 2005; Steinkrüger 1995). Crafted into a romantic mythology during the 19th century, the heretics were understood as martyrs of freedom, their beliefs enveloped in an esoteric halo. The troubadours, with their attractive poetry and courtly love, fueled the image of an educated, tolerant people opposing the barbaric Middle Ages (Biget 1979). Theirs is a history made up of memories and oblivions, carved out betwixt and between several ideological conflicts that have traversed French history over the past centuries, such as the clash between centralism and federalism or the different versions of anticlericalism. This is why I am not interested here in presenting a historic account of the Albigensian Crusade, but rather in going over the specific uses of this past in the case of Catalonia. The revival of political Occitanism during the 1960s marked the articulation of the Cathar imaginary with theories of local liberation in France (García and Genieys 2005, 28), a usage that was later and only marginally echoed in the Catalan Pyrenees.

In Catalonia the implications of the Cathar heresy were not widely discussed (Gascón 2003), but a scaled-down debate was established in the Pyrenees within a movement to revalue mountain society that developed during the 1980s (Ros i Fontana 1997). Recovering the medieval past by restoring ancient monuments, but mainly by producing epic narratives, allowed the social imagination to bring forth positive images that emerged against the backdrop of the reality of abandonment, depopulation, and economic collapse destabilizing the local economy and society (Del Mármol et al 2018; Vaccaro and Beltran 2010). The novel *Cercamón*, by Lluís Racionero (1982), was key for the deployment of a local Cathar mythology, based on the work of historian Ventura Subirats (1960) proclaiming that the annihilation of the

Christian heretics in Occitania was a political scheme to block the creation of a Catalan-Occitan nation on both sides of the mountain range, a new nation that could have eclipsed the power of the French monarchy and the papacy. *Cercamón* was widely read, considered by many as a "local Bible",[9] in which the romantic appeal of Catharism was seized to project an alternative imagination where the region became the center of a possible future that had never arrived. A celebration of Pyrenean identity, the book sketches the portrait of a sophisticated and enlightened culture that blossomed in the mountains and was devastated by the royalist powers. According to the novel, what would become the origin of Catalan identity evolved in the Pyrenees, in a well-suited parallelism with the national narratives of defeat against the Spanish Crown:

> [Blanca of Castile speaking] I must pave the way for future generations of my lineage to rule these nations. One danger lies ahead: that the Pyrenean and Occitan people found a new kingdom on both sides of the mountains. Thereupon, a realm capable of contending with us and France would spread from the Ebro to the Rhône. It is essential that neither the Francs nor the Castilians allow this to happen. (Racionero 1982, 119)

In this romantic representation, the Pyrenees are depicted as the center of the Catalan-Occitan nation that would have illuminated the darkness of medieval Europe. Placing the Pyrenees in a complex history that establishes a dialogue with contemporary national narratives helps build strategies of symbolic connections, claiming a role in the present. *Cercamón* became popular locally, imbuing young generations with a distinct sense of self-pride, reclaiming the otherwise neglected Pyrenean identity.

A decade later, the turn of events in southern France continued to have an impact on the Catalan Pyrenees. New publications approaching the Cathar past from a historical but also from a romantic perspective achieved some popularity in Catalonia (Dalmau 1997; Mestre 1994). However, the most important change was the development of merchandising and tourism fostering the Albigensian Crusade for a wider market of visitors (for France see García and Geneiys 2005). Some villages of the Alt Urgell chose to celebrate the Cathars in newly created events that would later be encompassed within the *Festival Càtar del Pirineu Català* (Cathar festival of the Catalan Pyrenees). In Josa de Cadí, the mayor put forward the idea of holding a Cathar symposium after being informed by a local historian and novelist, Esteve Albert, that the medieval lord of Josa had been a supporter of the heresy. It was 1996, several years before the hamlet was left empty after the death of the last permanent inhabitant, prompting many former residents – who had already moved away to nearby cities – to strengthen their efforts to keep the village afloat. From

---

[9] Heritage technician, 2007, personal interview.

then on, a strong solidarity emerged among the summer community, made up not only of former inhabitants but also of other people – Catalans from other regions who were looking for a place to go during the scorching summers in the cities and were persuaded by the other residents to buy and restore houses in Josa. In this context, the organization of the first Cathar gathering, to which the Centre d'Agermanament Català-Occità[10] was invited, was a clear attempt to recover the glorious past of the vanishing village community.

Nonetheless, the initiative was not unanimously welcome. Aside from the circles of Pyrenean intellectuals and middle classes living mostly in the capital of the district, the local inhabitants of depopulated and nearly abandoned villages from the higher valleys viewed the matter differently. For these people, the celebration of a distant past was perceived as foreign, only heightening the feelings of dispossession experienced through the gradual abandonment of their region. For many years, they opposed and ridiculed the celebration of what they called an "invented past", coming together in favor of the *festa major* and other local festivities. These conflicts must be also contextualized within long-term struggles between local families quarrelling about scarce resources – be it land, houses, heritages, or even rooted in the fierce conflict of the Civil War.

Several years later, a new context emerged when the area was reshaped as a tourist destination through a complex geopolitical dynamic (see Del Mármol et al 2018), providing a new purpose for the initially neglected Cathar gatherings. In 2001 it was rebranded as the Cathar festival, Josa being added to the recently created Cathar Trail (*Camí dels Bons Homes*) that joined different points in the Catalan Pyrenees marked as having had a Cathar past (a broad connotation, indeed). Designed for tourist purposes, the celebration brought together the few permanent inhabitants who were struggling to find a livelihood in the village, such as a recently opened local restaurant and a newcomer with a small handicraft venture based on local plants. The festival, together with other newly created celebrations in the valley (see Frigolé 2005) turned out to be the perfect showcase for the local handicraft and artisanal production fostering new ways of making a living. As Norum and Mostafanezhad (2016, 158) highlighted: "Perceptions of authentic others, whether human or non-human, from other times and other places, are powerful agents of othering and of legitimizing such others as sites of touristic value and attention."

---

[10] An association founded in 1977 with the aim of promoting Catalan–Occitan relations, focusing mainly on the common language, culture and history. For more information see: https://caoc.cat/caoc/qui-som/

A CRY FOR FREEDOM FROM THE PAST TO THE FUTURE

As we have seen, the origin of the Cathar festival is linked to a politically-motivated celebration that articulated Catalan identity in relation to the exile of the persecuted heretics. The former mayor, Tino, raised in a depleted Josa de Cadí, rummaged through the past until he found a specific point, mostly forgotten, which allowed him to place the hamlet in a brilliant role, harking back to the past with an eye on the future – building on the romantic recreation of the Cathar past forged in the south of France in recent decades, Tino created a dialogue that linked his political views with his desire of renewal for the village. Many local conflicts stepped in and hindered local acceptance among Josa's inhabitants and visitors, condemning the event to oblivion in its first years. But the celebration of last year's Cathar festival brought most people together. The idea of paying tribute to Jordi Turull as a common goal was met with joy. In this way, old uses of the past, boosted by local intellectuals in the 1980s, and developed into token tourist celebrations during the early 2000s, have found a second life as the expression of local imaginaries of independence within the current convoluted political situation.

Whereas in the late 2000s the Cathar festivals led me to refer to the major emphasis on spectacle within the context of tourist promotion, eight years later the festivities gave rise to new expressions and meanings. What was once felt by many as a commodified festival designed to attract tourists, detached from local engagement, turned into a platform for political discontent as well as a celebration of local identity. In an ethnography of the French Midi, Hodges (2009, 76) explored how heritage tourism "cohabits with and colonises modern memory practice at a micro-level." However, it does not preclude other possible uses. "Symbolic revaluation" is a critical concept in this author's ethnography, confronting how changing contexts may provide differing frames for the emergence of new symbolisms, utilizations or affects in relation to aspects or material elements from the past. Limiting the interpretation of heritage tourism practices to empty commodified experiences crafted for visitors is a way of diminishing the complexity of the variety of forms a society has to relate to the past, which, as Hodges remarked (2009, 78) "reveals their commonality of existential focus."

The performative politics of independence, together with the repudiation of what was largely felt as political repression in the form of strong retaliation to Catalan politicians, was met with the local feeling of community built over many years of mostly summer cohabitation that intermingle individual lives with the local experience of conviviality. This last experience largely contradicted a strict categorization of social inhabitants that strongly reject the label of "local" to people coming from other places (MacClancy 2015; Waldren 1996). But when Josa was on the brink of total abandonment and oblivion, it took a particular path in which the remaining settlers built bonds with newcomers, encouraging them to buy and rebuild houses, even if only as summer homes. This community came together to honor one of its own people, performing a political narrative while reinforcing local ties and the sense of belonging. The celebration outlived its original motives and, even though riddled with local conflicts, has become the most attended celebration in the hamlet to date, attracting visitors and tourists from all around.

Coming back to the event in 2018, the President of the Generalitat joined a guided hike from Gósol to Josa de Cadí organized by the Consell Comarcal de l'Alt Urgell in order to commemorate the 20th anniversary of the opening of the Cathar Trail (*Camí dels Bons homes*). Many villagers and local political representatives joined in, allowing for multiple parallelisms with the exile of the Cathar refugees from Languedoc, documented in historic sources as escaping the bloody massacres committed by the Crusades in the 13th century (Biget 1979). In fact, this trail evokes the exile, joining the Catalan trail with the French Cathar Trail originally created in 1980s (Menzel 2017). As previously mentioned, Cathars are portrayed as martyrs and symbols of independence, tolerance, and resistance both in historical and popular accounts (McCaffrey 2002). These narratives fit in perfectly with the recent experiences and official accounts of some sectors of Catalan society, depicted in terms of a modern nation determined to oppose Spanish repression. The recent path of referendums held both legally and illegally in the Catalan region is considered by the ruling and other pro-independence parties to open a path towards liberation for the Catalan people, a legacy to which they remain committed. In his speech during the official ceremony held at the village square, Torra proclaimed with a trembling voice:

> What did they do to be in prison? These people have complied with what we have asked them to do, [...] to give the voice to the people of Catalonia to be able to vote, to freely choose our future. And you find yourself here, at the heart of the Pyrenees, and you ask yourself why we Catalans do not have the right to choose our future.

After which he adamantly proclaimed:

> Today, I am taking on Josa's commitment to say enough is enough. Enough of this judiciary farce [...] [and asked] the people of Catalonia to symbolically start a march in defense of civil rights to overthrow these sentences. [...] We cannot tolerate having honorable politicians, *bons homes* and *bones dones* [...], remain imprisoned."

The Cathars emerged as an analogy of resistance and justice, while channeling a deep-rooted expression of regional and local history and identity ingrained in the traditional representation of the Catalan people. Turull's wife read aloud a letter the politician sent from prison for the occasion, among many tears from the people gathered in the *plaça*:

> I don't know how long it will take me to be with you again, to sit and chat on the steps of Cal Magre for a while[...] or to recommend to everybody that they buy Mercè and Raúl's cheeses, which are the best in the world. I don't know how long it will be because this is not about justice, but about punishment. Punishment at all costs. What I do know is that I will be adamant in my convictions without resentment nor bitterness. I will follow the path of the *bons homes* and the magnificent *dones* [...] Thanks, Josa, for so much. Thanks, Josa, for everything.

Festivals and celebrations as open-ended symbolic arenas allow for change and multiple projections of values and needs. The imprisonment of Catalan political figures amid the punitive blow inflicted by the Spanish Government after the Declaration of Independence in 2017, specifically affecting a "townsman of Josa", namely Jordi Turull, marked a turning point for the Cathar festival. The Cathar past once again became a political resource for reflecting on Catalan identity, self-identification, and nationalism. Linking cultural distinctiveness with national identity, the celebration mobilized local assets and managed to attract national attention with the visit of the Catalan President. In this process, Josa's inhabitants reveal the malleability of historical signifiers, denying both the commodification of newly created festivals that popped up just to attract tourism, and the conservative reading of a distant past mobilized to link the locality to a traditional image. Through the ongoing reshaping of the uses of the past, the Cathar festival allows for the mediation of local identity, the expression of national feeling as well as political desires, placing the recent past into a long-term perspective.

In this manner, the Cathars help demarcate the imaginary boundaries of Catalan history and identity, bringing together distant representations of victimhood and fatality that hark back to the mythical origins of the Catalan people back in the Middle Ages. The *Renaixença* consolidated this concrete selection of the past as the cradle of the country, based on the independent character of the feudal lords and the autonomous nature of the territory thus organized (Martel 2003). The century-long refusal of the Occitan counties to accept the centralized government of the French and Spanish Crown is harnessed as a fruitful analogy to substantiate the current state of affairs in the country. While widespread national efforts have focused on the celebration of the defeat of 1714, epitomizing the final defeat of the autonomous government of Catalonia subsequently absorbed by a centralized Spanish kingdom, Cathar history and its specific use illustrated here moves along similar lines. The significance of this particular selection lies in its ties with the region, foregrounding the central role played by the Pyrenees in the ancient origins

10. *Festa dels càtars* 2018. Source: Author.

of the country (Roma 2004), which are not represented in the widely celebrated events of 1714. The Cathars bring the Pyrenees to the fore, reclaiming a privileged part not only in the history of the country but in its contemporary struggles and eagerly awaited future as well.

In this same vein, the words of Jordi Turull to Anna Gabriel, former MP for the CUP (Candidatura d'Unitat Popular, Candidacy of Popular Unity) currently living in exile in Switzerland to avoid her prosecution for the crimes of rebellion and sedition, are a clear example. The letter[11] refers to the bond they both have with the people of Josa de Cadí (Anna Gabriel's family being close to many Joseans), and bring up the shared experience of repression and persecution beyond their ideological differences

> Now, in addition, there is also at stake the legacy of justice, democracy, and rights and freedoms that many of us thought to have been achieved and consolidated. And this should appeal to everyone, because these fundamental rights and freedoms that are being violated belong to everyone and are for everyone, not only for those we defend and who are committed to the independence of Catalonia [...] I am convinced that we will suffer and that it will not be easy, but also that in the end we will get there. We will turn this difficult situation into a great opportunity. The 21st century is for those of us who peacefully want to enhance justice, democracy, and rights and freedoms, and not for those who authoritatively undermine them day after day.

Resilience and determination, commitment and serenity, as well as the role of Catalan *seny* (common sense or reason) are repeatedly praised in the many letters between political figures of the independence movement, as well as the thousands of letters written to the political prisoners by unknown citizens in the context of the public "Write to the prisoners" campaign (see Ardèvol and Travancas 2019). These authors analyzed letter-writing as a political act:

> Letters articulate political protest through the circulation of affections, linking the intimate gesture of writing with public, large-scale action. Letter-writing, both as an individual practice and collectively, works outwards and inwards: to overcome fear, separation and suffering, and to open up to struggle, hope and freedom. (2019: 111)

Crameri (2015) analyzes civil pro-independence dynamics as a crucial aspect of independence politics in Catalonia, moving beyond simplistic notions of bottom-up/bottom-down dynamics and advocating for a more complex approach based on multidimensional movements. In this sense, civil celebrations, such as the one addressed in this chapter, offer excellent material for reflecting on the blurred boundaries between official politics and popular mobilization. Letter-writing, large group dinners, and a variety of social events honoring the political prisoners in Catalonia, including the Cathar festival in

---

[11] Available at https://www.vilaweb.cat/noticies/cartes-per-la-llibertat-turull-anna-gabriel/.

Josa de Cadí, are part of an "affective nationalism" as described by Militz and Schurr (2016): the act of shaping a nation through physical encounters and affections, both joyful and painful. Therefore, the nation is considered as something that is continually being shaped, formed, and experienced throughout the deployment of social events, political performance, and a variety of celebrations displaying a multifarious catalogue of creativity. The shared suffering and tears in the village square is one of these instances in which the nation is brought into existence (Ahmed 2004). As Waterton and Watson (2013, 10) remarked: "Bodies moving through interactions with heritage are changed, and some (though not all) of the felt affordances generated hold significance."

CONCLUSIONS

Festivities and celebrations, as well as newly crafted traditions, open up new horizons of meaning that remains accessible for the times to come. Nonetheless, the metaphor of the blank slate does not apply here, since its many possibilities are not indefinite, but closely regulated by local norms and restrictions. The Cathar festival, once a cry against depletion and abandonment, underpinned by vernacular images of identity facing opposition on the basis of local conflicts and vicinity issues, was later turned into a commodified celebration to display local production in the context of a tourist economy (albeit not devoid of local unrest). As time passed by since that distant 1996, the local community, consisting primarily of holiday residents, embraced every opportunity to celebrate their gathering during their summer holidays, the village festival being the major public event of this kind. 2018 opened up the opportunity for a different social experience, in the context of the independence movement and the imprisonment of political leaders, among whom was one of their own: Jordi Turull. Harking back to the Cathar past affords new channels to convey feelings of defeat and failure, and to turn them into narratives of possible futures. Much as the extermination of Catharism by the Inquisition led to new narratives of salvation in the form of various influences that spread at both sides of the Pyrenees, the current uses of the Cathar past suggest a path of redemption. Following Khalvashi (2018), I contended that the Cathars continue to mediate the conceptual worlds of the Catalan *procés* in this specific location in the Pyrenees. The recent political blow can thus be reimagined.

The 2020 festival was cancelled due to Covid-19 pandemic, as every major celebration in the valley and around the globe. But the festival will still be there for years to come, to be shaped and reconfigured on every occasion to serve as an arena for expression and affection, for conflict and sociality, to communicate and represent in each case for whoever wishes and manages to shape the event. It is easier to envision futures when they are built upon the past. The Cathars serve here as a template made of sound values from which to understand the ignominious present and build a brighter future. From failure and defeat, the Cathars fuel the hope for endurance, permanence, and continuity, an alternative narrative leading to a different future. If we focus "on the way that past conditions occupy the future, setting limits on the plausible" (Ahmann 2019, 12), we can grasp the relevance of recurring to a variety of pasts that could help build different future orientations that are crucial for imagining new plausible realities.

Nowadays, the Cathar Trail is prompting new parallelisms. Within the current context resulting from the impact of the global Covid-19 pandemic, the population is suffering long periods of lockdown and self-isolation. The situation has proved more challenging within densely populated urban settings, especially large cities such as Barcelona. The streets and metro stations in the city quickly began displaying appealing images of natural surroundings, promoting the virtues of rural landscapes, and revealing the market's malleability in facing new crises. The strict lockdown loosened its grips by the end of June 2020 – for the moment, at least – forecasting a new summer situation in which faraway destinations were out of the question (Réau and Guibert 2020). The most cherished urban experience, built upon a global imaginary of cosmopolitanism, multiculturalism, and opportunities underscoring the virtues of liberalism and global connectedness, turned into a viral trap. Exhausted urban dwellers were compelled to find relief in nearby rural settings, challenging the existing assumptions and imaginaries about distant places. The Cathar Trail, in a recent post in its website, summoned its readers to appreciate the value of life and the bare essentials, building an emotional analogy with the Cathars seven centuries ago: "We invite you to discover the relevance of those values, and perhaps, who knows, to unleash the *bon home* or *bona dona* within you."[12]

---

[12] http://www.camidelsbonshomes.com/, http://www.camidelsbonshomes.com/May 2020.

5

The Heritage of the Humiliated: Popular Resistance in Defense of the "*Bous*" in the Lands of the Ebro

MANUEL DELGADO, ROMINA MARTÍNEZ ALGUERÓ,
SARAI MARTÍN LÓPEZ

RECUPERATION AND BOOM OF CATALAN POPULAR CULTURE, BUT NOT ALL OF IT

In Catalonia, the last phase of Franco's dictatorship and the re-establishment of formal democracy led to an intense dynamic of recuperation and reinvention of popular festivities.[1] These were now highly participative festivities that implied the transformation of everyday life environments – like streets and squares – as well as the intense participation of ordinary people (Prat and Contreras 1984; Prats et al 1982). This revival of popular culture was common in European countries throughout the 1970s and 1980s (Boissevain 1992; Vovelle 1985, 187–203). However, in this part of Spain it had a special connotation associated with much contentious history that demanded Catalonia's cultural singularity be converted into political sovereignty.

---

[1] This chapter results from a research project titled *"Que no ens toquin els bous". The increase of bullfighting traditions and fighting for ones dignity in the Ebro region*. This project was led in 2019 by the Institut Català d'Antropologia with the support of the Institut Ramon Muntaner (IRMU) and with the collaboration of the Museum of the Terres de l'Ebre. Emma Fàbrega's translation was possible thanks to a grant of the Facultat de Geografia i Història of the University of Barcelona.

However, the recuperation of this festive atmosphere was used as an instrument for social cohesion and community identification. It was not a mere replica of what had been the customary Catalan universe before its deactivation – and in the best of cases appropriation – due to Franco's dictatorship. If we had to highlight some of the most singular traits of this restoral, which accompanied Catalonia throughout the advent of democracy after Franco's death, probably the most remarkable would be the displacement of the sources of festive repertoires. Now, what had been the predilection of romantic Catalanism for the *Catalunya vella* (Old Catalonia) (Prats 1989) – including the counties of Girona and Centre Catalonia – was translated into elements like the *castellers* (human towers), the sound of the wind instrument *gralla*, the *gegants* (giant representations of iconic personalities from a region) and the *diables* (groups of people that dress as devils and throw fireworks with music), which came from areas composed of el Garraf, Alt and Baix Penedès, Alt and Baix Camp, the Conca de Barberà, the Priorat, and the Camp de Tarragona – in other words, counties south of the capital, Barcelona, and that occupy a greater part of the province of Tarragona. Thus, we are speaking of a territory that extends, following the Mediterranean coastline, between Sitges and below Cambrils.

This transfer of the essential geographic nucleus of imaginary Catalanness from the counties around Girona to those in Tarragona and the Penedès demonstrates how symbols that endow a certain sense of identity are not "static categories, sclerotized, homogenous categories, but something alive, in a constant process of recreation and transformation", depending on the "diverse circumstances and independent factors that make up and give its precise, synchronic, and contextual content" (Pujadas and Comas D'Argemir 1991, 647). In this case, it was obvious that if it was indisputable from nationalist essentialism that Catalonia was eternal and immutable, the selection of testimonies to that truth could mutate depending on the times and the political trends.

Just like during the *Renaixença* period[2] and afterwards, the counties closer to the rest of Spain – Aragon and the Valencian Country – were once again excluded from this new redistribution of resources that can be homologated as Catalan popular and national culture. These counties included the counties of Ponent in the east and the counties of the Ebro in the south. The latter were significant, because southern Catalonia – the counties of Ribera of Ebro, Montsià, Terra Alta, and Baix Ebre – presented cultural peculiarities marked by its relationship with the rest of the Catalan territory. They were determined by the omnipresence of the Ebro River and its delta, its rice culture, the

---

[2] The *Renaixença* ("Rebirth") was the literary and linguistic renaissance that characterized the Romantic period in Catalonia.

memory of the grand battle that occurred there during the Civil War and, in the festive arena, the *jota*, the music bands ... and the *bous*.

The *bous* – *correbous* in the rest of Catalonia – are a form of participatory popular bullfighting based on the active intervention of participants. Unlike what happens in conventional races – *la corrida* – there is no separation here between the competitors and the animal. There are several varieties: the *bous al carrer* (bulls on the street), which consists of releasing a calf, ox, or cow into the streets in a confined urban route; the *bous a la plaça* (bulls in the square), in which a cow is let go in a square expressly constructed for those purposes; the *bou embolat* (bull with fireballs), a nocturnal modality that consists of putting fireballs in a device suspended from the horns of the animal and letting it lose in the square or in the streets of a town, always in a closed circuit; the *bou capllaçat, ensogat* or *amb corda* (tied up bull), is a technique in which the animal is tied by the lower part of its horns with a rope; the *bous a la mar* (bulls in the sea), in which part of the games with the animals takes place in the water of the beach or the port; and the *exhibició d'habilitats* (exhibition of skills) are competitions between *retalladors* (cutters) or *emboladors* (packers).

11. *Bous al carre*r in Horta de Sant Joan. September 2018. Source: Marc Sampé Compte.

It must be noted that, in Catalonia, a new and growing sensibility towards relationships with animals, and the simultaneously growing tensions in a political climate especially attentive to certain contentious symbolic and historic aspects with Spain, led to the abolition of the *fiesta nacional*, or *la corrida* professional (professional bullfighting) in 2010 (Brandes 2017, 2019; González Fernández 2022; Grisostolo 2017). This new spirit led to a gradual decline in most of the Catalan territories where participatory bullfighting festivals, *els correbous*, had been held. In the counties of Girona, those of Roses, Olot and Torroella de Montgrí have disappeared in recent years. Only that of Vidreres survives. In those of Barcelona, the one in Cardona persists, the one in the neighborhood of Llefià, in Badalona, has been suppressed, and the one in Santpedor is pending a referendum.

This tendency of the disappearance of the festivities with bulls – regulated or popular – registers an exception in the strong increase of various types of *correbous* in a cornered part of Catalonia – both in the sense of it being a corner and in the sense of it being forgotten – in the Terres de L'Ebre. In this region, and more exactly in its counties of the Montsià and Baix Ebre – areas nicknamed the *marineres* or in other words the sailors –the participatory bullfighting festivities not only resisted governmental restrictions, but also continued and even increased year after year due to a relative institutional approval that was firmly supported by the popular and political will at a local level. This increase contrasted with the rejection and practical extinction of the practice in the rest of Catalonia. That is how, in 2011, 208 *bous* were counted; in 2015, 214; in 2016 it went down to 195, but in 2017 it went up to 433 in a total of 202 days. In 2018, 439 authorized *bous* took place in 207 days in 27 towns. Within this total, 138 were *bous embolats* (bulls with fireballs) – 10% fewer than the year prior – and 43 *bous capllaçats* (tied-up bulls).[3] There are *correbous* in the areas of the Montsià, except Freginals, and in all of Baix Ebre, except el Perelló and l'Ametlla de Mar. In some places, the practices have been recovered, like in Aldover or in various neighborhoods of Tortosa. In other places the calendar of bullfighting festivities has been expanded, like in l'Aldea.[4]

---

[3] We do not have data for 2019 and 2022. In 2020 and 2021 there were hardly any *correbous* held because of the coronavirus epidemic.

[4] There is a minority sector of neighbors in the Ebro counties who are for the abolition of the *correbous*, and they consider this form of Ebro identity as disposable. They have formed groups like the Anti-bull Platform of the Terres de l'Ebre (Plataforma Anti-Taurina de les Terres de l'Ebre) or We All Are Town (Tots som poble). This position has a minimal political representation and is related to the leftist radical pro-independence parties like Candidatura d'Unitat Popular or CUP, whom have a very modest presence in the area, and who support the suppression.

The *correbous* have been a problematic issue in recent years, especially since October 1 when the Parliament gave a green light to Law 34/2010, which regulates traditional festivities with oxen and bulls that are mostly celebrated, as previously stated, in the Ebro counties of Baix Ebre and Montsià. The result of the vote that allowed the safeguarding of the celebrations with bulls was 114 votes in favor. In other words, the entire Parliament voted in favor, except for 12 votes against the motion cast by the political parties Iniciativa per Catalunya and EUiA – Eco-Socialist and Communist parties – as well as two socialist votes, and five abstentions. The new law generated a climate in favor of the bulls and their defense in the Ebro region. As previously stated, the *bous* multiplied, and by April 2015, 10,000 people filled the streets of Amposta with signs reading "Yes to the bulls" and "Respect traditions".

This parliamentary support for the Ebro bullfighting celebrations encouraged a campaign driven by the Agrupació de Penyes i Comissions Taurines de les Terres (Terres de l'Ebre Association of Bullfighting Clubs and Commissions) in November 2011, which asked UNESCO to declare the *correbous* an intangible cultural heritage of humanity. Within a few days, several southern municipalities had supported the initiative: Amposta, Sant Carles de la Ràpita, Ulldecona, la Sénia, Santa Bàrbara, Sant Jaume d'Enveja, Masdenverge, la Galera, Godall, Mas de Barberans, Deltebre, Xerta, l'Aldea, Paüls, Alfara de Carles, Horta de Sant Joan and Arnes. Bullfighting associations put forward their demands in strictly cultural and even ecological terms, and avoided any political connotations, but the localities from which they obtained institutional support had an electoral profile with a clear majority (between 85 and 100%) in favor of the independence of Catalonia. Highlighting the contradictory nature of this dynamic, in order to formalize its request to UNESCO, the bullfighting associations of Ebre – a reflection of a pro-independence political environment – had to do so by adhering to initiatives promoted at the level of the whole of the Spanish state by the Partido Popular, representative of the most radical Spanish nationalist right.

Contrary to this euphoria were the constant attacks from animal rights associations that were against these festivities, associations that were mostly alien to the territory. Some incidents even implied assaults by animal rights activists. In May 2017 the Parliament accepted a popular legislative initiative that asked for the suppression of *correbous*, responding to a poll made public in March 2012, which showed that 68% of Catalans were against these practices. This tug-of-war between those fiercely defending this popular festivity rooted in a certain part of the country, and their opposition by animal rights movements, the media, and the majority of the country according to the polls,

---

On a local level however – like Amposta– they argue for the modest elimination of some modalities of *correbous*.

was resolved on September 26, 2019, in a proposal for a resolution by the Parliament. This proposal urged the Generalitat, the Catalan government, to prohibit the *correbous* in all of Catalonia. The En Comú Podem party – linked to the Podemos political party in the rest of the state – started the initiative, which was approved by 50 votes in favor and 17 against, abstention being the option most of the Parliament took, with 61 parliamentarians. The health emergency caused by the Covid-19 pandemic led to the suspension of the *bous* festivities in 2020. Some were restored the following year. In the summer of 2022 the normal bullfighting calendar was re-established throughout the whole of the Ebro territory, without anyone, except animal rights groups, apparently seeming to remember the parliamentary decision taken three years earlier.

The fact that the majority of parliamentarians abstained was a shocking situation, resulting in the contradictory posture of left-leaning parties – like Esquerra Republicana de Catalunya, En Comù, Partit Socialista – which, as supporters of the abolition in general, saw how their representatives from the Ebro counties refused to vote against the festivity in question. This led to an institutional reaction at a local level similar to those in the initial days of October of the same year. Twenty mayors gathered from the Ebro region and Cardona – PdeCat, Catalan conservative nationalist; ERC, PSC and Movem, the En Comú party in the Ebro counties – in order to create a common front that would prevent the inconceivable disappearance of the *bous* from their towns and cities. In August 2022, the President of the Generalitat, Pere Aragonés, the highest regional authority, acknowledged that changes in the celebrations with *bous* – not to mention their eradication – would be difficult if they were perceived as an imposition from Barcelona.

The background of this contradiction – a traditional festivity on the road to extinction that is constantly under threat of being prohibited but that, simultaneously, endures and revives in a specific territory – is underpinned by a social support that understands that the festivities with bulls are non-negotiable as part of the Ebro identity. Usually, this feeling of belonging has been constructed under conflicting conditions of opposition. In this case, it was born out of Barcelona's political and economic centralism, which includes hegemonic models of essential Catalanness. In the initial phase, the campaign against restrictions established by law 3/1988 was key, as it prohibited a basic element of many expressions of the *correbous*: the public death of an animal (Loureiro Lamas and Sánchez García 1990; Padullés 2010, 2011). In the second phase, during the first two decades of the 21st century, the Ebro identity found itself strongly reaffirmed as many counties in the Delta area were forced into a fight against the Plan Hidrológico Nacional (or the National

Hydrological Plan) (Boquera Margalef 2009; Franquesa 2018),[5] a struggle of which the defense of the *bous*, which by then was already an authentic social movement, became a part.

THE OTHER "CATALANNESS"

The presence of popular bullfighting festivities in the Ebro counties was proof of the survival of what had been a long and extensive tradition of these types of celebrations across the Catalan territory. One of the keys of its ubiquity is Montsià and the Baix Ebre's shared borders with the province of Castellón, in the Valencian country, where popular festivities with bulls are common. Therefore, bullfighting in the Ebro counties does not question their Catalanness given the inclusion of the Valencian country in the cultural universe of what is understood as Països Catalans (the Catalan Countries). Ignoring or negating this historical and cultural evidence, the intense presence and popularity of bullfighting festivities in the Terres de l'Ebre was recognized as a type of anomaly that contradicted the supposed ethical modernization process of Catalan society expressed, among others, in the rejection of bullfighting festivities. The presence of popular festivities considered to be cruel by the Principality was viewed as an obstacle when constructing a national popular culture profile appropriate for the political interests of its elites, as these practices were associated with Spain.

The virtues officially attributed to the Catalan people were related to their dialoging, civic, and moderate temperament, including a European calling. In order to satisfy this "natural" Catalan character, which was incompatible with any festivity that implied any real violence (Delgado 1993), Catalan popular culture needed to appear as a festive illustration of common sense (or *seny* in Catalan) as an identifying quality of Catalans, apt to be exhibited as the living testimony of a society that detested excesses of all kinds. That is why it was necessary to erase all remnants of abundant and common bullfighting traditions – including bull races – across the country (Amades 1956, 113–114; González 1990). This rejection of bullfighting festivities has now become one of the most recurrent themes in anti-Spanish nationalism in Catalonia (Tkac 2014; Xifrà and Sriramesh 2019). This is how an illusion of a false "bullfighting region" was generated in the Terres de l'Ebre, a place where the active and

---

5   The Plan Hidrológico Nacional (PHN) was a project pushed by the Partido Popular – a right wing political party – to divert water from the Ebro river. It was approved by the Spanish Congress in 2005. This provoked big demonstrations across the affected counties, led by the Platform to Defend de Ebro (Plataforma en Defensa de l'Ebre).

continued presence of these popular festivities acted as an identifying trait of an isolated territory (Maudet 2006), in the manner of the Camargue or the French Landes, camouflaging the reality of a Catalonia that, until the 1960s, had been as invested in bullfighting as the rest of Spain.[6]

The Ebro exception in the festive realm confirmed the precarious accommodation of the southern Catalan counties to the accepted models of Catalanism that were institutionally promoted. This incongruence dates back to how the liberal nation-state developed during the 19th century, which was consolidated in Spain with the arrival of the Ordination of Provinces (1833), marking the start of the correspondence between borders and culture. Each administration tried to legitimize its geographical limits through a symbolic identification that combined the cultural diversity of each territory as undifferentiated cultural parameters within, and as differentiated as possible in relation to, its environment. This way, the administrative divisions started to create identity dynamics encapsulated within the provincial, regional, or even county perimeter (Sánchez Cervelló 2010). This is how cultural manifestations without recognition were cast aside, such as the Catalan-speaking environment of the Ebro riverbed, which is diluted due to its distribution between Castellón, the Aragonese Matarranya, and Tarragona (Collet 2012).

Therefore, there is a hegemonic Catalan nationalism that assumed an unquestionable, sole ethnic-cultural representation clearly contrasted with the Spanish state, linked to a new national-territorial reality that is accompanied by its corresponding cultural imaginary, designed with this very purpose. This nationalism bases its criteria on the significance of cultural elements such as the use of the Catalan language as what determines the belonging to a modern Catalonia (Clua i Fainé and Sánchez García 2014). In this sense, the standard grammatical Catalan model adopted from Pompeu Fabra only ratified this ignorance of the Ebro region, challenging *tortosí* as a linguistic variety that is not entirely Catalan.

We must recall that this affair provoked the reappraisal of the debate about the standard model of Catalan and the proposal that geographic variants should be recognized in the 1980s (Pradilla Cardona 2014). This call for plurality clashed with an identity politics imposed by conservative Catalanism – represented by Convergencia i Unió, a centrist political party of which Jordi Pujol, President of the Generalitat for many years, was a part.

---

[6] The defense of the *bous* in relationship to Barcelona's political centralism is very similar to the *curses camagueses* o *landeses* at the end of the 19th century in the name of "southern liberties" in the face of French Jacobin centralism. In fact, the *corridas a l'espagnole* were widespread in the French geography, including Paris, Lyon, Vichy, and Saint Malo (Bennassar 2000; Lafront 1977).

Born out of romantic *Renaixença* at the end of the 20th century, the conservative centrist Catalan party created its own notion of Catalanism, which was centralist and egalitarian. This was ironic, as the same political party pleaded for the Spanish state to recognize cultural plurality in Spain while they were not able to recognize the cultural plurality in their own region.

The language and customs of southern counties do not fit into this project of cultural unification. These counties are considered to be the culprits in causing impurity in the nationalist Catalan project due to their shared frontiers with the deep south that was in the nationalist Catalan imaginary the País Valencia (Valencian Country), lost to and "contaminated" by Spain, a country that has irrevocably absorbed it (Collet 2012). Bulls and *jotas* (a traditional dance in southern Catalan counties and other parts of Spain) were considered to be "Spanish" or, at least, more Spanish than Catalan, even though it was not always made explicit. Needless to say, this cultural stigma was accompanied by a marginalization that extended to areas such as politics and economics, which made the southernmost counties of the country a battered and residual land that was not only in the south of Catalonia but also it was the South in the symbolic sense that Mario Benedetti gave to this cardinal point in one of his most famous poems, "El Sur también existe" ("The South also exists"). Expressions of an old sense of grievance by both local authorities and ordinary people in that territory have been constant throughout the investigation reported here. Most of our informants embodied the image of the humiliated and insulted that gave the title to the famous novel by Fyodor Dostoevsky, the main reference of the great chronicler of Terres de l'Ebre in Catalan literature, Sebastià Juan Arbó (2001). It was this part of the country to which belonging to the rest of Catalonia was somehow denied. In fact, nowadays, when speaking of going "beyond the Ebro" people associate it with something that is no longer Catalonia. This is how the symbolic division came about between a rich and civilized north, where ending the remnants of unacceptable traditions was possible, and a marginal, poor, and savage south, where these very traditions were maintained and even increased in number and participation.

All of this must be contextualized in the middle of the independence process in Catalonia that was initiated in the beginning of 2010 and was violently truncated by the Spanish government in the autumn of 2017. This political atmosphere was reflected in the proliferation of *estelades* – the Catalan pro-independence flag – in bullfighting events in towns with mostly Catalan independence-leaning local governments. In fact, "*Terres de l'Ebre*" and "*ebrenc*" are relatively recent expressions that renew the resistance against the hegemonic model of Catalanism, through a secessionist, reactionary and anti-Catalan idea called Tortosinisme (a movement in Tortosa, capital of the

Baix Ebre).[7] Recently, the ways in which reactions against Catalan symbolic centralism unfold – including the vindication of bullfighting – are not presented as a renunciation of Catalanism, but as its radicalization. Tortosinisme revealed how the process of the affirmation and definition of Ebre identity (Valldepérez 2004) – inseparable from the bullfighting festivities – implied the reformulation of Catalanness.

FIGHTING FOR HERITAGE AND POPULAR RESISTANCE

The parliamentary protection of the *correbous* in 2010 was never done in the name of saving a type of heritage. Once they were redeemed from their original sin of violence, which no one seemed to remember, the legal recognition of *bous* was undoubtedly the consequence of pressure exercised by a majority of the population of the Delta del Ebro who, in spite of the hostile climate against their festivities, were unwilling to give them up. This was especially true in the Delta counties; here, the defense of their *bous* was also a defense of their long undermined cultural identity. However, this legal protection was never considered to be a designation of heritage value.

Effectively, Law 34/2010 makes no allusion to the preservation of the festivity either as tradition or heritage. On the contrary, it insists on limiting the right of its celebration to those areas where they could demonstrate their "traditionality". This ruling is similar to the French law of 1958 that protects the Landes and Camargues races as traditional in each area, while making sure that no new ones are created. With the same objective, legislative action in relationship to the *correbous* has been oriented towards avoiding its proliferation beyond the territories where it is already celebrated, prohibiting its appearance in other areas, which shows the implied assumption of legislators about the practice's extinction.

If in Law 34/2010 the term "heritage" appears in relation to the *correbous*, it is only in its preamble, but only to refer to their importance as "genetic heritage". Later, in the regulations implementing this law, Decree 156/2013, the word "heritage" does not appear either, and, instead, notions such as "tradition", "festival", "protection", "spectacle", or "respect" are used. Throughout the text, any consideration of the legislative framework on heritage in Catalonia is obviated, and the regulation is proposed at a governmental level – "security", "inspections", "offences", "infractions", "sanctions" ... – which is

---

[7] Tortosinisme was a political and cultural right-wing movement that developed in the south of Catalonia at the end of the 19th century and into the 20th century, which negated the catalanness of the Ebro river bank counties and claimed a specific administration at the margins of Catalonia (Agramunt Bayerri, 2019).

12. *Bous amb corda* in Ulldecona in August 2015. Source: Eduard Solà.

consistent with the fact that it is the Department of the Interior, with jurisdiction in governmental matters, and not the Department of Culture, that issued the regulation.

The latter is important. All the legal problems surrounding bullfighting festivals have been raised behind the backs of the institutional bodies theoretically competent in the matter, the Directorate General of Popular Culture and its highest consultative body, the Centre for the Promotion of Popular and Traditional Catalan Culture. For the official bodies in charge of managing the field of intangible heritage, bullfighting is intangible, but with the lower rank of "catalogued". The inventory of the intangible cultural heritage of the Terres de l'Ebre includes them, and the Catalogue of the Festive Heritage of Catalonia includes more than 40 *festes majors* (local festivals) with *correbous*, almost all of which have been incorporated since 2016. This was the result of the commitment to recognize the heritage value of the festivals with bulls announced by the then Director General of Popular Culture, Lluís Puig, currently (August 2022) in exile – persecuted by the Spanish authorities for his participation in the declaration of independence of Catalonia in October 2017.

In parallel, in the field of grassroots cultural associations, the bullfighting *colles* are by no means marginalized. On the contrary, the Agrupació de Penyes i Comissions Taurines de les Terres de l'Ebre is fully integrated in the ENS de l'Associacionisme Cultural Català, which brings together organizations that defend popular and traditional Catalan culture and is federated in the ICH NGO Forum, a platform accredited to advise the UNESCO Intergovernmental Committee for the Safeguarding of Intangible Cultural Heritage. However, in spite of this relative official recognition and the full acceptance of the bullfighting groups by the popular entities for the defense of traditional culture, no celebration with *correbous* appears in 2022 among the 65 festivals declared by the Generalitat to be of heritage relevance, those that are in need of protection and promotion.

It is true that, in recent years, the official cataloging of festivals and traditions as intangible cultural heritage has increased in Catalonia (Costa Solé and Folch Monclús 2014). Some of them, like the *Patum* of Berga (a traditional festival celebrated in Berga that involves popular dances and many pyrotechnics) or the *castells* (human castles) have achieved international recognition by UNESCO. However, the nature of intangible heritage as a concept is both the cause and the effect of a series of contradictions materialized in quarrelsome struggles, the case before us being a good example. These types of popular expressions, particularly those that imply the use of animals, manifest the dimension of the conflictive nature of intangible heritage and contribute to its problematization as an ambiguous category that is used in an arbitrary manner in the service of different causes and projects that search for legitimacy. As already noted, it is difficult to fit the *correbous* in the image the country offers, which consequently has led to the denial of it as heritage. This, in turn, is a direct result of its conceived inconvenience as a custom that is undesirable by Catalan legislation itself.

Even more unfeasible was the attempt to promote the *correbous* as intangible cultural heritage of humanity, because they are in direct contradiction with the values (such as animal welfare) of today's post-modern and post-materialistic societies (Boiso Cuenca 2021; Casal 2021; García Rubio 2021; Gómez Pellón 2017; Ridao Martín 2017).[8] There were already two dissuasive precedents: the withdrawal of the Italian state, in the face of animal protests, to its application to obtain the UNESCO seal for *il palio de Siena* (Scovazzi 2011) and criticism for having included Mexican *charrerias* in its inventory in 2016.

---

[8] The problem raised here is similar to that posed by cultural practices that have been marked as a sign of identity by certain communities and are incompatible with universal human rights, in this case with animal rights. The issue has been raised primarily by feminist critiques of cultural relativism (Maquieira d'Angelo 1999), and has been applied to the festive field in the Spanish state (Bullen 2000). But it is not discussed here that cultural traits can be questioned within the human groups themselves who possess them as a result of internal ideological struggles. That would not be the case. Here we are talking about external legal actions that are perceived as authoritarian and arbitrary.

The vindication of the bullfights of the Ebro delta as a world cultural heritage was presented within the Bullfighting-UNESCO campaign, promoted by the International Bullfighting Association to defend the bullfighting festivals of eight states: Colombia, Portugal, France, Mexico, Peru, Ecuador, Venezuela, and Spain, including Catalonia. None of these states, which are the bodies that should formally do so, endorsed the petition before UNESCO. In November 2020, the Intergovernmental Committee on the Intangible Cultural Heritage rejected a request from an individual, made by letter on behalf of the AIT, that bullfighting festivals from around the world be included in the urgent safeguard list. Shortly before, 985 animal welfare organizations and a number of prominent personalities approached the international body to urge that it should not grant protection to bullfighting.

It could not be otherwise. For Catalonia and for any other country in the world, the active presence of festivals that can be considered abusive towards animals in their territory is a factor of international discredit. In fact, the *correbous* would be an expression of what the UNESCO considers as

> cultures that may not be worthy of respect because they themselves have been shown to be intolerant, exclusive, exploitative, cruel and repressive. Whatever we may be told about the importance of "not interfering with local customs", such repulsive practices, whether aimed at people from different cultures or at other members of the same culture, should be condemned, not tolerated. (UNESCO 1995, 54)

Here is an example of the paradoxes of the authorized heritage discourse (Nielsen 2011), which is instituted by pointing at the forms of "unacceptable diversity" (Stowkowski 2009; Wright 1998).

The logic of the lists of intangible assets to be preserved according to UNESCO follows the logic of any list: it includes some things at the expense of excluding others (Hafstein 2009). When drawing up their inventories of the vernacular to be protected and extolled, those in charge of carrying out the selection decontextualize certain cultural realities to recontextualize them in relation to ethical and aesthetic parameters to be universally promoted. Indeed, UNESCO only considers worthy those elements that can contribute to its idealism of a humanity where social and territorial asymmetries have disappeared and have been replaced by an idyllic mosaic of cultural postcards that illustrate universal virtues. And the *correbous* cannot be part of this closed, Eurocentric utopia (Brumann 2018). After all, the universal values claimed by UNESCO are those of the global governance plans for which the international body is "the cultural arm, the visionary agency and the factory of ideas" (Meskell and Brumann 2015).

The issue of the Ebro *bous* deserves attention as it brings eloquence to determined problems that anthropology and, particularly, critical studies about heritage (del Mármol et al 2010) have considered by pointing out the controversial dimensions of the mechanisms of heritage stratus. Therefore, these appear charged with cracks, antagonisms, and contradictions, which are far from the kind and uncomplicated visions offered by their institutional or professional management, especially considering that they take place in a festive environment (López López 2020; Sánchez-Carretero 2013). The private and hidden intentions of heritagization always end up coming to the surface. Through what Joan Frigolé (2014) calls the "rhetoric of authenticity", heritage titles construct politically determined identity projections and/or contribute to territorial marketing purposes (Santamarina and Moncusí Ferré 2015). We know that what is listed as heritage is supposed to result from so-called expert criteria, but derives from business or institutional interests, or both. In the face of this, there are predictable dynamics of popular resistance that question what deserves to be highlighted as intangible heritage and what does not (Santamarina Campos and del Mármol 2020). These dynamics may involve a challenge to dominant moral values and adopt openly anti-hegemonic stances, like the case at hand.

CONCLUSIONS

In this chapter we discussed what criteria activate a certain cultural element as intangible heritage. We did so, following what Brumann (2014) called an agnostic perspective. This perspective sought to keep a distance from "beliefs of heritage", that is, beliefs that institutions or certain social segments hold about what was to be considered sacred – in other words, untouchable – regarding a cultural landscape they shared. In line with this framework, the 2003 UNESCO Convention for the Safeguarding of the Intangible Cultural Heritage intended to establish a new paradigm that was aimed at breaking with the European model of monumental heritage and valued manifestations of cultural life as practised by its bearers instead (Blake 2016). As such, this convention served to establish in a clear manner that the "intangible cultural heritage means the practices, representations, expressions, knowledge, skills – as well as the instruments, objects, artefacts and cultural spaces associated therewith – that communities, groups and, in some cases, individuals recognize as part of their cultural heritage." However, it turned out that those who got to decide what was to be safeguarded as sacred for communities, groups, and individuals were none of the latter; it was rather the experts who accepted or rejected what the states deemed venerable according to their own interests, which, often, were political and economic in their nature, in addition to being quite alien to the actual communities, groups, and individuals that were concerned.

But the specialists have not always had a guaranteed monopoly on the mark of heritage. As a discursive production, the enhancement of official heritage value may be disallowed for or ignored by certain social groups or inferior territories. Through adopting certain practices, they express not only who and what they consider that they are, but also the mistreatment of which they feel themselves to be the victims. The "immaterial" manifestations that hide all kinds of grievances and forgetfulness can be different from, and even incompatible with, what the authorized distributors of heritage excellence consider remarkable. Therefore, the Ebro region presents a case where heritage, a realm of knowledge that is meant to be idyllic, uncontestable, and theoretically safe from social or political gravitations at the exclusive hands of wise experts and commissions, actually appears to convey all kinds of social tensions and belligerence between actors with competing interests and identities.

In this sense, the unviable patrimonialization of the *bous* in the Ebro region beyond the local sphere permits us to illustrate what kind of cultural traits deserves to be isolated from the symbolic universe to which it belongs, to be praised as admirable and exemplary. For Catalan institutions, the virtue of intangible heritage must accord with what Llorenç Prats (1996, 295) called a virtual pool: a stock of symbolic references, articulated and activated as a congruent set in the service of a given identity discourse, appropriate to the interests of its promoters. From here, everything that does not fit in with this discourse of a "well-tempered" "us" will be doomed to exclusion, or persecuted, as in this case. *Correbous* do not belong with the range of symbols that a genuinely European country can be proud of, and do not fit in a tourist promotion brochure alongside *castellers* (human castles), *sardanas* (Catalonia traditional dance), Montserrat or *correfocs* (traditional pyrotechnic shows). Cases such as the popular defense of the *bous* on the banks of the Ebro show how intangible heritage can also become a political battlefield.

6

Communities without Festivities? Community Effects, Transformations, and Conflicts after Covid-19 in Catalonia

XAVIER ROIGÉ, MIREIA GUIL, LLUÍS BELLAS

Covid-19 has profoundly altered festive practices all around the world.[1] Public health regulations have imposed restrictions on public celebrations, compromising social rhythm and community relationships, and calling the real and symbolic objects connected with the lockdown period into question (Appadurai 1996). The "normality" of mass public rituals has had to be suspended due to restrictions connected with lockdown, social distancing, and new forms of social control (Mansilla 2020). This has translated into feelings of social frustration and community mourning caused by the suspension of festivities (Bindi 2021). Faced with the impossibility of performing their collective practices, communities have reacted in different ways, from cancelling festivals to holding them using alternative smaller or digital formulas, and in some cases conflicts of greater or lesser intensity have appeared. One could even say that the pandemic has resulted in many communities reacting with

---

[1] This study was carried out as part of a project entitled: "Patrimonio inmaterial y politicas culturales: desafios sociales, politicos y museológicos" (PGC2018-096190-B-I00), and "Patrimonio inmaterial y museos ante los retos de la sostenibilidad cultural" (PID2021-123063NB-I00), which was funded by the Spanish Ministry of Science, Innovation and Universities and the FEDER Program. Translation: Marc Duckett.

an attitude of resilience with new forms of use and negotiation of intangible heritage, stressing its political nature.

This chapter examines the social effects, debates, and conflicts experienced in festivals in Catalonia through ethnographic research performed from a dual perspective: on the one hand, online analysis of the debates and alternatives used to hold festivities; and, on the other hand, an ethnographic analysis of some cases studies in Catalonia through participant observation and interviews with people connected with these celebrations. Examination of the public actions performed during this short period of time is fertile ground to analyze the changes made to the concept of festivities, through a process of reconfiguration of traditions (Testa and Isnart 2020).

Our objective is to use the case of Catalonia to set out the theoretical scope and importance of processes to recreate heritage in relation to festive practices. We aim to show how festive practices are changeable and how human activities establish and manipulate their own differentiations and purposes in a ritual context (Bell 2007). From this point of view, we have formulated the hypothesis that the processes of change in festivals adopted in the past year have come at the expense of conflicts between the logic of lockdown and the logic of festivities. In this sense, festive practices have sometimes been stages not just for cohesion and solidarity but also the dramatization of social tensions.

THE IMPACT OF COVID-19 ON FESTIVITIES: FROM ALTERING COMMUNITY RHYTHMS TO FORMULATING NEW RITUAL PRACTICES

All festivals undergo constant processes of change and adaptation. In recent years, aspects such as globalization, the tourism boom, and heritage protection processes have generated new challenges to their forms of celebration and uses (Boissevain 1999; Crozat and Fournier 2005; Fournier 2019; Roigé et al 2019). The crisis caused by the Covid-19 pandemic has posed new challenges, strategies, and transformations for communities in holding festivities. For the foreseeable future, social distancing has put an end to the way festivities are held in public spaces, altering community rhythms and commencing a physical and virtual hybridization of festivities to make them "viable" in this past pandemic year. The three most hotly debated questions concerning the effects of the pandemic on festivities are: the impact on communities of not holding festivities; the disruption to festivals caused by public health restrictions; and the scope of substitution with digitization and its effects on celebrations.

Firstly, communities view cancellation for public health reasons as something painful and worrying, so it is a break with the past and tradition. Festivals are cyclical and cancelling them breaks with the reassuring certainty of repetition and community integration (Ariño 1998; Contreras 1978; Fabre 2006). However, interestingly, the pandemic period has stimulated the creation of new social rituals: one could say that the discourse of heritage has been used as a key element of resilience through new social practices based on and defended with the discourse of tradition.

The UNESCO (2020) report, produced from a significant sample of the effects of lockdown worldwide, concludes that although the pandemic had affected the rhythm of celebration of 94% of the festivals registered in the Representative List of the Intangible Cultural Heritage of Humanity, 59% of them carried out innovative actions to allow for continuity. The same report also highlights how intangible heritage has been used as a source of resilience to reconstruct social relationships and spiritual, psychological, and emotional support in the face of Covid-19. As García Canclini (1989) states, members of the community feel that they play the leading role in the material and symbolic organization of traditional festivals, and see them as something spontaneous. Therefore, cancellation has been seen as altering the community rhythm, and even as something destructive of community relationships, being perceived as an imposition by the political power on community and personal autonomy.

Secondly, there is the question of the disruption that Covid-19 generates for festive events. The public health measures not only restrict capacity; there are also difficulties with accessing the places, objects, and materials that intangible cultural heritage requires. Generally speaking, festivals involve performing practices that cannot be carried out in a pandemic situation (crowds of people, proximity, physical contact, and heavy social interaction). Since festivities set out to be activities that break down social barriers, with physical proximity that unsettles the social order (Delgado 2004), physical distancing rules have a profound effect on the essence of festivities. They also imply the triumph of an idea of closing down the community with the utopia of a *cordon sanitaire* (Gonzalez and Marlovits 2020). We do not know whether these impacts will be temporary or long-term, stretching into the future, as Davies (2020) wonders; whether more restrictions on celebrations will be imposed with a maximum number of permitted attendees; and we also do not know whether festive celebrations will be more "exclusive" or based on a new "collaborative economy". Moreover, one of the most important disruptions for festive celebrations is the economic effects, because not holding them implies a loss of income from the non-participation of tourists and not selling artisanal products. That also implies a risk for certain professions that depend on income from sales concentrated within a particular time of year.

Thirdly, there is the issue of digitization of intangible heritage. The use of virtual space already has a long history in inventories adapted to the UNESCO Convention for the Safeguarding of the Intangible Cultural Heritage. However, one interesting aspect in the Covid-19 period is that the virtual space appears to have opened up new possibilities for participation through mechanisms that allow communities to share content through social networks or virtual museums. In spite of the fact that some authors consider this greater participation to be nothing more than a utopia (Appiotti and Sandri 2020), the fact is that the pandemic period has opened up new opportunities to create projects based on participative means to articulate practices, knowledge, shared experiences, commonplaces and sceneries.

The cancellation or suspension of festivities has also involved social conflicts in many cases. Festivals have an essentially disruptive character and are intended as an escape from the everyday rhythm with behavior not accepted during the rest of the year (Boissevan 1992; Prat and Contreras 1984). During the pandemic, this character has produced various conflicts of greater or lesser intensity. However, in all cases, the need to decide whether or not to hold the festivity, or whether it should be postponed or held on a smaller scale, has implied the opening up of mechanisms for collective negotiation of intracommunity conflicts (Noyes 2006). These negotiations have generated conflicts between the authorities, who have decreed the suspension of festivities, and some members of the community, who have insisted on holding them. There have been many different responses: from practices broadcast through social networks with a humorous tone to celebrations involving conflicts that have even resulted in some cases in police intervention.

One could say that there has been (and continues to be) a degree of symbolic resistance by communities in the contradiction between social control justified for public health reasons and community resistance to accepting those prohibitions. Society has a need for ritual as a social release valve and, during the period of restrictions on festivities, this desire appears to be heightened. As Mansilla (2020) states, the suspension of local festivals should not be interpreted solely on the basis of public health issues, but also in relation to the social value of the festivity. In fact, festivities – which act as both a space for community affirmation, social demands, and a political arena bordering on social disruption – have been seen by the authorities as a potentially conflictive element contrary to the social distancing imposed during lockdown, and they have even stigmatized them. One interesting aspect of protesting by insisting on holding festivals is that this is an attempt to reclaim the shared significance of the streets, laden with values and meanings, which the public health rules have sought to snatch away from them.

The paradox of lockdown taking precedence over festivities is that, on the one hand, it has highlighted the fragility of intangible heritage, since the majority of mass festivals have been cancelled due to inaccessibility or restrictions (UNESCO 2020). However, on the other hand, this has given rise to an unprecedented process of resistance, reinvention, and creativity in festivities. To some extent, the pandemic period has involved a return to the added value of the past and has involved a call for recognition of living, intangible cultural heritage, which is based on the nostalgic exaltation of "what was" and now can only exist through creative, participatory experiences, always based on respect for the restrictions (Bindi 2021). Traditions have been redefined and given value by calling for a community model presented as an alternative within complex modern societies that are tending towards globalization (Ariño 1996). As we pointed out elsewhere (Frigolé and Roigé 2012), this call for recognition of the authentic, the traditional, the autochthonous connected with the local area is the other side of the coin in the globalization process. In this regard, it is interesting that during the pandemic, there appears to have been a call for recognition of the ideal of the neighborhood or the local community where the festival is held, which coexists with it and participates in it (Crozat and Fournier 2005), but with the paradox of it taking place during lockdown with social distancing and interconnectivity based on more globalized forms.

THE DIFFERENT ALTERNATIVES AND DEBATES CONCERNING THE PERFORMANCE OF FESTIVALS IN CATALONIA

In Catalonia, the use of festivities and folklore has often been an arena for political confrontation based on identities (Arrieta et al 2020). The current Catalan festive model began, to a large extent, by reinventing festivities through cultural policies developed in the 1980s, after the transition to democracy (Roigé 2016). Traditional festivities, together with heritage and local museums, were one of the key elements in reclaiming the streets during the transition to democracy and the socio-political reconstruction after Franco's dictatorship (Delgado 2003; Noyes et al 2003). This model of cultural management, which is fundamental in the assertion of Catalan identity, was a central element in constructing local and national identities after the economic crises of 1990 and 2008 (Guiu 2008; Kammerer 2014). In addition to all this, there is the political process that Catalonia has undergone in recent years within the framework of demands for political independence that, as we will see, in many cases made festivals a megaphone for these demands.

These elements, which we have outlined in summary, should be taken into account in our analysis for two reasons: on the one hand, to analyze the reactions and alternative forms of celebration that arose during 2020; and, on the other hand, because they have put Catalan cultural polices developed in recent years, especially in relation to festive practices, to the test. The impact of Covid-19 has given us an exceptional scenario to analyze the various responses adopted to festivals and to see how different perceptions about festivals have emerged much more clearly. In the case of Catalonia, there were various responses to the pandemic, which complement and may be combined with one another: 1) cancellation of the festivity; 2) holding it in a smaller format, with symbolic celebrations and reinvention of new practices; 3) celebrations based on the use of virtual space or other substitute mechanisms.

Although, generally, national and local authorities have tended to ban festive events and, therefore, suspend festivities, the idea of continuity has been used in many communities as an argument for not interrupting festivals and legitimizing them. In many towns, people were insistent in recalling that festive events have always been held, even during the Civil War, so festivities should be held come what may, in small formats or by changing the dates. These debates took place especially during the initial stages of the pandemic, in March 2020, decreased during the strictest lockdown, and then resumed in May/June of the same year, after the lockdown.

Most festivities were suspended and in all cases the municipal announcements had a similar tone: expressing sadness for the suspension together with calls for social responsibility, highlighting the atypical nature of festivities, and guaranteeing public health conditions. In this way, the small Olesa Town Council stated in its announcement on May 11, 2020:[2]

> we are living through extraordinarily complex times due to the situation caused by Covid-19, which has completely changed and modified our social relationships to contain the health crisis it has caused. [In view of this, the Town Council] has taken the difficult decision to cancel the 2020 Town Festival, which is traditionally held on the third weekend of July. [It regretted that] the festival is a key component of the social movement in our municipality, a mark of local identity, so this was a complicated decision that was very tough for everyone, but which was carefully analyzed and thought through. These times that we are living through require determination and solidarity, and we need to put municipal resources into managing the health crisis for the well-being of local residents. We would like to thank you for your understanding of this difficult decision. The Catalan Ministry of Culture will continue to work to uphold festive traditions, always prioritizing the population's health and safety.

In a similar tone, Boí Town Council justified the cancellation of the *Falles* (fire festivities) by stating that "the decision was very difficult because the *fallaire* [torch-carrying] sentiment is always present. However, health comes before everything and it is not possible to ensure a safe distance between members of the public". And it added, "the flame has not gone out and we hope to meet again in 2021 stronger than ever". It is interesting that although the two announcements concern very different festivities, they

---

[2] http://www.olesadebonesvalls.cat/actualitat/noticies/comunicat-de-suspensio-de-la-festa-major-dolesa-de-bonesvalls.html [viewed on January 23, 2021].

both refer to public health solidarity, while insisting that they will continue to work to uphold tradition.

The second response has been to hold the festivities in a smaller format, a mechanism that arises in contexts in which keeping the festivity "alive" is seen as an obligation, because it has "always" been done. In the town of Valls, for example, the town festival[3] was held with a hybrid program, in alliance with social networks and local television. The rituals were creatively adapted to the public health restrictions and broadcast via the Internet. Religious services, music concerts with *grallers* (traditional wind-instrument players], bell-ringing and a *Gegants* (giants) dance performance were held. Conversely, rituals such as *cercaviles* (parade) and *Castells* (human towers) were cancelled, since they could not be adapted to the social-distancing restrictions. In the same way, during some carnival celebrations, *cercaviles* were performed by the *Rei Carnestoltes* (the Carnival King) alone, while the inhabitants watched, suitably dressed up, from their balconies, as took place in the town of Vilanova del Camí. The celebrations were accompanied by festivity reinvention processes in which new rituals and family celebrations were created (Imber-Black 2020). In the same way, in this pandemic context, the creation of intangible heritage exhibitions accelerated, especially when museums were allowed to open from June 2020, because this kept the festivals alive within a museum context. Many towns held "emergency" exhibitions at which the inhabitants could "contemplate" the material part of the festivities. For example, in Vilanova i la Geltrú an exhibition recreated a *cercavila* from the town festival with material objects from the festivals and texts together with video clips of interviews with festival participants and ritual dances through social networks.

The third response was virtual. As in all countries, domestic lockdown led to extensive use of screens, social networks, and mobile devices. The Virus Popular[4] (Folk Virus) YouTube channel is a paradigmatic example of disseminating and broadcasting intangible heritage during lockdown. The channel was launched by a group of communication and intangible heritage professionals. It produced a long series of debates, forums, and talks each week with the participation of tradition-bearers for gastronomy, dance, theater, uses of nature, and gender perspective in intangible cultural heritage. Creativity also flowed among the managers of intangible cultural heritage, who dedicated themselves to creating adapted and virtual, but also hybrid, programming. There were many virtual strategies, including participatory spaces on social networks and broadcasts of parades on social networks or local TV, especially during the Three Kings Parade, for example in Vic (one of the most important

---

3   https://tarragonadigital.com/alt-camp/balanc-festa-major-sant-joan-valls-2020 [viewed on January 23, 2021].
4   https://www.viruspopular.cat/ [viewed on January 23, 2021].

festivals in the Catalan festival calendar). In some cases, festival programming included an authentic program of events mimicking the usual celebration: Ripoll Town Festival had a virtual opening speech, live children's storytelling, music concerts on balconies, broadcasts of ritual dances, and even a dance session on balconies with music broadcast through social networks. As Imber-Black (2020, 920) states, numerous festive, family life-cycle rituals have been adapted to the virtual format: "Zoom" rituals.

As these cases highlight, the pandemic has given rise to a series of strategies, such as those we have just set out, which are based, from our point of view, on two elements: on the one hand, avoiding the complete absence of celebration, i.e., not breaking the cyclical nature of the festivities; and, on the other hand, respecting the public health measures that the pandemic requires. Striking a balance between these two elements has not always been easy.

ETHNOGRAPHY OF THREE CASES DURING COVID-19

The holding of any festival in the pandemic context highlights the great capacity that festivals have for adaptation, reinvention, and resilience. Three ethnographic examples, studied in greater depth, allow us to better understand the debate that took place within groups of organizers to deal with the pandemic. As we will see, different strategies were followed.

The Raiers Festivity

In our first example, the festive celebration went ahead, albeit with some format changes. The *Raiers* (timber raftsmen) festivity is held every year on the first Sunday of July in La Pobla de Segur, a municipality with 3,000 inhabitants in the Catalan Pyrenees, and a hub for various basic services. Although there is a long historical tradition of going down the river on timber rafts, the *Raiers* festivity is relatively recent in origin. There was a first attempt in 1972 and, later, in 1979, it resumed in the format we know today. It was established as part of promotional activities carried out at the end of Franco's dictatorship to draw tourists to the town, resulting in the invention of the festivals we are analyzing. The festivity is based on commemorating an ancient trade in the area, the transport of timber down the Noguera Pallaresa river, by *raiers*. The timber is felled in the Pyrenean forests and is floated from there down to the sawmills, but the journey used to be much longer, all the way down to the Mediterranean (Giménez 1995; Portet 1996). From the first quarter of the 20th century, when hydroelectric dams were built and goods transport roads were improved, this trade declined and then disappeared.

As we have said, this festivity began in 1979 in La Pobla de Segur and, almost a decade later, another town in the area, Coll de Nargó, also started to do it. The festivity gradually became more popular in Catalonia as a whole, until it became considered a Traditional Festivity of National Interest in 2003. In addition, internationally, the Association of International Timber-Raftsmen[5] (Portet 1996) was created. Various countries are preparing an application to have this trade included in UNESCO's Representative List of the Intangible Cultural Heritage of Humanity.[6]

The continuity of the celebration in 2020 was justified on the grounds of supporting the registration application. The president of the Coll de Nargó Association said in the press that "he hoped that going ahead with the celebration with all appropriate safety measures would be a point in our favor in achieving this recognition".[7] In fact, both Coll de Nargó and La Pobla de Segur went ahead with their respective celebrations, adapting them to the required public health measures and holding most of the planned activities: the descent of the *rais* (timber raftsmen), the *espardenyada* (a mountain hike tracing the timber raftsmen's return path), a live music concert, a firework display, and an *arrosada* (rice-based meal).

In response to the pandemic, they did not consider cancelling the celebration but instead adapted it to follow the safety rules.[8] However, the organizers highlight that they had to go through many procedures and provide a great deal of documentation with plans to control the capacity of festive venues and specify the public health measures that each activity would comply with to avoid crowds. The mountain hike was performed in family groups and the concert consisted of a musical performance that moved through different points in the town to prevent audience crowds from building up. The descent of the river followed the same itinerary, but the people watching it were spread among different points along the river. However, the main new feature in 2020 was the live broadcasting of the descent.

Fire Festivals in the Pyrenees

In the case of the fire festivals in the Pyrenees, the alternatives to the public health restrictions ranged from not holding them to holding them in a smaller format. These festivities, which are included in UNESCO's Representative

---

5 http://www.raftsmen.org [viewed on January 23, 2021].
6 Latvia, Spain, Austria, Czech Republic, and Germany. In Catalonia, the towns of Pobla de Segur and Coll de Nargó, both of which are in the Catalan Pyrenees, have registered; although Spanish towns in other autonomous communities have also done so.
7 https://www.segre.com/noticies/guia/2020/08/13/coll_nargo_prepara_els_rais_112652_1111.html [viewed on January 23, 2021].
8 Interview with the vice-president of the organizing association, February 21, 2021.

List of the Intangible Cultural Heritage of Humanity in 2015,[9] take many different forms in different areas, although in this case we will focus only on those held in the Catalan Pyrenees. They are held in mountainous areas with a very small population and an economy based on cattle-raising and mountain tourism. In the Pallars Sobirà and Alta Ribagorça valleys, the festivity (held on Saint John's Eve, June 23–24) has a very similar structure, *falles* (lit torches) are carried from a high point on the mountain down to the town. Once they reach the town, the torches are thrown in the fire, which may be a bonfire or a tree trunk erected somewhere in the town. In contrast, in the case of Val d'Aran, the focus of the festivity is the *haro* (a splintered spruce more than five meters tall in the town square). During the celebration, music and dances accompany the fire-burning ritual.

In Pyrenean towns, the idea of local community is very important, and the festivals are a fundamental symbolic element in constructing the community. Although there is documentary evidence that they have existed for many centuries, the festivities' popularity has increased since the 1980s as a consequence of processes to assert local and Catalan identity after Franco's dictatorship. In fact, since then, this celebration has been used to assert the local identity of each area, whether the district, valley, or town itself (Guil 2019). For example, the Alta Ribagorça valley promoted these festivals within the framework of the creation of a specific *comarca* (a Catalan administrative unit that groups various municipalities together – a district) in 1988 as an element of the valley's identity (Grau 1995). The same happened in other areas, such as the town of Isil, where the festivity was very soon recognized as a "traditional festivity of national interest" (Riart and Jordà 2015), and Les (in Val d'Aran, a territory in Catalonia with an Occitan language and identity, which is administratively decentralized), which used the festivals as a way of asserting its Occitan identity. Subsequently, since the 2000s, these local heritage initiatives began to be interconnected with those held in Spain, France, and Andorra to assert a cross-border Pyrenean identity and thus be able to submit an international application to UNESCO.

In the pandemic context, in spite of them being part of the same declaration of intangible heritage, each town's response to the situation was different. For example, in some towns in the Pallars valleys, the organizers of these festivals produced a video that was shared on social networks, announcing that each group would hold a "symbolic" event and asked people from other towns and tourists to stay away: "Don't come, stay home, do it for us, do it for our

---

[9] It is an international application that includes celebrations in various towns in the Spanish, French, and Andorran Pyrenees.

people. We will be back.".[10] This video is interesting in that it asserts "the local identity" of the festivity, and calls for it to be held in a version only for people from the town, as a form of community reaffirmation. Each town organized the festivity differently, although generally the event consisted of a *baixada* (walking down the mountain with torches) with very limited numbers of participants, between three and 30 people.

In the case of the Boí valley, towns jointly announced the cancellation of the festivities, although the town of Vilaller, near Vall de Boí, held a "symbolic" event that consisted of burning a small *falla* (torch) on the balconies or patios of homes that the town council had given out to residents together with a bottle of wine and a piece of *coca* (traditional pie). In this case, they cancelled the descent with the torches, since there were usually large crowds involved. In Valle de Aran they decided to cancel the burning of the *haro* (splintered spruce trunk). This also sparked a debate about what would happen to the trunk, since each year, one week after it was burned, a new trunk was set up in the town square and would remain there all year round, as a symbol of local continuity, just as the trunk from 2019 was still standing there. However, they proposed a set of activities on social networks, and other activities such as how to make a miniature *haro*.

Cervera Aquelarre

In this last example, the festivity resulted in open conflict. In the town of Cervera, with a population of 9,350 inhabitants, which is located in inland Catalonia, each year a neo-carnivalesque festival is held in which around 40,000 people take part in devil "worship", invoking the *Mascle Cabró* (Baphomet, devil billy-goat). The festivity was invented in 1978, shortly after the end of the dictatorship in Spain (1975), on the initiative of a group of young people who called for a pagan festival that was not connected with the Catholic nationalistic festivals of the dictatorship (Prats 2007). The group wanted to hold the ritual event in the historic town center in a street called Carreró de les Bruixes (Witch Alley) and through an association of ideas (alternative festivity, witches' coven, etc.), the festivity was called an *Aquelarre* (Witches' Sabbath).

Since then, in the last week of August, the city has been immersed in a collective transgression night after night with the Baphomet, devils and witches as symbols (Delgado 1992). The first four days are self-organized by various local groups: on Monday, the young people hold a night-time folk festival on the streets; on Tuesday, the shopkeepers organize an evening event

---

[10] https://www.facebook.com/CatedraPirineus/videos/2843929685736519 [viewed on January 23, 2021].

to raise funds with tapas and local devil dances; on Wednesday, the festivity is recreated in the original format from 1978 in Witches' Alley; and, finally, on Thursday, the women from the festival groups take control of the street with performances and *Correfocs* (pyrotechnic processions with dancing devils). They confront the men dressed in white, shouting "They shall not pass" (an anti-fascist slogan). From Friday to Sunday, the local groups and the town council hold three core days of festivities, which are much more institutionalized and attended en masse by festival tourists. On Friday, a performance promoting feminist demands and a parade of dragon dances is held. Saturday is the most important day of the celebration with a mass *cercavila* through the center filled with fantastic characters, percussion and *Correfocs* through the narrow streets in the center. The festivals end in the early hours of Sunday morning with the invocation of the billy-goat, his orgy with the witches, and the ritual with which the festivals culminate: the *Escorreguda* of the Baphomet (the simulated ejaculation of the anti-Christ's "semen" over the crowd).

During the 40 years it has been held, the local population has structured the ritual processes of this newly-created festival based on the model of an urban carnival (Harris 2003; Testa 2019) together with elements from other traditions and imaginaries: paganism, witches' Sabbaths, Corpus Christi ritual dances such as giants, dragons and devils, *Correfocs*, music festivals, and even Afro-Brazilian *Batucada* percussion. The set of rituals has been expanded with *Fira del Gran Boc*, the largest esoteric fair in the south of Europe, and the *Aquelarret*, a kids *cercavila* in the image of the *Patum infantil de Berga* (Berga children's *Patum*).

Covid-19 had a devastating impact on these public festivals. The high participation of local people and tourists from other areas interacting for seven days in a row were two factors that made it unviable in times of Covid-19. In addition to the factor of extreme social interaction, we should add the political instability of the local government, which was made up of a coalition of parties of different leanings. A vote of no confidence just three months before the festivity spoiled relations within the local administration and hampered local groups' requests. Although an initial smaller version of the festivity was designed with static events and bleachers to limit audience capacity, this option did not succeed when the new municipal government came into power in June 2020. The new left-leaning, pro-independence town council announced the complete cancellation of the events[11] in the usual format, although it allowed the possibility of local groups proposing events "provided they are adapted to

---

[11] https://www.ccma.cat/324/la-covid-tomba-laquelarre-de-cervera-que-no-se-celebrara-per-primer-cop-en-43-anys/noticia/3026835/ [viewed on January 23, 2021].

the current public health measures".[12] Small-sized events were thus proposed, which were viable in the epidemiological situation and offered the possibility of holding an *Aquelarre* that was "more local than ever", i.e., without tourists.[13]

The new program was intended to "keep the spirit of the *Aquelarre* alive", but it did not last long. The very week of the "lockdown" *Aquelarre* (the last week of August 2020), the government of the Catalan autonomous community decreed ten days of public health restrictions due to the increase in Covid-19 patients. This required the cancellation of all planned activities, to be replaced with alternative, theoretically safe forms. Although the official program was cancelled, self-organized initiatives arose that gave rise to various conflicts. Local organizations protested with a controlled performance demonstration, but some groups of young people held uncontrollable night-time *botellones* (crowds of people gathering to drink alcohol in the open-air) in locations in the town hidden from sight. These dynamics reached their climax on the Saturday with a large-scale *botellón* that ended with police charges.[14] The mayor made a statement condemning these night-time festivities, saying that it was unacceptable to jeopardize people's health "in such a stupid manner".[15]

The uncontrolled, crowded nature of neo-carnivalesque festivals such as the *Aquelarre* resulted in serious conflicts when it was cancelled, due to the significance the folk celebration has for the local people. The organizers of the festivity attempted, with their own resources, to arrange a competing program of events adapted to Covid-19, but they were unsuccessful when the festivity was cancelled by the authorities. The protests were to be expected, taking into account the almost riotous character of the festivity (Delgado 2003) and its transgressive nature. The local community reacted with collectively organized riots.

These three examples have allowed us to see more closely how various aspects have had an impact on festive celebrations in addition to public health decisions: political circumstances, and the significance of the festivity within the community. What the three ethnographic cases have in common is the collective will to continue to hold the festivity in spite of the pandemic situation, with capacity for adaptation and resilience, innovations, and reaffirmation of the local identity over external presence. The three cases are festivals

---

[12] https://www.lavanguardia.com/local/lleida/20200623/481933014252/cervera-suspende-aquelarre-2020-coronavirus.html [viewed on January 23, 2021].
[13] https://www.lleida.com/noticia_canal/cervera-treballa-fer-possible-una-edicio-especial-de-laquelarre-amb-el-coronavirus [viewed on January 23, 2021].
[14] https://www.elperiodico.com/es/sociedad/20200831/alcalde-cervera-condena-encuentros-nocturnos-redes-8093976 [viewed on January 23, 2021].
[15] https://lleidadiari.cat/comarques/cervera-registra-trobades-nocturnes-joven-aquelarre-festa-major [viewed on January 23, 2021].

with a high level of participation by people from outside the community. It is interesting that all of the communities argued that the festivals could be held provided only people from the town itself took part, i.e., by retreating within the community. However, the three cases differ in the strategies followed. While in the first case (*Raiers*), the festivity was held in a form rather similar to the format of other years, in the second case (*Fiestas del Fuego*) they were either cancelled or held in a smaller format. And in the third case (*Aquelarre*) holding the festivity resulted in fierce conflicts, which is an issue we will deal with in the final section.

LOCKDOWN CELEBRATIONS AND CONFLICTS

Conflicts due to cancellation or changes in the form of holding festivals also emerged in other Catalan towns, in a more or less perceptible way. The logic of festivals is often articulated as a free space with a certain opposition to institutions and political governance (Orozco 2020). Precisely for this reason, festivals have become an exceptional space to observe all kinds of conflicts, from gender to the management of public space through identity and tourism (Delgado 2004). Festivals are significant moments in the life of a particular community but, at the same time, they involve tensions, the intensity of which may support or destabilize the hegemonic order and its functional imaginaries (Testa 2014a, 66).

As in our last ethnographic example, Cervera, the tension caused by not holding the festivals translated into incidents when some members of the community tried to hold them in spite of them being banned. Cancellation of festivals has been seen as a form of social control and domination (Domene 2017) and has created a degree of communal social frustration expressed in the form of more or less spontaneous demonstrations, protests, and performances. To some extent, these protests expressed discontent with the mechanisms of power and social control, as has frequently been noted in relation to festivals (Brandes 1988), a reclaiming of the streets (Delgado 2004). Issues such as local or national identity, the use of public space, and the political use of festive rituals have emerged as triggers for conflict situations.

In the case of *La Patum*, the core of the conflict was the political issue related to national independence. *La Patum* is a festivity that takes place in the town of Berga, registered in UNESCO's Representative List of the Intangible Cultural Heritage of Humanity, which in recent years has had heavy political content, asserting Catalan nationalism (Noyes 2003). In this case, a pandemic-adapted program was planned ("The lockdown Patum"), but the cancellation of the crowded ritual dance performances translated into various political conflicts. At the time when the festivity usually began in Plaça de

Sant Pere (the town square), there was a spontaneous outbreak of applause. However, it was, above all, the night-time performance of a spontaneous dance through the streets, the *Salts de Maces* (an exhibition of devil dances), that sparked greater debate, especially due to the participation of a municipal councillor, a member of the CUP radical left and pro-independence party. Her disobedience caused great controversy, and the other political groups in the town council issued a statement calling for the resignation of the participating councillor, who was also the vice-president of the council. On the following days, the police had to bring in reinforcements to prevent crowds from gathering. In the end, the councillor was removed from the vice-presidency due to her "irresponsible" behavior, after appearing in a video that had a great impact on social networks. This led to the cancellation of the rest of the scheduled events due to the difficulty of guaranteeing public order.

In other cases, the conflict was related to local identity and the use of public space. Performance of the ritual dances during the town festival was prohibited in Reus, but the organizing associations responded with a protest performance in the street.[16] On the very day of the festival, accompanied by music from mobile phones and loudspeakers, people started to perform the various festival dances (*Ball dels Nanos, Ball de Cercolets,* and *Ball de Pastorets*). The opportunity was taken to make a speech with the cry "*Visca la Festa Major!*" (Long Live the Town Festival!), attracting more and more participants. There was also a *tronada* (setting off of fireworks) processions of *grallers* (Catalan wind-instrument players) and *timbalers* (drum players), which were interrupted by the municipal police, although afterwards the mayor authorized them, provided the regulations were followed.

As we saw in the example of Cervera, cancellation of the festivity even gave rise to confrontations with the police. Something similar happened in the town of Vilafranca del Penedès, where crowds gathered in the streets to celebrate the Sant Fèlix town festival. This also produced a political confrontation with people who accused the town council of being too permissive.[17] The town council thus issued an urgent announcement on August 29, 2020, stating:

> [I]n response to the images of crowded events that took place on Saturday in the streets of the town, the Town Council wishes to express its disagreement with the holding of these festive events and calls upon everyone to act responsibly to avoid any situation that goes against all of the Covid-19

[16] https://www.diaridetarragona.com/reus/VIDEOS-Sant-Pere-viu-un-llument-dels-grups-festius-i-una-Tronada-improvisada-20200629-0034.html [viewed on January 23, 2021].

[17] https://elcaso.elnacional.cat/ca/successos/video-festa-major-vilafranca-penedes-multitud-concentrada-tronada-cercavila-coronavirus_36794_102.html [viewed on January 23, 2021].

prevention measures [...] [T]his year, we are experiencing some very different festive days. The Town Festival has been cancelled, but the festive spirit lives on within us. However, it is very important for us to act responsibly in response to the public health crisis we are experiencing.[18]

Conflicts of this kind, which were reproduced in various municipalities, led to some town councils cancelling planned "symbolic" festivals as they could not guarantee public order.

The same parameter was seen in all cases: a municipal prohibition on holding the festival, a group of people who ignored the prohibition and held the festival, controversy in the municipality and on social networks, accusations of irresponsibility (generally levelled at young people), and political debates. We can raise three questions regarding the examples set out. Firstly, these debates were mixed up with political debates (such as independence for Catalonia). Secondly, one can see that, in protest actions, the amplification of local demands appears to stand in opposition to a global pandemic discourse, as a way of breaking with the imposition of restricted and homogenized leisure (Suari 2020). Thirdly, there is a common pattern of accusations levelled at young people, as the main perpetrators of "anti-social" attitudes. In any case, these "alternative" demonstrations show us how festivals have the capability of becoming a space for resistance and transgression (Gutiérrez 1997).

CONCLUSIONS

As Delgado (2003) points out, festivities are a kind of sacred space sheltered within time, the equivalent of a temple or monument in the spatial dimension, a refuge (or a storm) in which humans dramatize the ultimate meaning of existence as a social being and the conditions that make it possible. The experience seen during the pandemic is an outstanding analysis laboratory that allows us to see how rituals and festivals are adapted and modified, demonstrating the processes used to reconfigure tradition (Testa 2020b).

In the Catalan case, during this pandemic period, local traditions, especially in their festive or public versions, have acted as a strong cultural glue, sometimes as a veritable social raison d'être (Testa 2020b), by way of responding to the global experience of the pandemic. Far from being stopped, festivals and rituals have adapted to the new situation and given rise to new forms of celebration. These "lockdown" festivals have maintained a set of elements considered "representative" of festivals (Imber-Black 2020) to ensure their continuity. However, at the same time, this representativeness

---

[18] https://festamajor.vilafranca.cat/noticies/lajuntament-fa-una-crida-la-responsabilitat-de-tothom [viewed on January 23, 2021].

has been conditioned by the pandemic and has given rise to both expansion and reduction of their elements. Virtuality has become a fundamental tool in transmission of the celebration. However, it is not virtuality that ensures continuity, but instead the presence of a set of representative elements for each celebration, which, as we have seen, vary in each context, but which will possibly also be part of future celebrations. In any case, subsequent analysis will make it possible to analyze, in greater detail, the elements that have become most "representative" and those that will end up being part of new festive rituals in the coming years.

At the same time, the conflicts and controversies we have set out in this chapter confirm the character of social disorder that characterizes festivals with opposition between the authorities seeking to control them and those who take advantage of the symbolic character and appeal to tradition to reclaim the streets and public spaces that were closed or restricted (Low and Maguire 2020). Conflicts and negotiations were part of all of these practices, as any type of narrative in which the "value of tradition" opposes apparently objective public health decisions and, above all, legal prohibitions (Bawidamann et al 2020, 8). In this sense, festivals have functioned not only as a vehicle for feelings and consensus, but also as elements of challenge and resistance (Testa 2014a, 64).

It is still too soon, after our first urgent ethnography, to determine the extent to which this period will affect the forms in which festivities are held in the future (Davies 2020). However, in any case, in Catalonia during lockdown, the debates about festivities and negotiations on holding them confirm the interrelationships between identity, the use of public space, and the political use of traditional festivals.

7

Bon Profit! Food as National Identity in Catalonia

VENETIA JOHANNES

INTRODUCTION: FOOD AND IDENTITY IN CATALONIA

On the evening of Tuesday, 9 January 2018, the chef Ada Parellada held an event at her *Semproniana* restaurant in Barcelona. It was a special charity supper, open to the general public, called the *El Sopar Groc* (the Yellow Supper), where all the food would be yellow. The event was held several months after the constitutional crisis that had rocked Spain in the autumn of 2017, when pro-independence protests in the Catalan Autonomous Community (CAC) lead to civil unrest, arrest of public figures, and a long-awaited explosion of tensions between the Catalan regional and Spanish central government. The supper, themed on the colour yellow that had become a symbol of the recent protests, gathered funds for the legal case for a number of the recently imprisoned politicians and public figures, and raised awareness of their plight.

This instance of the use of food in support of Catalan independence is one of many that I saw during my research into the relationship between Catalan national identity and food culture. However, this relationship goes much further than independence politics. In this chapter, I consider whether Catalans express their national identity through food and, if so, what are the ways in which they do so. I begin with an overview of the academic literature that inspired my research, with a particular focus on defining the terms in use in this chapter. I follow this with another literature review, this time of Catalan cookbooks, which provides a short history of Catalan cuisine and demonstrates the importance of these texts to the simultaneous development of Catalan cuisine and national identity. This goes into some of the basic practical elements of Catalan cuisine, and how they relate to other elements of

Catalan identity, such as *seny*. The next section deals with the gastronomic calendar and the importance of travel and national identity performance. Finally, I conclude by considering the complex relationship between food and contemporary independence politics.

INTERSECTIONS BETWEEN FOOD, NATIONALISM, AND IDENTITY

My research responds to the late anthropologist Josep Llobera's call for a better understanding of nationalisms through the anthropological study of their 'subjective feelings or sentiments' (Llobera 2004, 188). He argued that 'We cannot make a scientific inventory of the social facts of nationalism, for the simple reason that we lack the basic building blocks: good monographic studies of nations' (Llobera 2004, 184). As an anthropologist, what Llobera meant by monographic studies was ethnographies, that is to live among a group under study for an extended period of time to understand that group's social structure, beliefs and way of life, as opposed to a historical, political, or literature-focused approach. While there has been greater interest in nationalist movements since he published this statement in 2004 (and, indeed, since the duration of my research from 2011 to 2018), the importance of understanding these movements still rings true, especially in an era when such movements are experiencing a global resurgence.

The Catalan political theorist Montserrat Guibernau provides the most useful definition of nationalism for the Catalan case: 'a human group conscious of forming a community, sharing a common culture, attached to a clearly demarcated territory, having a common past and a common project for the future, and claiming the right to rule itself' (Guibernau 2002, 3). Note the final point about self-determination, which does not require a state, and until recent years Catalan secessionism was historically weak (Keating 1996). Another theory highly relevant to the Catalan case is that of political theorist Benedict Anderson in his *Imagined Communities* (1983), where he defines a nation as 'an imagined political community – and imagined as both inherently limited and sovereign', with cultural roots as the source of its power. Most members of the nation will never meet other members, thus requiring elements such as education, print capitalism, and other elements of shared culture to create the nation in the minds of its members.

One approach to understanding nationalist movements and ideology is by studying the everyday lived realities of such movements. Food, as an everyday necessity, is a useful tool for this endeavour. Catherine Palmer (1998), inspired by Billig (1995, who first coined the term 'everyday nationalism'), considers food to be one of three 'flags' or cultural objects with which national sentiments are associated in everyday practice (the others are the related concept of the body and landscape). Anthropologist Jeremy MacClancy, based on experiences in the Basque country, suggests that 'turning foodstuffs and dishes into bearers of national identity is a down-to-earth way to make an otherwise abstract ideology more familiar, domestic, even palatable' (MacClancy 2007; 68). These references to the importance of food in nationalism provide examples of early interest in the topic; however, they did not fully recognise or explore its potential, and food was still regarded as a sidenote in nationalism studies rather than a focus.

More recently, Atsuko Ichijo and Ronald Ranta have made an explicit focus on the relationship between nationalism and cuisine, concluding: 'Practising and asserting national identity through food means making choices and decisions that provide direct links to […] the nation's perceived or imagined history, social traditions, culture and geography' (Ichijo and Ranta 2016, 8). They are inspired by sociologist Michaela DeSoucey, who coined the term 'gastronationalism' to describe this process, where 'the use of food production, distribution, and consumption to demarcate and sustain the emotive power of national attachment' (DeSoucey 2010, 433), and that any assault against these foods is an assault against the nation itself. This in turn built upon Priscilla Ferguson's (1988) notion of 'culinary nationalism' in the development of French cuisine as a vehicle for French national identity.

There are limits to Ichijo and Ranta, and DeSoucey's work. While useful, Ichijo and Ranta's approach dichotomises social reality, categorising instances of gastronationalism based on the influence of the nation-state, when social reality is more complex. It is also harder to apply in cases where there are competing state actors. Related to this, DeSoucey's work is largely concerned with the role of official, organisational actors. Gastronationalism therefore refers more to official recognition and promotion of the nation through food than the thoughts and sentiments of individuals.

By contrast in my work, I have emphasised the opinions of individual Catalans in the context of their Catalan identity. I therefore include a broader range of behaviours in my interpretation of gastronationalism, including recognised Catalan culinary behaviours where official recognition is unimportant to Catalans. When I refer to 'Catalan cuisine', I refer to a set of recognised culinary procedures, characteristics, and ingredients to create certain food products. 'Catalan food culture' is a broader term encompassing both cuisine and the social behaviours surrounding its preparation and consumption.

Theorising the relationship between food and nation has received increased attention in the last decade (Long 2021). Much work here has focused on Central and South America, such as Jane Fajans' on Brazil (2012), Hanna Garth's edited volume on the Caribbean (2013), and Steffan Igor Ayora-Diaz's work on the Yucatan in Mexico (2012), the latter providing some parallels with Catalonia. Portugal (Sobral 2014), Bulgaria (Yotova, 2014), and Lithuania (Mincyte 2008) have also provided research in this area. In 2019, an edited volume by Ichijo et al (2019), *The Emergence of National Food*, provided in-depth explorations of the role of food in the nation-state in 14 cross-global case studies. In another recent edited volume, *Culinary Nationalism in Asia* (2019), editor Michelle King defines culinary nationalism to be a 'dynamic process of creation and contestation' (King 2019, 2), an approach that well understands the changeable and performative nature of food in national contexts, although the dichotomisation with what she perceives as a more static 'national cuisine' is perhaps artificial. Questions of food heritage and national and state interests are considered by Di Giovine and Brulotte (2014) in *Edible Identities: Food as Cultural Heritage*.

The plethora of recent explorations of food and the nation demonstrate this is a fruitful area for understanding contemporary nationalisms. As folklorist Lucy Long has remarked: 'As symbolic object and activity, food is often mobilized, intentionally and unintentionally, as a medium for enacting one's place within nation' (Long 2021). Returning to Catalonia, I found that food itself was often present in the literature on Catalan nationalism and identity, but not a focus in itself. Folklorist and ethnologist Dorothy Noyes (2003) discussed the importance of food for enculturation and belonging in her field site of Berga, in her seminal ethnography, *Fire in the Plaça*. Anthropologist Alexander Robertson has also referred to food in his works on his long relationship with the region, specifically the town of Mieres. He describes food as 'the essence of conviviality in Catalonia', and references the 'binding power' of commensality (Robertson 2010, 72), yet still does not focus exclusively on it. The evidently important role of food in the literature suggested there was more to this subject, and it could be a novel way to understand how Catalan identity is lived and experienced. Other more recent writers on the subject of Catalan cuisine are H. Rosi Song and Anna Riera, who have done an excellent job of studying the culinary identity of Barcelona in their book *A Taste of Barcelona* (2019), which explores the culinary history of Barcelona and the surrounding regions, as well as providing some insights into Catalan cuisine in the contemporary era. It does tend to gloss over the at-times conflictual relationship between Barcelona and the rest of Catalonia. While the official capital of Catalonia, Barcelona today is considered a less 'Catalan' city, with its greater use of Castilian and notably lower support for Catalan independence.

My primary fieldwork took place over 15 months, from June 2012 to September 2013, which allowed me to experience the festive and gastronomic year and be present at most major annual events in the Catalan cultural calendar. My main field site was the city of Vic, 60 kilometres (37 miles) north of Barcelona, a place known for its traditional Catalanism (and, more recently, pro-independence politics). Since 2013 I have also made several shorter visits to both Barcelona and Vic, the most recent of which was in January 2018. This visit was the source of more recent findings following the political crisis in autumn 2017. As an anthropologist, my primary research methodology was that of ethnography, and its associated research methods of the ethnographic interview and participant observation, as well as image elicitation and analysis of written materials and media.

COOKBOOKS AND THE CREATION OF CATALAN CUISINE

When starting a discussion of Catalan cuisine, there are two natural starting points: one is the basic sauces, the other is cookbooks. In this instance, I will begin with cookbooks, due to the important role they have had in shaping and categorising Catalan cuisine, and to create a perspective through time. The role of cookbooks in creating national cuisines is one that has been recognised across several countries (Anderson 2013 in Spain; Appadurai 1988 in India; Ferguson 1988 in France; Fragner 1994 in Iran; Sobral 2014 in Portugal). Catalonia is no exception, and a brief analysis of cookbooks demonstrate the standardisation of Catalan cuisine in the 19th century, an important time for the development of Catalanism in general. Song and Riera (2019) have also recognised the important role of cookbooks in Catalan culinary and social history. Cookbooks also show how food became a symbol or metaphor of the ideals of Catalan nationalism up to the present day, making them what Arjun Appadurai has called 'revealing artefacts of culture in the making' (Appadurai 1988, 22). One should also underline the symbolic importance of these cookbooks as historic and cultural objects, particularly medieval works. This is because the Catalan language is the crucial and primary expression of Catalan national identity (Crameri 2000; Hargreaves 2000), as well as claims to a separate history (Llobera 2004). Thus, literature in Catalan from historic eras has a special reverence as a representation of that time. Medieval works in particular are a source of pride for many Catalans as they are relics of the royal courts of the Catalan-Aragonese empire, a perceived golden age in Catalan national history (Keown 2011a).

It is impossible to give a complete overview of the variety of cookbooks throughout Catalan history, so I will only give a brief overview of the most important here. This is especially true for the 19th and 20th centuries when many were published, and I speak here of cookbooks whose authors explicitly link their cookbooks to the Catalan national project. A natural starting place is the medieval cooking manuals of the *Llibre de Sent Soví* of 1324 (also called *Libre de totes maneres de potatges de menjar*), and later the famous *Libre de Coch* of 1520 by Robert de Nola, the first printed cookbook in the Catalan language.

Many contemporary chefs and writers who I interviewed saw *Llibre de Sent Sovi* itself as a demonstration of the antiquity of Catalan cuisine, through the presence of an early form of some essential sauces in Catalan cuisine, such as the *sofregit* and the *picada*. The view that Catalan cuisine has this unbroken tradition from the medieval golden age to the present day draws parallels to the notion that the Catalan nation has its origins in the medieval past. This view has been especially promoted in the Generalitat-sponsored campaign to recognise Catalan cuisine as a UNESCO intangible heritage, where these cookbooks have been essential in backing up claims to antiquity and uniqueness.

After these texts, few cooking manuals on cuisine in Catalonia appeared until the 19th century. Some chefs I spoke with saw this as reflective of the general decline in Catalonia's fortunes during the intervening centuries, with the centralisation of power in Madrid as the 16th and 17th centuries progressed, civil unrest, and the humiliations of the end of the War of the Spanish Succession and the Nueva Planta decrees of 1716.

The first Catalan cookbook of the modern period, *La Cuynera Catalana*, is a bridge between medieval cuisine and that of the present day (Martí Escayol 2004), the sign of a rebirth in Catalan cuisine in the context of incipient 19th-century Catalanism (the *Renaixença*). Originally a series of pamphlets published from 1833 to 1835, it was finally compiled into a full edition in 1851. Still revered today, the text is unusual as it was written exclusively in Catalan. Most historians date the Catalan *Renaixença* to 1833, with the publication of *Oda a La Pàtria* (*Ode to the Fatherland*) by Carles Aribau. *La Cuynera Catalana* began serialisation only two years later, when the *Renaixença* was still in its infancy. Considering the context, to publish a serialised book entirely in colloquial, unstandardised Catalan was a bold undertaking, one likely influenced by moves in Catalan literary culture. In choosing to publish in Catalan, the author is aligning with the ideals of *Renaixença*. Similar to the incipient work of folklorists and historians of that time, this cookbook recorded popular Catalan cuisine of the era, while also being a practical and useful tool in the kitchen.

This dual role of practical cookbook and record of Catalan culture was a characteristic of many of the later cookbooks published in the 19th and early 20th century. One such work was the 1907 cookbook *La Cuyna Catalana* (*Catalan Cooking*) by Josep Cunill de Bosch. It is with this work that cooking begins to be explicitly linked with the project of Catalan nationhood. The author described cooking as 'the greatest transcendence, both for the individual and the community' (Cunill de Bosch 1908, 7). The book begins its introduction by referring to national dishes typical of Catalans, particularly the *escudella i carn d'olla* (a meat and vegetable stew), and makes explicit connection to Catalan popular culture. Sixteen years later, in 1923, the authors of the *Art de*

Ben Menjar make similar statements. The authors of the book were Adriana and Sara Aldavert, the daughters of journalist and Catalanist politician Pere Aldavert (Armengol 2015), writing under the pseudonym 'Marta Sàlvia'. This fact underlines the book's gastronationalist credentials, demonstrating the importance that the Catalan intelligentsia of the time placed on Catalan cuisine. Both books refer to antiquity and the historical past of Catalonia within the Mediterranean, placing the cookbooks within the context of an evolution from a historic past, so important to a Catalan nationalism where claims to a separate identity are strongly based on history.

In *Art de Ben Menjar*, the authors intend to appeal not to refined palates, but to contribute to the good preparation of dishes 'at the hearths of our native land', i.e. Catalonia. This use of 'our native land', and the image of the hearth is a potent emotional one, connecting the home and kitchen with the nation. The presence of these pro-Catalan phrases, the background of the authors, the subtitle of the book, and the implied historical connectedness all suggest the influence of Catalanist ideas of the time in cookbooks.

No discussion of Catalan cookbooks is complete without mention of Ignasi Domènech, chef and cookbook writer (1874–1956). Much of his extensive output was published in Castilian (standard) Spanish. However, he also had a substantial body of work in Catalan, including popular works such as *La Teca* (literally *The Grub*, 1924) and *Àpats* (*Meals*, 1930). These icons of 20th-century Catalan cuisine are popular icons in the present day. During my fieldwork, every household I knew had at least one of his books (generally *La Teca*), which were often displayed and discussed. It is probable that many of the most popular dishes today gained their privileged position thanks to inclusion in *La Teca*. While this book was a practical cooking manual, his second most popular work, *Àpats*, is more complex. It is a recipe book, but also contains sections that are less relevant to cooking, e.g. information on the Catalan gastronomic calendar (more on that later in this chapter), a history of popular Barcelonan restaurants, and past menus he prepared for important political and cultural events. It should be seen as an elaborate 'coffee table book' in today's parlance, to be read in one's spare time, primarily by a bourgeois readership. It is not just a recipe book, but is also intended to contribute to knowledge about Catalan cooking and its cultural traditions.

The apogee of the alignment between Catalanism and Catalan cuisine came in the form of Ferran Agulló's *Llibre de la Cuina Catalana*, published in 1928, a work written purely with the intention of glorifying cuisine as a rallying point of Catalan nationalism. Agulló was not a chef; he was a well-respected member of the intelligentsia and political elite of the era, associated with the right-wing Lliga Catalana. In the introduction to his book, he throws down the gauntlet for his defence of cuisine as a repository of Catalan identity: 'Catalonia, just as it has a language, a right, customs, its own history and a political ideal, so it has a cuisine. There are regions, nations, peoples, who have a special, characteristic dish, but not a cuisine. Catalonia has that' (Agulló 1999, 11).[1]

This work is intriguing from a contemporary perspective, as many of the features that Catalans today express as central to their cuisine are already present in this book. This includes the openness and adventurousness of Catalan cuisine to new influences, symbolic of Catalonia itself as an open, modern nation. He also discusses daily meals and festive occasions (the gastronomic calendar again), before going into the main dishes and sauces.

The prosperity of this era was to end abruptly with the Spanish Civil War of 1936–1939. The succeeding anti-Catalan Franco government was keen to eradicate all signs of separate Catalan identity. While publications in Catalan were largely forbidden, this was relaxed in the 1960s and 1970s. Re-editions of popular and religious works, including cookbooks were permitted. In fact, some new Catalan cookbooks were permitted because of their supposedly non-political nature (Hall 2001). Ironically, this meant that one of the few ways that the Catalans could have access to new literature in their language was through cookbooks. Many families kept treasured Catalan libraries hidden in their homes (Llobera 2004), and cookbooks formed part of these libraries, helping to preserve cultural knowledge and the Catalan language. Indeed, one of my informants, a university professor, recalled that he learned to read Catalan during his childhood through his mother's copy of *La Teca*. The book was kept in pride of place in their kitchen, and its presence there, as well as the Catalan meals cooked from it, were a way to covertly perform Catalan identity and resist Francoist oppression.

Two of the works published in this era deserve mention, *200 Plats casolans de cuina catalana*, (*200 Homemade Dishes from Catalan Cuisine*, 1969) by Antoni Dalmau, and *Cuina Catalana* (*Catalan Cuisine*, 1971) by Maria del Carme Nicolau. In the introduction to their books, these authors make explicit remarks about Catalan cuisine's separate identity, through landscape, regional diversity, and even language. To have made these statements in other contexts would have been suspect, even dangerous. Yet in a seemingly unthreatening cookbook, covert expressions of Catalanism could sneak through censorship.

With the end of the Franco dictatorship in 1975, Catalan language and identity was now an acceptable and celebrated medium for publication, including cookbooks and magazine and newspaper articles. There had already been some tentative attempts at promoting Catalan culinary identity, for example with the 1975 *Assortiment Gastronomic de Catalunya*, organised by Josep Lladonosa i Giró. After 1977, there was an explosion of literature on Catalan cuisine, and one which has continued to this day, exemplified in the

---

[1] All translations from the original Catalan are my own.

work of Josep Lladonosa i Giró, Nestor Luján, Manuel Váquez Montalbán, Núria Baguena, and Jaume Fàbrega, to name but a few. In the last few years, with the rise of a new independence movement, expressing Catalan identity has begun to stretch to all parts of everyday life, and cookbook publishing is no exception. At gastronomic and national festivals, any Catalanist bookstall is incomplete without a sizeable cookery section peddling the popular titles of the last few years, and new editions of the older works.

SAUCES, STEWS AND SYMBOLS: THE BASIC ELEMENTS OF CATALAN CUISINE

Now is a good moment to turn to the practical elements of Catalan cuisine, the key components and main dishes. For some of my informants, the very selection of a limited number of elements to present here is an insult to the wide *receptari* (recipe collection) and regional diversity of Catalan cuisine. However, for space reasons I need to limit the discussion here to the fundamental sauces of the *sofregit* and the *picada*, and two important 'national' dishes, the *escudella i carn d'olla* and the *pa amb tomàquet*. I have chosen these because they were mentioned and debated most frequently in informant discourse and also were often discussed in culinary literature (both in cookbooks and in popular media), as exemplifying some important elements of Catalan culture.

Whenever I began any discussion about Catalan cuisine during fieldwork, there were four things that almost always appeared first: the *sofregit*, the *picada*, the *allioli*, and the *romesco*. These are sauces that are the foundations of Catalan cuisine, firstly because of their claims to distinctiveness, and secondly because of their essential role in 'flavouring' a dish to make it Catalan, both literally and figuratively. I discuss the first two in detail here, as today they are considered more important for distinctiveness than *allioli* and *romesco*, which have been more commercialised by the food industry and can now be found outside Catalonia. The *sofregit* is the starting point of any dish, made up in its most basic form of onion, garlic, parsley, and tomato. The *picada* is a grainy paste of herbs, spices, and ground nuts with some liquid, added at the end of a meal. One of my informants, the editor of Catalan food magazine *Cuina*, defined Catalan cuisine as 'something that starts with a *sofregit* and ends with a *picada*, and in between, things happen!'. The *sofregit* and *picada* are often considered representative of Catalan cuisine's long history. Early forms of the *sofregit* (without tomato) and *picada* can be found in medieval cookbooks, such as the *Llibre de Sent Sovi* of 1324 and the *Llibre de Coch* of 1520. Using foodstuffs originating in the Americas, like chocolate, is not perceived as contradicting this sense of continuity. In fact, quite the opposite, as it is an example of the perceived adaptability and openness of Catalan cuisine.

13. *Picada*, a grainy paste of herbs, spices, and ground nuts with some liquid, added at the end of a dish's preparation in Catalan cuisine. Source: Author.

A dish that was mentioned in the previous section was the *escudella i carn d'olla*. *Escudella i carn d'olla* is a stew of various ingredients, a selection of meats, a bone, sausage, meatballs (*pilota*), vegetables, rice, *fideus* (tiny pasta sticks) and/or large pasta pieces (*galletes*). It was once a subsistence dish, created from whatever food was available. The cookbook writers in the previous section often referred to the Catalan's love of the dish, treating it as *the* national dish, a view that was shared by many of my informants. While sharing many characteristics and ingredients with similar stews throughout Europe, there are several features that Catalans point to that make it unique. It is connected to Catalan national history and rural identity, but also to the industrialisation of the region through its popularity with working women in the 19th century. While eaten through the year, it is strongly associated with Christmas. Thus its manner of consumption is different from similar dishes in neighbouring cuisines. It is therefore also consumed almost exclusively in communal and familial settings, giving it a strong association with commensality. Finally, the *escudella* is a culinary manifestation of an ideal aspect of the Catalan character, namely *seny*. A word that is difficult to translate, it suggests a sensible, rational, down-to-earth attitude, a business-like and hard-working approach to life (Hargreaves 2000). *Seny* is also encapsulated in the ideal of thriftiness, an attitude expressed in the popular saying, 'We make use of everything'. *Seny* is an emic concept, used by Catalans as an ideal standard of behaviour deployed at appropriate moments. Foods that have their origins in subsistence cuisine provide the most frequent opportunities for Catalans to encounter *seny* and thriftiness in everyday life.

The food that most typifies *seny* is *pa amb tomàquet*. This is made by rubbing a ripe tomato into a slice of bread, ideally using hard bread that is a few days old and otherwise inedible, allowing the juices to soften the bread. Then, oil and salt are added to taste, and sometimes a little garlic rubbed in. Most informants claimed to eat it every day, or at least every other day, either as a snack or a light meal. Of all the signature dishes identified by Catalans, *pa amb tomàquet* is probably the most regularly eaten and ubiquitous, being found in everyday sandwiches, to festive side-dishes, to snack plates in Catalan homes when there is a Barça match (on these occasions alongside other signature Catalan products like Estrella Damm beer and *llonganissa*).

Pa amb tomàquet is also claimed to be unique to Catalonia, though its spread to other regions of Spain has altered this conception somewhat. Now the emphasis is more on the process of making it, that of rubbing the tomato into the bread, rather than pouring on squashed or sliced tomato, which is done in other regions. As with the *escudella*, it is the process (cooking) and its position in culinary culture that are considered bastions against the risk of homogeneity. Moreover, *pa amb tomàquet* is recognized as distinctly Catalan by non-Catalans elsewhere in Spain. It is therefore a point of self-identification that is reinforced by interactions with non-Catalans.

Its component ingredients contribute to this recognition. The tomato, as both a central component of Catalan cuisine and a product from the Americas, symbolises the ideal of an integrationist cuisine open to new influences, and of Catalan nationalism as ideally open, willing to accept all those who wish to learn Catalan, adopt Catalan culture, and self-identify as Catalan (Llobera 2004). Bread is a basic staple in Catalonia and has received some attention with the recognition of *pa de pagès* (peasant's or farmer's bread) as a food with Protected Geographical Indication (PGI) within the EU. Its description even states explicitly that it is ideal for *pa amb tomàquet*, officially enshrined as part of a 'traditional' foodway. Oil too is a matter of pride as one of Catalonia's main exports, and the fact that it varies hugely from region to region makes it an example of the ideal of regional diversity and variety. *Pa amb tomàquet* can also be found in all parts of Catalonia. This role as a cultural unifier is particularly important in Catalan food culture due to the inherent diversity in regional cuisines, which might otherwise contradict the claim of Catalan culinary unity, something that I discuss in the next section.

THE GASTRONOMIC CALENDAR AND PERFORMING IDENTITY

The gastronomic calendar is a central tenet of Catalan food culture, specifying that certain foods are eaten on certain days or in certain seasons. The ways in which food and festivity are associated are often considered unique or defining characteristics of Catalan culinary culture. This is not to say that the practice of associating the two is unique to Catalonia (it can be found worldwide), but the foods that are associated with different annual events are essential to claims of gastro-cultural uniqueness. Most Catalans realise that they usually eat the same foods as neighbouring countries. This is so even for popularly recognised Catalan dishes, such as *escudella i carn d'olla* and *canelons*. However, what has marked them out as different was their application in Catalan cuisine thanks to the gastronomic calendar.

These associations are normally related to seasonally available produce or secularised religious feast days. In the case of the former, the celebration of religious feast days is characterized by food, rarely by any religious feeling. For contemporary Catalans, such days provide another connection with a historical and idealized past. For instance, a key part of the celebration of Lent in contemporary Catalonia continues to be the consumption of cod dishes, so much so that February to March is called the *temporada de bacalla* (cod season) in restaurants, markets, media outlets, and everyday interactions. This is recognised and performed even by Catalans that I knew who were non- (or even anti-) religious.

Other foods also have associations with particular days or times of the year because of their seasonal availability, such as the *calçots* (spring onions) in February, herbs and fruits in May and June, mushrooms in October, chestnuts in November etc. The popular summer festival bread, *coca* decorated with sugared fruits, was originally topped with seasonal fruits and nuts such as cherries, strawberries and almonds. Mushrooms are a popular food in Catalonia, as is the autumnal (and less common spring) activity of *busca-bolets* or mushroom finding (also called *caça-bolets*, mushroom hunting). Catalans point to this as another distinctive element of their culinary culture. Heavier foods can be found in the winter months, which is considered to be a seasonal variation because of climate rather than the availability of produce. This can be seen at Christmas, when the universally recognised dish is the *escudella i carn d'olla*, suited to large gatherings and the colder weather; the Christmas leftovers are reused on St Steven's Day (26 December) as the fillings for *canelons* or stuffed pasta rolls, another food that typifies a national ideal of *seny*.

Today, neither seasonality nor religious prohibitions have the influence on contemporary food availability they exerted in former times. However, the association of the resulting gastronomic calendar with the past has lent it a new significance in light of the renewed awareness of Catalan culture in everyday settings that has been brought about by the pro-independence movement.

The gastronomic calendar is also relevant in another way for experiencing the nation. When consuming dishes on particular days associated with the gastronomic calendar, there is awareness on an individual level that throughout the rest of Catalonia other Catalans are eating the same dishes. Much like language or the collective celebration of national days, following the gastronomic calendar creates a connection between the individual and the greater Catalan nation through the shared consumption of the same foods. It is a culinary expression of Anderson's concept of imagined communities, as Catalans imagine other members of the Catalan nation consuming the same festival foods and partaking in the same festive moment.

This is exemplified by a Good Friday meal I ate with an older couple, Pep and Rosa-Maria. The main dish on the menu was a cod and egg dish, *Bacallà de Divendres Sant* (Good Friday cod). Although Pep and Rosa-Maria were not religious, they still insisted on making reference to the continued sway of Lent until it ended that Sunday, so as to respect the gastronomic calendar. The dish itself respects seasonality in its other ingredients, such as spinach and beans, and the large quantity of springtime eggs. Pep also pointed out that the dish included a *sofregit*, proof of its identification as Catalan. In describing what this dish meant to him, Pep summed up the real importance, the central tenet of the gastronomic calendar in Catalan gastronationalism: 'There is a connection at the level of all Catalonia. You feel linked to a culture; we're all doing the same this Good Friday.'

I had heard similar feelings implied during shared festive meals throughout fieldwork (for instance, eating *escudella* and *canelons* at Christmas time, and *Coca de Sant Joan* for St John's Eve), but it was Pep who expressed it so succinctly and so clearly. This situation also bears resemblance to other contexts. For instance, Fajans (2012) notes the prevalence of the *feijoada* dish for Saturday lunch, such that Brazilians can partake of a shared essence and identity through the consumption of the same food at the same time.

Related to this knowledge of shared foods via the gastronomic calendar, it is worth mentioning another element of Catalan food culture, namely the importance of regionality of food, and of demonstrating knowledge of this regional variety. Food is a medium through which local identity is expressed at the county and regional levels, so much so that many Catalans seem to hold a culinary map of their country in their minds, associating food, people, place, and season. This culinary map is part of a system of knowledge about Catalonia, which Catalans use to demonstrate their knowledge of their nation. This includes knowledge of regional recipes and specialities, or markets and fairs. It also includes performing and applying this knowledge through physically travelling through Catalonia and visiting different places, an activity called *excursionisme* that had its origins in 19th-century nationalism. One of these activities is the act of mushroom hunting that I mentioned earlier, since a successful *boletaire* requires enough knowledge of mushroom lore and familiarity with territory. Showing and performing such knowledge through actions and discussions with other Catalans (often over food) reasserts and demonstrates a sense of being Catalan. I participated in this performance, when I was able to talk with authority about different regional cuisines, and my own experiences of travel across Catalonia for my research. The act of journeying across Catalonia, experiencing the territories and regional intricacies of the nation first-hand, is likewise a significant performance of national identity. That this activity is called *fent país*, literally 'making country', is testament to the essential role of this activity in both national identity creation and performance.

The connection between *territori* (the Catalan interpretation of *terroir*), regional dishes and the EU quality systems (e.g. Protected Denomination of Origin, PDO or Protected Geographic Indication, PGI) is a complicated one. Most Catalans take a pragmatic approach that if these recognitions promote Catalan business interests, then they are useful and seen positively. Catalans are also proud of PDOs (or similar labels), even if conversely many well-loved Catalan foods do not have this recognition. The Catalan government regularly use PDOs in touristic marketing, in a classic example of what Ichijo and Ranta (2016) call a top-down promotion of national foods. At the same time, attempts by the Catalan government to engage with the rural (an ideal which has a strong place in Catalanism), through regional foods and PDOs to 'package' the Catalan nation has met with mixed success (Davidson 2007).

THE POLITICISATION OF CATALAN FOOD

During the fieldwork I conducted in 2012–2013, many of my informants were cautious about explicitly connecting food to the independence movement. They saw the secessionist movement as a political wing of Catalan nationalism, not a cultural one that is associated with cultural manifestations like food. While this situation may sound odd on first reading, it is a consequence of the sometimes tortuous relationship between culture and politics in Catalan identity since the 19th century. Multiple political movements in Catalonia and even Spain have sought to emphasise their support for Catalan culture for their own ends, to greater or lesser degrees of scepticism from Catalans themselves. This was evident during the Primo Dictatorship (1923–1930), the Spanish Civil War (1936–1939), and even recently during the Spanish Constitutional Crisis of 2017. Indeed, it has been suggested that Catalan identity endured because it was not the preserve of a single political affiliation (Crameri 2000), a feature shared with other banal nationalisms (Billig 1995).

The policy of most chefs and food-industry operatives on this subject follows a popular Catalan saying: 'At the table, never talk about politics'. At the same time, food in Catalonia is often deployed as a cultural symbol at appropriate moments, to express protest in subtle and clever ways. For instance, Spain's National Day on 12 October has become a Catalan antifestival through the celebration of *botifarrades* or sausage-eating events, as an insult to the Spanish state. To *fer la botifarra* has vulgar connotations as a rude gesture, the implication being that by eating sausages on this day one is performing this gesture to Spanish nationalists, instead of celebrating Spanish identity. Sausages are also another popular national food in Catalonia, due to their regional specificity that celebrates rural identity, regional landscapes and microclimates (the *llonganissa de Vic* is a particularly famous example), and also as another food that manifests *seny*.

The presence of the Catalan national flags (the *Senyera* and proindependence *Estelada*) on food is an interesting development in recent years and is particularly noticeable on foods associated with two Catalan national days, the *Diada de Sant Jordi* (23 April), and the *Diada* (11 September). The discussion of these foods is relevant for understanding the development of potential new national foods, and the complex and often contradictory attitudes that surround the use of national identity to promote foods and products in the commercial sphere. Until recently, these festive days did not have a widely recognised food associated with them according the to the gastronomic calendar. This has changed with the creation of *pans de Sant Jordi* (Saint George's bread), a savoury bread flavoured with cheese and *sobrassada* sausage in the form of a *Senyera*, and the *pastís de Sant Jordi* (St George's cake), a cream cake decorated with images associated with the saint. For the

14. *Pastís de la Diada* from a Barcelona bakery on sale during the *Diada*, decorated with Catalonia's national flag, the *Senyer*a. Source: Author.

September *Diada*, a similar cake can be found in cake shops and bakeries, this time emblazoned with *Senyeres* and *Estelades* in sugar and fondant. It has also become common for other food products decorated with the flags to be available at this time, such as biscuits and croissants. The first *pans de Sant Jordi* were allegedly produced in the Fleca Balmes in Barcelona in 1987. The origins of the *pastís de Sant Jordi/de la Diada* are less clear. The Barcelona Cakemaker's Guild presented a cake like this to the President in exile of the Generalitat in September 1977, while there are references to a 'Sant Jordi' cake in the late 1920s (Rondissoni 1927).

As a food product emblazoned with the Catalan flag, one of the most powerful symbols of Catalan national identity, I had expected it to be revered in a similar way to other Catalan foods. To my surprise, my informants had mixed reactions to these new foods, and questioned the motivations of their producers. Were they a representation of genuine support for Catalan identity, and (in the cases of those cakes with *Estelades*) of pro-independence sentiments by businesses? Or were they a money-making ploy to take advantage of the current political situation? Many of my informants believed it was the latter. Some professed to a lack of familiarity with them outside Barcelona, demonstrating the at-times condescending view of the city as a place where Catalan identity is weaker, despite being the Catalan capital. One informant in her 20s remarked they were 'all marketing, invented [...] not traditional', and another older activist remarked they were 'total marketing' for the bakeries. Despite the reservations and negative attitudes to many of these cakes, it was interesting that many of my informants admitted to buying these cakes and similar products. The same activist who made the comment above added that 'once we are independent, then we'll have to have a cake' to mark Catalonia's independence day in the gastronomic calendar. It is also interesting to note that in a recent cookbook, *El Receptari Groc* (Òmnium Cultural 2018), which I discuss in further detail at the end of this section, two recipes included desserts decorated with the *Senyera*, suggesting a softening of attitudes, or different attitudes in pro-independence or political contexts. Perhaps, in a generation, these foods will become traditional foods, as has happened with other 'traditional' Catalan foods that originated in the 20th century (for a further discussion of these foods, see chapter 5 in Johannes 2019).

The traumatic events of autumn 2017, which I described in the introduction, had a deep effect on the mood within Catalonia. When I visited Catalonia in January 2018, many friends and acquaintances described feeling a sense of shock, which has manifested itself in relationships with food. According to some of my informants, in September and the early days of October, there were noticeably more food products sporting Catalan flags (the *Senyera*) and Catalan companies emphasised their Catalan connections and identity as a selling point to promote their products. After November there was a conspicuous decline in this kind of promotion, as shops and producers seemed to hide the *Senyeres* in fear of a potential backlash from disappointed and jaded consumers.

One of the most visible results of the events of October 2017 has been the presence of yellow ribbons in public places. This has become a new symbol of support for independence, as a symbol of the 'Free Political Prisoners' campaign led by Òmnium Cultural. This campaign has spawned several awareness and fund-raising initiatives, some of which have focused on food. At Christmas, one was the *Nadal Groc* (Yellow Christmas), where supporters were encouraged to place a yellow scarf or ribbon over an empty chair during the Christmas meal to represent one of the Catalan politicians or public figures imprisoned for rebellion. The symbolic potential of this act should not be underestimated. An aspect of the Catalan independence movement was being explicitly linked with an important festive moment in the Catalan gastronomic calendar, where food is central to its celebration – and not just any food, but recognised national dishes such as *escudella*, *canelons* and other popular seasonal dishes. In creating a symbolic chair for significant members of the nation one can sense the creation of a fictive kinship with these individuals through the Catalan nation by providing them with a place at the Christmas table, a place for the strengthening and celebration of commensality and family ties.

Another manifestation of the symbolic importance of the colour yellow was through the *Sopars Grocs* (yellow suppers) described at the start of this chapter. The originator of the idea, Barcelona chef Ada Parellada, created a five-course menu where each dish used yellow foods, including dishes such as scrambled eggs, battered cod with mustard sauce, and lemon cake with caramelised *crema catalana*. While not typical dishes of Catalan cuisine, the supper itself was another example of the unifying power of food in political contexts. As a result of the event, Parellada experienced a harassment campaign, yet also an upsurge of support when she made this known on Catalan news media. Ironically, the harassment campaign raised awareness of the *Sopar Groc* across Catalonia, and the event was transformed into a focus of the 'Free Political Prisoners' campaign. The event inspired further 'yellow dinners' in restaurants and private homes. The restaurant-based *Sopar Groc* movement resulted in the creation of a recipe book by participants, with proceeds being donated to Òmnium's campaign. The prologue was written by one of the imprisoned activists, Jordi Cuixart, who continues to be chairman of Òmnium Cultural. In it, he expresses some enlightening views on the relationship between culinary and political identity in Catalonia:

> Because in the end in the most complicated moments culture is always the best tool, the best antidote against intolerance […] Catalan cuisine and the world over is a motive of collective self-love. Men and women of the areas of the Països Catalans, valiant and transgressive [people] have never been afraid to experiment based on their origins or from the things brought from other cultures, to find new pleasures for the senses. (Òmnium Cultural 2018)

His first sentence encapsulates the attitude towards food and politics that I mentioned earlier, that of no politics at the table, and the importance of keeping culture (including food) separate from politics. While they may be linked, food can be a balm against the conflict engendered by politics. He continues the words of many other Catalanists who have written on food, such as Ferran Agulló, while also referencing the past (a crucial aspect of Catalan nationalism) and national character.

CONCLUSION

Jordi Cuixart's comments reflect the attitudes of many of the people I knew and interviewed during my fieldwork in Catalonia. While politics may be a source of division, Catalan culinary culture is a unifying force. Even where there are debates and disagreements about the precise nature and technicalities of Catalan cuisine (and I have been present at many!), for there to even be such a discussion implies an agreement between disputants that Catalan cuisine exists, and that they both have enough knowledge and common ground on the subject to dispute. Related to this, such discussions are a way of performing Catalan identity, as Catalans demonstrate national knowledge, but also continually interrogate and reformulate what it is to be a Catalan.

Another finding was that food provides a nexus of associations with other areas of Catalan culture and identity. It connects with national language and literature (such as cookbooks), national character, social history, festivals, landscape, and territory. The intersections of these different associations of the nation with its food creates a combination of symbols that continually enforce and flag (Billig 1995) Catalan culinary identity. Not unlike Fajans' (2012) Brazilian *feijoada*, through consuming festive foods and shared dishes, yet also being aware of territorial variations, Catalans are involved in creating an imagined community through food.

The aim of my work overall (and, in some ways, this chapter) is to give insight into the lived experiences and everyday culture of Catalans going through a traumatic moment in their history, as they live amid a national, social, and political movement. It is, in a sense a work of cultural history. Reading history, especially those on nationalism, one tends to forget the lives of ordinary individuals, who lived in those eras and experienced its tumult.

Afterword:
Beneath the Nation: Collective Creation and Civic Need

DOROTHY NOYES

It is more than spectacular. The giant bubbling pan of an *arrossada* on the ground, stirred by a team of cooks; the fiery river of a *correfoc* passing through a narrow street; the triumph of a tiny child raising her hand at the top of a swaying human tower. No foreigner leaves Catalonia unimpressed by the vitality and pervasiveness of traditional popular culture. The camera can capture the splendid forms, but the atmosphere is what matters most, overwhelming the body and then incorporated. The simmering rice begins as sound and aroma; it becomes savor and inner warmth. The fire, mediated by smoke and sparks, startles the breath and marks skin and clothing. The tower is felt underneath as an enveloping tissue of pressures, even rising up from the paving stones, that linger in joints and muscles. Always the boundaries of the self must yield, in exhilaration and terror, to powerful stimuli and the agency of others.

COLLECTIVE CREATION

Contemporary innovation is often contrasted to modern invention as a distributed, cumulative effort. It depends on networked, mutually visible actors who exchange ideas and compete to outdo one another; it progresses by iteration and negotiation.

The persistent, vernacular, collective forms we call "tradition" or "folklore" also take shape through distributed invention, but their social base is different. To be sure, open-source technologies, music scenes, and social movements do not come from nowhere; indeed, they typically emerge from less focused vernacular practice. Nonetheless, they depend on the voluntary engagement of a self-selected group. It is different with the creations of scarce-resource, non-liberal societies – a category that includes Catalonia and most of the world during most of its history. Eating is not optional, and cuisines develop from both the material resources and the social arrangements at hand. Social interaction in shared space is not optional, and is rife with conflict and contradiction. Festival and ritual practice build on everyday sociability, just as cuisine builds on everyday commensality, to formalize, stylize, reflect upon, and reshape the realities on which they depend. In this sense, participation in folk culture is general, but the reverse of homogeneous. *Escudella* and carnival both make use of what there is. In reciprocity, *escudella* and carnival make themselves available to anyone who can make use of them.

The complexity of festival, ritual, and cuisine requires them to be sustained by continual practice. The cookbook offers a supporting script, and festival records can assist the reconstruction of certain effects, but a *castell* cannot rise from the study of a video. The production and reproduction of popular culture depends on traditional knowledge, an embodied "feel for the game". This is acquired through socialization and repetition within a context providing the material, social, and spatial resources required. Crises of war and pandemic can interrupt this transmission. It can be more seriously undermined by shifts in economic activity, residential patterns, the governance of public space, ideology, the distribution of wealth and power, and not least climate and the natural environment. Yet traditional forms exhibit surprising resilience, for they have absorbed the ingenuity of innumerable actors adapting them to innumerable circumstances and purposes, large and small, across time and space. These diverse sedimented agencies help traditions to resist capture by any single actor or interest.

CONSCRIPTING POPULAR CULTURE

The nation-state, however, is an interest not easily resisted, even if you think you are in the wrong one. Despite the realities of empire, migration, and global capital, the nation has for 200 years maintained itself as the apparently natural framework for human belonging. From the 19th century onward, dictionaries, folktale collections, and literary canons have been produced to make the case for distinctive nations that merit political recognition. Catalonia possesses all of these cultural objectifications, but nationalists have often pointed to persistent traditional repertoires as still more compelling demonstrations of the *fet diferencial*.

Depending on the moment and the antagonist, arguments from popular culture highlight various elements, construct various origin narratives, and derive various conclusions for the future, but all draw force from the embodied experience of participants. Whether eating a meal, climbing a mountain, chasing a bull, or building a tower, a recurrent shared practice instils rhythms and impulses that are felt "to come up from the blood" (Noyes 2003, 132). Practice also ties the body to the natural and built environment: the foraged mushrooms, the trodden pavement. In this way, as Venetia Johannes says, participating in any of these activities (or arguing about them) is a way to *fer país*: to fortify Catalonia as a shared lifeworld. The historic territory of the principality is small enough to be more than a purely imagined community: regular weekend excursions to taste a specialty or see a festival can easily generate a sense of proprietorship in the whole, and this *excursionisme* was a greater impetus to popular Catalanism than the literary revival of the *Renaixença*.

Catalanist intellectuals, like intellectuals anywhere, have rarely trusted popular culture to speak on its own. Interpretation and intervention conscript local tradition into national projects and discipline it to move more closely in step with national rhythms, just as, after the achievement of the nation-state, local bodies will be conscripted and trained in national militaries. Modernization took place at both levels, cultural and corporeal. The serial publication and the vernacular language of the 1830s *Cuynera catalana* were pragmatic adaptations to the limits of income and literacy among the women of the early industrial era. Such print culture contributed to the constitution of a working-class public, solicited by a wide range of competing social movements and encouraged to cultivate modern forms of self-consciousness in the process. Johannes shows how the codification of traditional knowledge in cookbooks came to model a moral economy of Catalan citizenship in which qualities such as *seny* and thrift, and, later, openness and cosmopolitanism, were highlighted. On such a foundation of national culinary modernity – supported by the infrastructures of industrial and then consumer capitalism – the avant-gardism of a Ferrán Adriá could assert itself, while locavore revivals might dig back beneath to recover specific *terroirs* and techniques.

Public ritual and festival must be perpetually reformed to accommodate local orders to the shifting narratives of state power and regional aspiration. The nationalist narrative famously both energizes and denies this process, through "invented tradition" (Hobsbawm and Ranger 1983). The supposed historicity and continuity of Catalan celebrations have long been expressed in refurbished decor, extravagant origin legends, and ingenious "recuperations" of putative former practices, including the Solsoní *mata-ruc* discussed here by Alessandro Testa. Solsona's Carnival is typical of post-Transition festival recuperations in its valorization of a popular, transgressive past; this democratic version of Catalanism inverted the aristocratic medievalizing typical of elite-driven festival invention in the late 19th century, the age of "industrial feudalism". Camila del Màrmol's chapter highlights the more esoteric medievalism of high Pyrenean cultural invention in the 1980s, which made common cause with Occitanist revindications on the other side of the border in response to a different set of concerns. The tiny permanent population of Josa del Cadí comprises individuals who find not just the Barcelona conurbation but small county seats such as Solsona and Berga too noisy, messy, commercial, and corrupt. Accordingly, Josa's communal creations have pushed beyond the extremes of existing social formations, even in the context of seeking touristic development. In the 1980s Josa emphasized the future, with a summer "Festival of Music, Cybernetics, and Nature". At the turn of the millennium, as Camila del Màrmol describes, the town resorted to the deep, barely documented but vividly reimagined Catharist past. After the 2017 referendum, del Màrmol shows how this imaginary of a concealed heretic past provided an idiom for valorizing the independentist prisoners as bearers of the same pure spiritual community that lay hidden in the high mountains: an uncontaminated source from which a struggling nation could be refounded.

Several chapters of the collection recognize the longstanding local competition to provide a representative anecdote for the nation through popular culture. In the late 19th century this reflected a contest for influence among different economic elites. With the concentration of the textile industries along the rivers descending from the Pyrenees, the northeast territory of "Old Catalonia", with its symbolic advantages of early reconquest from the Arabs and present proximity to Europe, became, in the term of James W. Fernandez (1988a), the "metonymic misrepresentation" of Catalonia, as Andalusia has always been for Spain. With that primacy established, the small episcopal city of Solsona could develop the consciousness of national centrality described by Alessandro Testa despite its rural surround and distance from Barcelona. Like its festival rival Berga, Solsona played an important role in the Transition's revival of civic celebration and, like Berga, it recognized festival participation as labor, voluntarily assumed and therefore rewarded with *de facto* local citizenship. The *bata* of the Solsona *comparses* is a descendant of the rural worker's smock, but now a visible shibboleth of belonging. As Testa suggests, the hazing process that confers the *bata* is a powerful commitment mechanism: the *gent tancada* of central Catalonia pride themselves on the *mala entrada i mala sortida*, difficult entry and difficult exit, to their communities. At the same time, Testa, Vaczi, and others have observed that theoretical inclusivity conceals corporeal barriers: the centrality of pork, alcohol, and bodily intimacy to many traditional practices demands too much from many Muslim community members.

Delgado, Martínez Algueró, and Martín López point to an important turn in symbolic geography after the 1970s, when the textile and mining industries sustaining the patriarchal Catalanism of Old Catalonia fell into terminal decline just as Spain moved towards democracy. The new Catalan political and business elite required new icons and repertoires; young people eager to assert their own agency and vision provided them. Barcelona and the coastal zone to the south, with their perceived dynamism and Mediterranean cosmopolitanism, became the foci of promotion, with Barcelona's theater culture, the gay scene in Sitges, and the creative festival revivals in Vilanova i la Geltrú, Reus, and Tarragona (cf. Erickson 2011). Above all, the intense expansion of the New Catalan practice of human-tower-building offered a new emblem for national aspirations. Instead of the hierarchy and endemic rebellion of Old Catalan giants, mules, and devils, the *castells* modelled social life as a dynamic, agglutinative process of collective effort towards ever-higher achievements, with a growing competitive edge; they even offered a vernacular correlative to Barcelona's avant-garde architectural vocation. Mariann Vaczi illuminates the allegorical utility of these spectacular constructions for promoting independentism to the European gaze, but more subtly for participants themselves, precariously balancing *seny i rauxa* to attain ever more improbable outcomes. Discovering the value of all genders, ages, and body types to the complex formations needed to undergird and erect higher towers (Vaczi 2023), the *castells* seem genuinely to ground and validate a progressive national vision. Still, the towers often fall: there are risks inherent in tying the nation to a "wish image".

For, however popular its New Catalan emblematization, the new Catalanist vision of the political class has been more neoliberal than progressive; it has excited resistance in its turn, on multiple fronts. This can be seen not just in social movements but, more inchoately, in festival. The purification project of independentist Josa provides one instance; Delgado, Martínez Algueró, and Martín López describe an inverse case, the bull revival along the southwestern border of the principality. Here, for the local population, the river Ebro has not constituted an edge but a focus of economic activity, fostering demographic, linguistic, and cultural exchange with neighboring regions. Singled out by Catalanists not just as Spanish but as backwards and un-European, the *correbous* channeled resistance to discipline from afar. Still more than the donkey and mule effigies of central Catalonia, the intractability of the living bull could assert a refusal of domestication, even by the "right" nation-state. In this sense, the *terres de l'Ebre* offer a fractal reduction of the Catalan irritant within Spain.

The burgeoning of *correbous* along the Ebro in the 2010s coincided with a growing independentist turn in heartland celebrations. The partisan appropriation of traditional ritual is of course nothing new, but in the early years of democracy organizers had resisted it. Festive gatherings were treated as performative equivalents of the new Constitution: spaces of *convivència* where all stances might meet and all must find a possibility of belonging. As Spanish politics polarized, however, the undercurrents between protest and festival that had been evident during the Transition returned to prominence. Independentist flags joined the Catalan ones, and a shift in participation began, with the self-exclusion of dissidents and – in contrast to the Francoist period – the limited presence of new immigrant populations. The shift was not always evident to continuing participants, for whom the experience felt the same as ever. They moved between their local festivals and Barcelona's September 11 demonstrations, enjoying the long-familiar sensation of self-enlargement in a focused crowd; they helped to organize the prohibited 2017 referendum in clandestinity much as the anti-Franco protests of their school years had been organized. The affective force of these activities blinded them to the change in context. Many middle-aged Catalans from the independentist *comarques* were profoundly shocked and hurt when the referendum was not received by Europe as an authentic democratic assertion of the general will.

Traditional popular culture was more fully flattened and homogenized after the referendum, and new ceremonies also emerged. Testa notes that Solsona's Carnival in 2018 was completely focused on Article 155 and the prisoners. The *Patum* of Berga now opens with the unfolding of a giant *estelada* and the singing of the nationalist hymn "Els Segadors", once performed only rarely, on highly charged occasions; once instituted, this practice was soon declared as "beginning to be a tradition" ("Una estelada gigante" 2019). Following Michael Billig (1995), we might think of the broader proliferation of flags, hymn, and yellow ribbons as banal independentism. The "war of the ribbons" described by Testa occurred throughout Catalonia during the early imprisonment of the referendum leaders and became a purely binary, quantitative struggle for visual dominance. Those in the ideological middle increasingly stayed at home and kept silent, a defensive strategy against bitter divisions in both communities and families.

Aesthetically and affectively richer were the new rituals of solidarity with the prisoners. The "yellow suppers" described by Johannes reflect the avant-gardism of Barcelona's food culture, but also signal, on the lower frequencies, the purist tendencies of independentism, for Catalan cuisine, with its pounded sauces and the slow simmering *convivència* of heterogeneous ingredients, is famously brown (Andrews 1988, 6). Mourning processions outside the Lledoners prison where the male leaders were held drew on a long tradition of façade performances challenging the legitimacy of political enclosure (Noyes 1995); at the same time they channelled pain and expressed identification with the sufferings of fellow believers. Some dissident Catalan commentators expressed discomfort with the explicitly Catholic, even penitential atmosphere of these observances, and worried about the cultivation of a victim mentality they felt was not fully warranted. If the *castells* somatize the quest for independence as constructive and forward-moving, as Vaczi argues, the processions instead marked the transformation of "*el procés*" into endless circular motion.

FROM REPRESENTATION TO RESILIENCE AND REFLECTION

The Covid-19 pandemic served as a call to order. When communal meals, festivals, and rituals were no longer possible, people were reminded of their most basic functions: the excitation of pleasure, the sharing of resources, the stimulation of the economy, the competition for prestige, the reminder of interdependence, the sense of collective continuity in place. Xavier Roigé, Mireia Guil, and Lluís Bellas note the widespread distress and disorientation when lockdown shut down both public space and collective time – when the body itched to dance and the community could not respond. The authors' typology of compensatory measures reflects perennial tensions between discipline and self-assertion as well as a long-cultivated capacity to improvise within constraints; the pandemic in these respects epitomized rather than inverted ordinary social life. But the satisfaction of devising virtual solutions did not compensate for the loss of multisensory co-presence. In this sense, two foundational impulses seem to have asserted themselves: to reconfigure the *cordon sanitaire* of confinement into an affirmative "retreat within the community" and to sustain the "representative" set of festival elements as existential reassurance for all who identify with them.

Roigé, Guil, and Bellas invoke the concept of resilience, the popular concomitant of neoliberal disruption (Noyes 2016, chapter 16); the relationship of resilience to popular culture recurs in these chapters. Vaczi considers the social support systems generated within the *colles castelleres*, especially during the economic crisis of the 2010s and again during the pandemic. This affordance of *associacionisme* descends less from the Catalanist tradition than from the worker organizations of the early industrial period and the neighborhood associations of the late Franco regime. It can be understood in part as a conscious effort to preserve or reconstruct, on more egalitarian lines, the old economic reciprocities that underlay traditional festival in the provincial capitals.

Delgado, Martínez Alguero, and Martín López note that the inhabitants of the Terres de l'Ebre are not exclusively preoccupied with the configuration of some future Catalonia. In 2015, *correbous* helped to mobilize the Platform to Defend the Ebro, a revolt against a massive Spanish hydroelectric project that would have put the region in company with innumerable global sacrifice zones, and indeed reproduced Franco-era development projects at larger scale.

(After the defeat of the project, the platform has moved on to address the far more enveloping threat of climate change.) Activist mobilizations of tradition are, however, more than counterbalanced by pragmatic collaborations with neoliberal frameworks. Both municipal and regional administrations have been eager to convert festivals and culinary specialties into resources for struggling local economies, notably through the "intangible cultural heritage" framework concretized in the 2003 UNESCO convention.

Such instrumentalizations of popular culture are more concerned with present challenges than with projects for the future. By the same token, to take Clifford Geertz's famous distinction, the reflective dimension of popular culture has as much to do with "models of" as with "models for" (1973). Carnival engages explicitly with immediate issues and actors, sometimes to humiliating effect, as Testa demonstrates. More stable, nonverbal traditions were historically no less anchored in everyday struggles. When I experienced the *Patum* of Berga in the years before the transformative Barcelona Olympics of 1992, it was no utopia: it was an analysis. Typifying endemic tensions along multiple axes of social difference, during the Transition to democracy it had helped participants to confront their fears of engaging in perilous public space. Later it encapsulated the tense, sweaty intimacy of *convivència* in the early democratic period. In that period, in contrast to more interventionist moments in its history, festival governance was anarchic, with norms negotiated in situ among diverse actors and interests; in this sense, too, it was an intensification and stylization of everyday street life. When institutional democracy and societal affluence changed the rules of coexistence, the *Patum* also changed, with conflict displaced to organizational and interpretive frameworks, and active management from above.

All of this is to say that neither cuisine nor festival are, *per se*, "about" the nation-state. Their immediate uses are immediate and unfixed: to nourish, console, stimulate, and impress; to socialize, exhilarate, capture, contest, and imagine. The nation need not be a referent for any of these processes: selves, economies, classes, theologies, sexualities, generations, and aesthetic form itself are as important. And representing is rarely as important as trying out and working through; any interpretation is by its nature reductive, a first alienation from immediacy. The nation-state remains, however, a powerfully mobilizing modern fantasy for destroying alienation and fusing representation, reality, and the space of action, especially in a territory with a historical name, knowable at human scale.

Still, the nation-state is not solving many problems lately. Despite the hoped-for clarity of the 2017 referendum, there is no consensus on the Catalan ground as to which nation-state constitutes an authentic expression, the social reality to be expressed by that nation-state, or what a national project should be. In the meantime, challenges on the ground require multiple scales of attention, from the *barri* to the planet, with no obvious solutions at any of these. As traditional culture is conscripted for political or economic gain it is typically reified, less amenable to processing the new. This leaves scope for new vernacular invention, which must contend in the first instance with its own constitution and agency. Solutions exist on a continuum from the *botelló*, the shapeless drinking assembly summoned by social media to a convenient space, to small-scale, highly designed festivals of sustainable exchange or interpersonal reconciliation. At the first extreme, a generational right to presence is asserted in space closed off by lockdown, regulation, privatization, or economic exclusion. At the other, sincere efforts to imagine larger orders may hope to achieve immanent self-governance of a sustainable kind, a resource for further development.

Something in the middle is needed: a space of collective reflection among different stances and interests. In theory, this is provided by the public sphere of liberal democracy, the hard-won achievement of the Spanish Transition. But in Spain, as elsewhere, that resource is proving insufficient. Folklore is a longer-standing public sphere, in which corporeal typification rather than verbal generalization is the vehicle of debate. Lacking the precision that is the standard of rational argument, traditional performance offers flexibility and deniability. Things can be said with the body that cannot safely be put into prose. Accordingly, to release popular culture from service to the nation – to let it be simply splendor, savor, and exhilaration – would free it to do its true civic work: the slow, continual re-formation of social foundations, aimed not at ideological consensus but at social consensus (Fernandez 1988b). I am not holding my breath for this outcome. Still, in her chapter Mariann Vaczi highlights a perennial "quixotic" tendency in Catalan popular culture, ever pushing back against seemingly inevitable alienation. Noting the hybrid implication of her adjective, we can hope.

Bibliography

"Una estelada gigante y 'Els segadors', los protagonistas de la Patum de Berga." 2019. *El Nacional*, 21 June. https://www.elnacional.cat/es/politica/estelada-gigante-segadors-protagonistas-patum_396841_102.html.

A.a.V.v. 1995. *25 Sermons del Carnaval de Solsona: de l'any 1971 al 1995*. Solsona: Pellicer i Associació de Festes del Carnaval de Solsona.

A.a.V.v. 1994. *Solsona, 400 anys d'història: miscel·lània : [1594–1994]*. Solsona: Ajuntament de Solsona.

Abrisketa, Olatz G. and Marian G. Abrisketa. 2020. "It's Okay, Sister, Your Wolf-Pack Is Here": Sisterhood as public feminism in Spain." *Signs: Journal of Women in Culture and Society* 45(4): 931–953.

Agramunt Bayerri, Agustí. 2019. "El tortosinisme i el passat dissenyat." *Plecs d'història local* 172: 5–7.

Agulló, Ferran. 1999/1928. *Llibre de la cuina catalana. (Presentació de Lloreç Torrado)*. 9th ed. Barcelona: El Pedrís.

Ahmann, Chloe. 2019. "Waste to energy: Garbage prospects and subjunctive politics in late-industrial Baltimore." *American Ethnologist* 46(3): 328–342.

Ahmed, Sara. 2004. *The Cultural Politics of Emotion*. London, New York: Routledge.

Ajuntament de Berga 2014. "La Patum, a l'exposició 'La festa popular, la catalanitat cívica', que es podrà veure a partir d'avui a Manresa", http://www.ajberga.

Ajuntament de Solsona 2018. "Solsona avui", https://www.ajsolsona.cat/la-ciutat/historia-i-tradicio/solsona-avui (accessed November 2019).

cat/frontal/noticies/detall.php?noticia=1083&apartat (accessed August 2020).

Aldomà i Buixadé, Ignasi and Romà Pujadas i Rúbies. 1987. *L'economia del Solsonès: aprofitament integrat dels recursos comarcals*. Barcelona: Caixa d'Estalvis de Catalunya.

Amades, Joan. 1956. *Costumari català. El curs de l'any*. Barcelona: Salvat.

Anderson, Benedict. 1983. *Imagined Communities: Reflections on the Origin and Spread of Nationalism*. London and New York: Verso.

Anderson, Lara. 2013. *Cooking Up the Nation: Spanish Culinary Texts and Culinary Nationalization in the Late Nineteenth and Early Twentieth Century*. Woodbridge: Tamesis.

Andrews, Colman. 1988. *Catalan Cuisine: Europe's Last Great Culinary Secret*. New York: Atheneum.

Appadurai, Arjun. 1996. *Modernity at Large. Cultural Dimensions of Globalization*. Minneapolis, MN: University of Minnesota Press.

Appadurai, Arjun. 1988. "How to make a national cuisine: Cookbooks in contemporary India." *Comparative Studies in Society and History* 30: 3–24.
Appadurai, Arjun. 1981. "The past as a scarce resource." *Man* 16(2): 201–219.
Appiotti, Sébastien and Eva Sandri. 2020. "Innovez! Participez! Interroger la relation entre musée et numérique au travers des injonctions adressées aux professionnels." *Culture & Musées* 35: 25–48.
Ardèvol, Elisenda and Isabel Travancas. 2019. "Cartas para la libertad: afectos y acción política en tiempos digitales." *Quaderns-e* 23(2): 99–113.
Argelaguet, Jordi. 2021. "The relevance of language as a predictor of the will for independence in Catalonia in 1996 and 2020." *Politics and Governance* 9(4): 426–438.
Ariño, Antonio. 1998. "Festa i ritual: dos conceptes bàsics." *Revista d'etnologia de Catalunya* 13: 8–17.
Ariño, Antonio. 1996. "La utopía de Dionisos. Sobre las transformaciones de la fiesta en la modernidad avanzada." *Antropología* 11: 5–19.
Armengol, Cristina. 2015. "L'escriptura de la cuina." *Vilaweb*, 31 January. https://www.vilaweb.cat/noticia/4229514/20150131/lescriptura-cuina.html (accessed 20 January 2023).
Arrieta, Iñaki, Joan Seguí and Xavier Roigé. 2020."Folklore, museums and identity politics in Spain: 1931 to present." *International Journal of Heritage Studies* 26(4): 387–400.
Ayora-Diaz, Steffan Igor. 2012. *Foodscapes, Foodfields and Identities in Yucatán*. New York, Oxford: Berghahn Books.
Bakhtin, Mikhail M. 1984a. *Rabelais and His World*. Translated by Helene Iswolsky. Bloomington: Indiana University Press. First published 1965 (orig. *Tvorcestvo Fransua Rable i narodnaja kultura srednevekovja i Renessansa*. Moscow: Chudožestvennaja literatura 1965).
Bakhtin, Mikhail M. 1984b. *Problems of Dostoevsky's Poetics*. Translated by Caryl Emerson. Minnesota: University of Minnesota Press (orig. *Problemy poetiki Dostoevskogo*. Moscow: Sovetskij pisat).
Barrera, Andrés. 1985. *La dialéctica de la identidad en Catalunya. Un estudio de antropología social*. Madrid: CIS.
Barrio, Astrid, Oscar Barberà and Juan Rodríguez-Teruel. 2018. "'Spain steals from us!' The 'populist drift' of Catalan regionalism." *Comparative European Politics* 16(6): 993–1011.
Barthes, Roland. 2012. *Mythologies*. New York: Hill and Wang.
Barthes, Roland. 1979. *The Eiffel Tower and Other Mythologies*. New York: Hill and Wang.
Bawidamann, Loïc, Laura Peter and Rafael Walhert. 2020. "Restricted religion. Compliance, vicariousness, and authority during the Corona pandemic in Switzerland." *European Societies* 23(sup1): S637–S657.
Bel, Germà. 2015. *Disdain, Distrust and Dissolution: The Surge of Support for Independence in Catalonia*. Eastbourne: Sussex Academic Press.

Bel, Germà. 2013. *Anatomía de un desencuentro. La Cataluña que es y la España que no pudo ser*. Barcelona: Destino.
Bel, Germà, Xavier Cuadras-Morató and Toni Rodon. 2019. "Crisis? What crisis? Economic recovery and support for independence in Catalonia." *Regional Science Policy & Practice* 11(5): 833–848.
Bell, Catherine (ed.). 2007. *Teaching Ritual*. Oxford: Oxford University Press.
Bellmunt i Figueras, Joan. 1994. *Fets, costums i llegendes: El Soldonès II*, Lleida: Pagès.
Benjamin, Walter. 1969 [1935]. "The work of art in the age of mechanical reproduction." In *Illuminations*. Edited by Hannah Arendt, 1–26. New York: Schocken Books.
Bennassar, Bartolomé. 2000. *Historia de la Tauromaquia: Una Sociedad del Espectáculo*. Valencia: Pre-Textos.
Berliner, David. 2005. "The abuses of memory: Reflections on the memory boom in anthropology." *Anthropological Quarterly* 78(1): 197–211.
Bertolotti, Maurizio. 1991. *Carnevale Di Massa 1950*. Turin: Einaudi.
Biget, Jean-Louis. 1979. "Mythographie du Catharisme (1870–1960)." *Cahiers de Fanjeaux* 14: 271–342.
Billig, Michael. 1995. *Banal Nationalism*. London: Sage Publications.
Bindi, Letizia. 2021. "Fiestas confinadas. Comunidades patrimoniales, practicas colectivas y distanciamiento social." *Patrimonios confinados. Retos del patrimonio inmaterial ante el COVID 19*. Edited by Xavier Roigé and Alejandra Canals, 119–128. Barcelona: Universitat de Barcelona.
Blake, Janet. 2016. "Development of UNESCO's 2003 Convention: creating a new heritage protection paradigm?" In *The Routledge Companion to Intangible Cultural Heritage*. Edited by Michelle Stefano and Peter Davis, 35–45. London and New York: Routledge.
Blok, Anton. 1998. "The narcissism of minor differences." *European Journal of Social Theory* 1(1): 33–56.
Boiso Cuenca, Miguel. 2021. "Análisis del delito de maltrato animal (art. 337 CP)." *Derecho Animal. Forum of Animal Law Studies* 12(1): 82–111.
Boissevain, Jeremy. 1999. "Notas sobre la renovación de las celebraciones populares públicas europeas." *Arxius de Sociologia* 3: 53–68.
Boissevain, Jeremy. 1992. *Revitalizing European Rituals*. London: Routledge.
Boquera Margalef, Montserrat. 2009. *Primer la sang que l'aigua: els pilars d'una nova identitat ebrenca*. Benicarló: Onada.
Bourdieu, Pierre. 1994. *Raisons pratiques: Sur la théorie de l'action*. Paris: Seuil.
Bourdieu, Pierre. 1978. "Sport and social class." *Social science information* 17(6): 819–840.
Boylan, Brandon M. 2015. "In pursuit of independence: The political economy of Catalonia's secessionist movement." *Nations and nationalism* 21(4): 761–785.
Brandes, Stanley. 2019. "El malestar de las corridas en la España actual (y la relación del mismo con el encaje de los españoles en Europa." *Revista de Estudios Europeos* 73: 97–108.

Brandes, Stanley. 2017. "Bullfighting and its discontents." *Studia Iberica et Americana* 4(4): 137–154.
Brandes, Stanley. 2009. "Torophiles and torophobes: The politics of bulls and bullfights in contemporary Spain." *Anthropological Quarterly* 82(3): 779–794.
Brandes, Stanley. 1990. "The Sardana: Catalan dance and Catalan national identity." *Journal of American Folklore* 103(407): 24–41.
Brandes, Stanley. 1988. *Power and Persuasion: Fiestas and Social Control in Rural Mexico*. Philadelphia, PA: University of Pennsylvania Press.
Breen, Colin, Sara McDowell, Gemma Reid and Wes Forsythe. 2016. "Heritage and separatism in Barcelona: The case of El Born Cultural Centre." *International Journal of Heritage Studies* 22(6): 434–445.
Brow, James. 1990. "Notes on community, hegemony, and the uses of the past." *Anthropological Quarterly* 63(1): 1–6.
Brownell, Susan. 1995. *Training the Body for China: Sports in the Moral Order of the People's Republic*. Chicago, IL: University of Chicago Press.
Brubaker, Rogers and Frederick Cooper. 2000. "Beyond 'identity'." *Theory and Society* 29: 1–47.
Brumann, Christoph. 2018. "Anthropological utopia, closet Eurocentrism, and culture chaos in the UNESCO world heritage arena." *Anthropological Quarterly* 91(4): 1203–1233.
Brumann, Christoph. 2014. "Heritage agnosticism: A third path for the study of cultural heritage." *Social Anthropology* 22(2): 173–188.
Buck-Morss, Susan. 1989. *The Dialectics of Seeing: Walter Benjamin and the Arcades Project*. Cambridge, MA: MIT Press.
Bullen, Margaret L. 2000. "Hombres, mujeres, ritos y mitos. Los Alardes de Irún y Hondarribia." In *Perspectivas feministas desde la antropología social*. Edited by María Teresa del Valle, 45–78. Barcelona: Ariel.
Burg, Steven L. 2015. "Identity, grievances, and popular mobilization for independence in Catalonia." *Nationalism and Ethnic Politics* 2(3): 289–312.
Byrne, Steven. 2020. "Language attitudes, linguistic authority and independence in 21st century Catalonia." *Journal of Multilingual and Multicultural Development* 41(8): 702–717.
Caillois, Roger. 1961. *Man, Play, and Games*. Champaign, IL: University of Illinois Press.
Camus, Albert. 1955. *Myth of Sisyphus*. New York: Vintage International.
del Carme Nicolau, Maria. 1971. *Cuina Catalana*. Publisher unknown.
Casal, Paula. 2021. "Whaling, bullfighting, and the conditional value of tradition." *Res Publica* 27(3): 467–490.
CEO (Centre d'estudis d'Opinió). 2018. *Baròmetre d'Opinió Política. 1a onada 2018*. Barcelona: Generalitat de Catalunya. http://upceo.ceo.gencat.cat/wsceop/6668/Dossier%20de%20premsa%20-885.pdf (accessed 12 October 2020).

Clifford, James. 1986. "On ethnographic allegory." In *Writing Culture: the Poetics and Politics of Ethnography: A School of American Research Advanced Seminar*. Edited by George E. Marcus, 98–121. Berkeley: University of California Press.

Clua, Montserrat. 2014. "Identidad y política en Cataluña: el auge del independentismo en el nacionalismo catalán actual." *Quaderns-e de l'Institut Català d'Antropologia* 19(2): 79–99.

Clua, Montserrat. 2008. *Cultura, ètnia i nació: una aproximació a l'estudi del nacionalisme des de l'antropologia social*. PhD Thesis. Bellaterra: Universitat Autònoma de Barcelona. http://www.tdx.cat/handle/10803/32154 (accessed 15 September 2020).

Clua i Fainé, Montserrat and Sánchez García. 2014. "Més enllà de la identitat: noves conceptualitzacions per a vells problemes?" *Quaderns-e de l'Institut Català d'Antropologia* 19(2): 1–9.

Collet, Raimon. 2012. "Fronteres de la comunitat, comunitat de frontera: el cas del Sènia." *Revista d'etnologia de Catalunya* (38): 149–153.

Colom Montero, Guillem. 2021. *Quim Monzó and Contemporary Catalan Culture (1975–2018). Cultural Normalization, Postmodernism and National Politics*. Cambridge: Legenda.

Colomer, Josep M. 2017. "The venturous bid for the independence of Catalonia." *Nationalities Papers* 45(5): 950–967.

Comas, José Maria. 2003. "Spain: The 1978 Constitution and Center-Periphery Tensions." In *Europe's Old States in the New World Order*. Edited by Joseph Ruane, Jennifer Todd and Anne Mandeville, 38–61. Dublin: University College Dublin Press.

Contreras, Jesús. 1978. "Les festes populars a Catalunya com a manifestació de la identitat catalana." *Mayurqa: revista del Departament de Ciències Històriques i Teoria de les Arts* 18: 217–224.

Conversi, Daniele. 1997. *The Basques, the Catalans, and Spain: Alternative Routes to Nationalist Mobilisation*. Hurst, Reno, NV: University of Nevada Press.

Costa Solé, Roger and Rafel Folch Monclús. 2014. "El patrimoni cultural immaterial a Catalunya. Legislació, actualitat i reptes de futur." *Etnologia. Revista de etnologia de Catalunya* 39: 57–72.

Crameri, Kathryn. 2015. "Political power and civil counterpower: The complex dynamics of the Catalan independence movement." *Nationalism and Ethnic Politics* 21(1): 104–120.

Crameri, Kathryn. 2012. "History written by the losers: History, memory, myth and independence in twenty-first century Catalonia." *Hispanic Issues Online* (11): 35–51.

Crameri, K., 2008. *Catalonia: National Identity and Cultural Policy, 1980–2003*. Cardiff: University of Wales Press.

Crameri, Kathryn. 2000. *Language, the Novelist and National Identity in Post-Franco Catalonia*. Oxford: Legenda.

Creed, Gerald, 2011, *Masquerade and Postsocialism: Ritual and Cultural Dispossession in Bulgaria*. Bloomington & Indianapolis: Indiana University Press.

Crespi-Vallbona, Montserrat and Greg Richards. 2007. "The meaning of cultural festivals." *International Journal of Cultural Policy* 13(1): 103–122.

Crozat, Dominique and Laurent Sébastien Fournier. 2005. "From festivals to leisure: Event, merchandizing and the creation of places." *Annales de geographie* 3: 307–328.

Csordas, Thomas J. 1990: "Embodiment as a Paradigm for Anthropology." *Ethos* 18(1): 5–47

Cuadras-Morató, Xavier and Toni Rodon. 2019. "The dog that didn't bark: On the effect of the Great Recession on the surge of secessionism." *Ethnic and Racial Studies* 42(12): 2189–2208.

Cunill de Bosch, Josep. 1908. *La Cuyna Catalana: Aplech de fòrmules pera prepara tota mena de plats ab economia y facilitar, propi pera servir de guia a les mestresses de casa y a totes les cuyneres en general.* 1st ed. Barcelona: Llibreria de Francesch Puig.

Dalmau, Antoni. 1997. *Terra d'Oblit: El vell camí dels càtars.* Barcelona: Columna.

Dalmau, Antoni. 1969. *200 Plats casolans de cuina catalana.* Barcelona: Editorial Millà.

Davidson, Robert A. 2007. "Terroir and Catalonia." *Journal of Catalan Studies* 1(1): 39–53.

Davies, Karen. 2020. "Festivals Post Covid-19." *Leisure Sciences* 43(1–2): 1–6.

Delanty, Gerard. 1999. "Die Transformation nationaler Identität und die kulturelle Ambivalenz europäischer Identität. Demokratische Identifikation in einem post-nationalen Europa." In *Kultur. Identität. Europa. Über die Schwierigkeiten und die Möglichkeiten einer Konstruktion.* Edited by R. Viehoff, R. T. Segers, 267–288. Frankfurt am Main: Suhrkamp.

Delgado, Manuel. 2004. "Tiempo e identidad. La representación festiva de la comunidad y sus ritmos." *Zainak* 26: 77–98.

Delgado, Manuel. 2003. "Carrer, festa i revolta: els usos simbòlics de l'espai públic a Barcelona (1951–2000)." *Revista d'Etnologia de Catalunya* 18: 143–148.

Delgado, Manuel. 1999. *El animal público.* Barcelona: Anagrama.

Delgado, Manuel. 1993. "El seny y la rauxa. El lugar de la violencia en la construcción de la catalanidad." *Antropología* 6: 97–130.

Del Valle, Teresa. 1994. *Korrika: Basque Ritual for Ethnic Identity.* Translated by Linda White. Reno: University of Nevada Press.

De Nola, Robert. 1969/1520. *Libro de Cozina.* Introduction, notes and vocabulary by Carmen Iranzo. [Place of publication unknown]: Taurus Edicions.

De Riquer i Permanyer, Borja. 1996. *Per a una història social i cultural del catalanisme contemporani.* Paris: Éditions Hispaniques.

DeSoucey, Michaela. 2010. "Gastronationalism: Food traditions and authenticity politics in the European Union." *American Sociological Review* 75(3): 432–455.

Di Giovine, Michael A. and Ronda L. Brulotte. 2014. "Introduction: Food and foodways as cultural heritage." In *Edible Identities: Food as Cultural Heritage.* Edited by Ronda L. Brulotte and Michael A. Di Giovine, 1–28. Farnham: Ashgate.

Domene, José F. 2017. "La función social e ideológica de las fiestas religiosas: identidad local, control social e instrumento de dominación." *Dialectología y Tradiciones Populares* 72(1):171–197.

Domènech, Ignasi. 1930. *Àpats: Magnific manual de cuina pràctica catalana, adequate a tots els gustos i el més variat i seleccionat de Catalunya*. 1st ed. [Place and publisher unknown].

Domènech, Ignasi. 1924. *La Teca: La Veritable Cuina Casolana*. 10th ed. Barcelona: Quintilla i Cardona. S.L.

Douglas, Mary. 1970. *Natural Symbols*. London: Barrie & Rockliff / Cresset.

Douglass, Carrie B. 1984. "Toro muerto, vaca es: An interpretation of the Spanish bullfight." *American Ethnologist* 11(2): 242–258.

Dowling, Andrew. 2018. *The Rise of Catalan Independence: Spain's Territorial Crisis*. London and New York: Routledge.

Dowling, Andrew. 2014. "Accounting for the turn towards secession in Catalonia." *International Journal of Iberian Studies* 27(2–3): 219–234.

Edles, Laura Desfor. 1999. "A culturalist approach to ethnic nationalist movements: Symbolization and Basque and Catalan nationalism in Spain." *Social Science History* 23(3): 311–355.

Elias, Norbert and Edmund Jephcott. 1994. *The Civilizing Process*. Oxford: Blackwell.

Erickson, Brad. 2011. "Utopian virtues: Muslim neighbors, ritual sociality, and the politics of *convivència*." *American Ethnologist* 38: 114–131.

Fabre, Daniel. 2006. "Le patrimoine culturel immatériel. Notes sur la conjoncture française." *La perte durable*, Rapport d'étude de Gaetano Ciarcia. Paris: Mission à l'ethnologie, Ministère de la culture: 29–51.

Fajans, Jane. 2012. *Brazilian Food: Race, Class and Identity in Regional Cuisines*. London, New York: Bloomsbury.

Fehérváry, Krisztina. 2013. *Politics in Color and Concrete: Socialist Materialities and the Middle Class in Hungary*. Bloomington: Indiana University Press.

Ferguson, Priscilla Pankhurst. 1988. "A cultural field in the making: Gastronomy in 19th-century France." *American Journal of Sociology* 104(3): 597–641.

Fernandez, James W. 1988a. "Andalusia on our minds: Two contrasting places in Spain as seen in a vernacular poetic duel of the late 19th century." *Cultural Anthropology* 3: 21–35.

Fernandez, James. 1988b. "Isn't there anything out there that we can all believe in? The quest for cultural consensus in anthropology and history." Paper read at the Institute for Advanced Study School of Social Science, Princeton NJ.

Fernàndez, Josep-Anton. 2020 "'Virilitat del país': Gender, immigration, and power in Jaume Vicens Vives's Notícia de Catalunya." *Hispanic Research Journal* 21(2): 143–158.

Fournier, Laurent Sébastien. 2019. "Traditional festivals." *Journal of Festive Studies* 1(1): 11–26.

Fragner, Bert. 1994. "Social reality and culinary fiction: The perspective of cookbooks from Iran and Central Asia." In *A Taste of Thyme: Culinary Cultures of the Middle East*. Edited by Sami Zubaida and Richard Tapper, 63–71. London: I.B. Tauris.

Franquesa, Jaume. 2018. *Power Struggles: Dignity, Value, and the Renewable Energy Frontier in Spain*. Bloomington: Indiana University Press.

Frigolé, Joan. 2021. "Para pensar 'El Procés' desde de la Antropología social." In *Símbolos en la ciudad. Ensayos en homenaje a María Cátedra*. Edited by Pedro Tomé, María Valdés and Consuelo Álvarez-Plaza, 281–296. Valencia: Tirant lo Blanch.

Frigolé, Joan. 2014. "Retóricas de la autenticidad en el capitalismo avanzado." *ÉNDOXA: Series Filosóficas* 33: 37–60.

Frigolé, Joan. 2005. *Dones que anaven pel món. Estudi etnogràfic de les trementinaires de la Vall de la Vansa i Tuixent (Alt Urgell)*. Temes d'etnologia de Catalunya; 12. Barcelona: Generalitat de Catalunya.

Frigolé, Joan and Xavier Roigé (eds). 2012. *Globalización y localidad. Perspectiva etnográfica* Barcelona: Edicions Universitat de Barcelona.

García, Marie-Carmen and Genieys, William. 2005. "L'invention du Pays Cathare: Essai sur la constitution d'un territoire imaginé." Paris: L'Harmattan.

García Canclini, Néstor. 1989. *Culturas híbridas: estrategias para entrar y salir de la modernidad*. Mexico: Grijalbo.

García Rubio, Fernando. 2021. "La tauromaquia patrimonio cultural inmaterial entre su protección y persecución." *Revista Aragonesa de Administración Pública* 57: 221–263.

Garth, Hannah. 2013. "Introduction: Understanding Caribbean identity through food." In *Food and Identity in the Caribbean*. Edited by Hannah Garth, 1–15. London and New York: Bloomsbury.

Gascón, Carles. 2003. *Càtars al Pirineu Català*. Lleida: Pagès Editors.

Geertz, Clifford. 1973. "Religion as a cultural system." In *The Interpretation of Cultures: Selected Essays*, 87–125. New York: Basic Books.

Generalitat de Catalunya. 2014. *White Paper on the National Transition of Catalonia. Sythesis*. Barcelona: Departament de la Presidència, Generalitat de Catalunya. http://economia.gencat.cat/web/.content/70_economia_catalana/Subinici/Llistes/nou-estat/catalonia-new-state-europe/national-transition-catalonia.pdf (accessed 28 October 2020).

Giddens, Anthony. 2003. *Runaway World: How Globalization Is Reshaping Our Lives*. London and New York: Routledge.

Giménez, Enric. 1995. "L'Explotació forestal al Pallars durant el segle XVIII: els raiers." *Drassana: revista del Museu Marítim* 4: 16–21.

Gómez Amat, Daniel. 2007. *La patria del gol: fútbol y política en el Estado español*. Irun, SP.: Alberdania.

Gómez, Aurora Morcillo. 2015. *En cuerpo y alma: ser mujer en tiempos de Franco*. Madrid: Siglo XXI de España Editores.

Gómez Pellón, Eloy G. 2017. "Los problemas del patrimonio inmaterial: uso y abuso de los animales en España." *AIBR. Revista de Antropología Iberoamericana* 12(2): 147–168.

González, Antoni. 1990. *Bous, toros i braus. Una tauromàquia catalana.* Tarragona: El Mèdol.
Gonzalez, Roberto J. and John Marlovits. 2020. "Life under lockdown: Notes on Covid-19 in Silicon Valley." *Anthropology today* 36(3): 11–15.
González Fernández, José Luis. 2022. "Toros y política en el siglo XX: una pasión correspondida." *Historia Contemporánea* 68: 263–293.
Graham, Stephen. 2016. "Vanity and violence: On the politics of skyscrapers." *City* 20(5): 755–771.
Grau, Joan. 1995. *La Nit de Sant Joan.* Barcelona: Editorial Columna.
Grau i Martí, Jan. 1996. *Gegants!* Barcelona: Editorial Columna.
Grisostolo, Francesco E. 2017. "La tauromachia come arena di scontro sulle competenze nell'Estado autonómico." *DPCE Online* 29(1). http://www.dpceonline.it/index.php/dpceonline/article/view/379 (accessed 10 March 2020).
Guibernau, Montserrat. 2014. "Prospects for an independent Catalonia." *International Journal of Politics, Culture, and Society* 27(1): 5–23.
Guibernau, Montserrat. 2013. "Secessionism in Catalonia: after democracy." *Ethnopolitics* 12(4): 368–393.
Guibernau, Montserrat. 2004. *Catalan Nationalism: Francoism, Transition and Democracy.* London: Routledge.
Guibernau, Montserrat. 2002. *Between Autonomy and Secession: The Accommodation of Catalonia Within the New Democratic Spain.* Brighton: Sussex European Institute.
Guil, Mireia. 2019. "Les falles de les Valls d'Àneu, un patrimoni aneuenc." *Nabius* 17, 92–95.
Guiu, Claire. 2013. "Ces fêtes qui 'font pays'. Systèmes festifs et développement territorial en Catalogne" *Espaces. Tourisme et loisirs* 311: 76–85.
Guiu, Claire. 2008. "Ritual Revitalization and the Construction of Places in Catalonia, Spain", *Journal of Mediterranean Studies* 18(1): 93–118.
Gutiérrez, Ramón. 1997. "La fiesta secular: tradición, obsecuencia y transgresión." *Historia* 30(1): 173–187.
Guttmann, Allen. 1978. *From Ritual to Record: The Nature of Modern Sports.* New York: Columbia University Press.
Hafstein, Valdimar. 2009. "Intangible heritage as a list: from masterpieces to representation." In *Intangible Heritage.* Edited by Laurajane Smith and Natsuko Akagawa, 93–111. London and New York: Routledge.
Hall, Jaqueline. 2001. *Convivencia in Catalonia: Languages Living Together.* Barcelona: Fundacio Jaume Bofill.
Hargreaves, John. 2000. *Freedom for Catalonia?: Catalan Nationalism, Spanish Identity, and the Barcelona Olympic Games.* Cambridge: Cambridge University Press.
Harris, Max. 2003. *Carnival and Other Christian Festivals: Folk Theology and Folk Performance.* Austin: University of Texas Press.
Harvey, David. 1992. *The Condition of Postmodernity: An Inquiry into the Origins of Cultural Change.* Cambridge MA & Oxford UK: Blackwell.

Herb, G. Henrik and David H. Kaplan. 1999. *Nested Identities: Nationalism, Territory, and Scale.* Lanham, MD: Rowman & Littlefield.

Herzfeld, Michael. 1997. *Cultural Intimacy. Social Poetics in Nation-State*: London and New York: Routledge.

Herzfeld, Michael. 1991. *A Place in History: Social and Monumental Time in a Cretan Town.* Princeton, NJ: Princeton University Press.

Hobsbawm, Eric, and Terence Ranger (eds). 1983. *The Invention of Tradition.* Cambridge: Cambridge University Press.

Hodges, Matt. 2009. "Disciplining memory: Heritage tourism and the temporalisation of the built environment in rural France." *International Journal of Heritage Studies* 15(1): 76–99.

Hughes, Robert. 1992. *Barcelona.* New York: Vintage.

Humlebæk, Carsten and Mark F. Hau. 2020. "From national holiday to independence day: Changing perceptions of the 'Diada,'" *Genealogy* 4(31): 1–24.

Hutchinson, John. 2013. "Cultural nationalism." In *The Oxford Handbook of the History of Nationalism.* Edited by John Breuilly, 75–96. Oxford: Oxford University Press.

Ichijo, Atsuko and Ronald Ranta. 2016. *Food, National Identity and Nationalism: From Everyday to Global Politics.* Basingstoke and New York: Palgrave Macmillan UK.

Ichijo, Atsuko, Venetia Johannes and Ronald Ranta. 2019. *The Emergence of National Food: The Dynamics of Food and Nationalism.* London and New York: Bloomsbury.

Imber-Black, Evan. 2020. "Rituals in the time of COVID-19: Imagination, responsiveness, and the human spirit", *Family Process* 59(3): 912–921.

Isnart, Cyril and Alessandro Testa. 2020 "Reconfiguring tradition(s) in Europe: An introduction to the special issue." In *Re-enchantment, Ritualization, Heritage-making: Processes Reconfiguring Tradition in Europe.* Edited by Cyril Isnart and Alessandro Testa. Special issue of *Ethnologia Europaea* 50(1): 5–19.

Johannes, Venetia. 2019. *Nourishing the Nation: Food as National Identity in Catalonia.* New York – Oxford: Berghahn Books.

Johannes, Venetia. 2018. *"El calendari gastronòmic:* Culinary nationalism in Catalan festivals." *Ethnoscripts* 20(1): 58–78.

Juan Arbó, Sebastià. 2001. *Terres de l'Ebre.* Barcelona: Grup 62.

Kammerer, Nina. 2014. "Catalan festival culture, identities, and independentism." *Quaderns-e de l'Institut Català d'Antropologia* 19(2): 58–77.

Keating, Michael. 1996. *Nations Against the State: The New Politics of Nationalism in Quebec, Catalonia, and Scotland.* Basingstoke: Macmillan.

Keown, Dominic (ed.). 2011a: *A Companion to Catalan Culture.* Suffolk: Tamesis – Boydell & Brewer.

Keown, Dominic. 2011b. "Introduction: Catalan culture: Once more unto the breach?" In *A Companion to Catalan Culture.* Edited by Dominic Keown, 1–12. New York: Tamesis.

Keown, Dominic (ed.). 2011c: "Contemporary Catalan culture." In *A Companion to Catalan Culture*. Edited by Dominic Keown, 13–39. Suffolk: Tamesis – Boydell & Brewer.

Khalvashi, Tamta. 2018. "The horizons of Medea: Economies and cosmologies of dispossession in Georgia." *Journal of the Royal Anthropological Institute* 24(4): 804–825.

King, Michelle. 2019. "Introduction: Culinary nationalism in Asia." In *Culinary Nationalism in Asia*. Edited by Michelle King, 1–20. London: Bloomsbury ebook.

Klandermans, Bert. 1997. *The Social Psychology of Protest*. Chichester: Wiley.

Kundera, Milan. 1984. *The Unbearable Lightness of Being*. London: Faber & Faber.

Lafront, Auguste. 1977. *Histoire de la corrida en France: du Second Empire à nos jours*. París: Julliard.

Lanternari, Vittorio. 1981. "Spreco, ostentazione, competizione economica. Antropologia del comportamento festivo." In *Festa. Antropologia e semiotica. Relazioni presentate al convegno di studi «Forme e pratiche della festa», Montecatini Terme, 27–29 ottobre 1978*. Edited by C. Bianco and M. Del Ninno, 132–150. Florence: Nuova Guaraldi.

Lesh, Kerri. 2019. "Size matters: The values behind Basque food, font and semiotics." *BOGA: Basque Studies Consortium Journal* 7(1): article 3.

Leoussi, Athena and Steven Grosby. 2007. *Nationalism and Ethnosymbolism: History, Culture and Ethnicity in the Formation of Nations*. Edinburgh: Edinburgh University Press.

Little, Oliver 2019. "Catalonia national day rallies: The saga continues." *Catalan News*, 10 September. https://www.catalannews.com/politics/item/catalonia-national-day-rallies-the-saga-continues (accessed January 2020).

Llobera, Josep R. 2004. *Foundations of National Identity: From Catalonia to Europe*. New York and Oxford: Berghahn Books.

Llobera, Josep R. 1997. "Aspects of Catalan kinship, identity, and nationalism." *Journal of the Anthropological society of Oxford* 28(3): 297–309.

Llobera, Josep R. 1994. *The God of Modernity: The Development of Nationalism in Western Europe*. London: Bloomsbury Academic.

Llobera, Josep. 1990. "The historical identity of Catalonia." *Critique of Anthropology* 10(2–3): 3–10.

Llorens i Solé, Antoni. 1987. *Solsona i el Solsonès en la historia de Catalunya*. II vol. Lleida: Virgili & Pagès.

Llosa, Mireia et al. 2014. "La Patum, primera declaració de Patrimoni Immaterial de la UNESCO a Catalunya, deu anys després." *Revista d'etnologia de Catalunya* 39: 134–141.

Long, Lucy M. 2021 "Introduction: Culinary nationalism." *Western Folklore* 80(1): 5–14.

López López, Juan de Dios. 2020. "Limpia, fija y da esplendor. Falsedad y autenticidad en las representaciones patrimoniales de la fiesta." *Pasos* 18(4): 683–691.

Loureiro Lamas, Celso, and Ana M. Sánchez García. 1990. "Patrimonio cultural, patrimonio natural." *Cuadernos de Etnología y Etnografía de Navarra* 22: 321–329.
Low, Setha and Mark Maguire. 2020. "Public space during COVID-19." *Social Anthropology* 28(2): 309–310.
MacClancy, Jeremy (ed.). 2015. *Alternative Countrysides. Anthropological Approaches to Rural Western Europe Today*. Manchester: Manchester University Press.
MacClancy, Jeremy. 2014. "What's up? What's going down? Goitiberak in the Basqueland." In *Playing Fields*. Edited by Mariann Vaczi, 85–104. Reno, NV: Center for Basque Studies Press.
MacClancy, Jeremy. 2007. *Expressing Identities in the Basque Arena*. Suffolk: James Currey Limited (Boydell & Brewer).
Majumdar, Margaret A. 2007. *Postcoloniality: The French Dimension*. London: Berghahn.
Manning, Erin. 2007. *Politics of Touch: Sense, Movement, Sovereignty*. Minneapolis: University of Minnesota Press.
Mansilla, José. 2020. *La pandemia de la desigualdad. Una antropología desde el desconfinamiento*. Barcelona: Bellaterra.
Maquieira D'Angelo, Virginia. 1999. "Antropología, género y derechos humanos." *Anales del Museo Nacional de Antropología* 6: 13–48.
del Mármol, Camila. 2019. "Cultivating disconnection: Imaginaries of rurality in the Catalan Pyrenees." In *Imaginaries of Connectivity: The Creation of Novel Spaces of Governance*. Edited by Luís Lobo-Guerrero, Suvi Alt and Marteen Meijer, 177–198. London: Rowman and Littlefield.
del Mármol, Camila 2010. "Cátaros: entre memorias y olvidos. Usos del pasado en el Pirineo catalàn y occitano." *Ibix Annals del Centre d'Estudis Comarcals del Ripollès* 6: 321–335.
del Mármol, Camila, Celigueta, Gemma and Vaccaro, Ismael. 2018. "Socioeconomic transitions and everyday life changes in the rural world: Pyrenean households and their contemporary economic history." *Journal of Agricultural Change* 18(3): 677–693.
del Mármol, Camila, Joan Frigolé, and Susana Narotzky. 2010. *Los lindes del patrimonio. Consumo y valores del pasado*. Barcelona: Icaria/ICA.
del Mármol Cartañà, Camila and Xavier Roigé Ventura (eds). 2014. *El patrimoni immaterial a debat*, monographic issue of *Etnologia. Revista de etnologia de Catalunya* 39.
Martel, Pere. 2003. "Els Jocs Florals, el Felibritge i la Renaixença." In *Càtars i Trobadors. Occitània i Catalunya: renaixença i futur*. Edited by M. Miquel. Barcelona: Generalitat de Catalunya.
Martí Escayol, Maria Antonia. 2004. *El Plaer de la Xocolata: La història i la cultura de la xocolata a Catalunya*. Barcelona: Cossetània Edicions.
Martí i Pérez, Josep. 1994. "The sardana as a socio-cultural phenomenon in contemporary Catalonia." *Yearbook for traditional music* (26): 39–46.

Marx, Karl. 1969. "The Eighteenth Brumaire of Louis Bonaparte." In *Selected Works*, vol. 1. By Karl Marx and Frederick Engels. Moscow: Progress Publishers.
Maudet, Jean-Baptiste. 2006. "Le taureau marque son territoire (festivités taurines et identités territoriales du Sud-ouest européen à l'Amérique Latine)." *Annales de geographie* 650(4): 361–387.
Mauss, Marcel. 1923–1924. "Essai sur le don. Forme et raison de l'échange dans les sociétés archaïques." *L'Année Sociologique. Nouvelle série* 1: 30–186.
McCaffrey, Emily. 2002. Imaging the Cathars in Late-Twentieth-Century Languedoc. *Contemporary European History* 11(3): 409–427.
McRoberts, Kenneth. 2001. *Catalonia: Nation Building Without a State*. Oxford: Oxford University Press.
Menzel, Ariadne. 2017. "Hiking and history: The various meanings of the Cathar trail in the south of France." *Anthropological Notebooks* 23(3): 109–132.
Meskell, Lynn and Christoph Brumann. 2015. "UNESCO and new world orders." In *Global Heritage: A Reader*. Edited by Lynn Meskell, 22–42. Oxford: Blackwell.
Mestre, Jesús. 1994. *Els càtars: problema religiós, pretext polític*. Barcelona: Edicions 62.
Miguélez-Carballeira, Helena. 2017. "El imperio interno: discursos sobre masculinidad e imperio en los imaginarios nacionales español y catalán del siglo XX." *Cuadernos de Historia Contemporánea* (39): 105–128.
Militz, Elisabeth and Caroline Schurr. 2016. "Affective nationalism: Banalities of belonging in Azerbaijan." *Political Geography* 54: 54–63.
Mincyte, Diana. 2008. "Food culture, globalization, and nationalism: Zeppelins in the Lithuanian imagination." *Working Paper, National Council for Eurasian and East European Research*. https://www.ucis.pitt.edu/nceeer/2008_823-15n_Mincyte.pdf (accessed 20 January 2023).
Mueller, Sean. 2019. "Catalonia: The perils of majoritarianism." *Journal of Democracy* 30(2): 142–156.
Muñoz, Jordi and Marc Guinjoan. 2013. "Accounting for internal variation in nationalist mobilization: unofficial referendums for independence in Catalonia (2009–11)." *Nations and Nationalism* 19(1): 44–67.
Muñoz, Jordi and Raül Tormos. 2015. "Economic expectations and support for secession in Catalonia: Between causality and rationalization." *European Political Science Review* 7: 315–341.
Nació Solsona. 2013. "30 anys de bata vermella i capa verda." *Nació Solsona*. https://www.naciodigital.cat/naciosolsona/noticia/6492/30-anys-bata-vermella-capa-verda (accessed November 2020).
Nielsen, Bjarke. 2011. "UNESCO and the 'right' kind of culture: Bureaucratic production and articulation." *Critique of Anthropology* 31(4): 273–292.
Norum, Roger and Mary Mostafanezhad. 2016. "A chronopolitics of tourism." *Geoforum* 77: 157–160.
Noyes, Dorothy. 2016. *Humble Theory: Folklore's Grasp on Social Life*. Bloomington: Indiana University Press.

Noyes, Dorothy. 2011. "Festival and the shaping of Catalan community." In *A Companion to Catalan Culture*. Edited by Dominic Keown, 207–228. Suffolk: Tamesis – Boydell & Brewer.
Noyes, Dorothy. 2006. "The Judgment of Solomon: Global protections for tradition and the problem of community ownership." *Cultural Analysis* 5: 27–56.
Noyes, Dorothy. 2003a. *Fire in the Plaça: Catalan Festival Politics After Franco*. Philadelphia: University of Pennsylvania Press.
Noyes, Dorothy. 2003b. "In the blood: Performance and identity in the Catalan transition to democracy." *Narodna umjetnost-Hrvatski časopis za etnologiju i folkloristiku* 40(1): 64–80.
Noyes, Dorothy. 1995. "Façade performances in Catalonia: Display, respect, reclamation, refusal." *Southern Folklore* 52: 97–120.
Ofer, Inbal. 2017. *Claiming the City and Contesting the State: Squatting, Community Formation and Democratization in Spain (1955–1986)*. London and New York: Routledge.
Òmnium Cultural. "Catalans want to vote – Human towers for democracy." *YouTube*. https://www.youtube.com/watch?v=m8YTJPJQevw.
Òmnium Cultural. 2018. *El Receptari Groc*. Barcelona: Viena Edicions.
Orozco, Aura Patricia. 2020. "El Carnaval de Negros y Blancos, patrimonio cultural del sur de Colombia en contexto de pandemia." *Mediaciones* 25(16): 109–204.
Padullés, Jofre. 2011. *Bous de Mort. El Corre de Bou de Cardona i la Cultura Popular Taurina de Catalunya*. Tarragona: El Mèdol.
Padullés, Jofre. 2010. "El Corre de Bou de Cardona: consideracions prèvies a una recerca etnográfica." *Revista d'etnologia de Catalunya* 37: 122–125.
Palmié, Stephan and Charles Stewart. 2016. "For an anthropology of history." *HAU: Journal of Ethnographic Theory* 6(1): 207–236.
Palmer, Catherine. 1998. "From theory to practice: Experiencing the nation in everyday life." *Journal of Material Culture* 3: 175–199.
Pink, Sarah. 1997. *Women and Bullfighting: Gender, Sex and the Consumption of Tradition*. Oxford: Berg.
Portet, Àngel. 1996. "Els raiers: el transport fluvial de la fusta del Pirineu a la Mediterrània." *Plecs d'història local* 62: 968–971.
Pradilla Cardona, Miguel À. 2014. "Dinàmiques sociopolítiques i procés d'estandardització a les comarques de la diòcesi de Tortosa." *Caplletra* 5: 95–127.
Prat, Joan and Jesús Contreras. 1984. *Les festes populars*. Barcelona: Llar del llibre.
Prat i Guilanyà, S Sebastià. 2012. "El suport a la independència de Catalunya. Anàlisi de canvis i tendències en el període 2005–2012." Barcelona: Papers de Treball del CEO.
Prats, Josep. 2007. "L'Aquelarre de Cervera. Una festa del segle XX." *Arts. Revista Del Cercle de Belles Arts de Lleida* 28: 24–28.
Prats, Llorenç. 1996. "Antropología y patrimonio." In *Ensayos de Antropología Cultural*. Edited by Joan Prat and Àngel Martínez, 294–299. Barcelona: Ariel.
Prats, Llorenç. 1989. *El mite de la tradició popular*. Barcelona: Edicions 62.

Prats, Llorenç. 1988. *El mite de la tradició popular. Els orígens de l'interès per la cultura tradicional a la Catalunya del segle XIX*. Barcelona: Edicions 62.
Prats, Llorenç, Dolors Llopart and Joan Prat. 1982. *La cultura popular a Catalunya*. Barcelona: Fundació Serveis de Cultura Popular.
Pujadas, Joan and Dolors Comas D'Argemir. 1991. "Identidad catalana y símbolos naturales." In *Antropología de los pueblos de España*. Edited by Joan Prat et al, 647–652. Madrid: Taurus.
Racionero, Lluís. 1982. *Cercamón*. Barcelona: Caixa d'Estalvis de Catalunya.
Réau, Bertrand and Christophe Guibert. 2020. "Ocio fordista. Dossier: Turismo año cero." *Le Monde diplomatique en español* July.
Resina, Joan Ramon. 2017. *The Ghost in the Constitution: Historical Memory and Denial in Spanish Society*. Oxford: Oxford University Press.
Riart, Oriol and Sebastià Jordà. 2015. *Les falles del Pirineu. L'Alta Ribagorça i el Pallars Sobirà*. Lleida: Pagès Editors.
Ricoeur, Paul. 1994. "Imagination in discourse and in action." In *Rethinking Imagination: Culture and Creativity*. Edited by Gillian Robinson and John Rundell, 87–117. London: Routledge.
Ridao Martín, Joan. 2017. "Toros: entre l'espectacle públic, el patrimoni cultural i la protecció animal." *Revista catalana de dret públic* 54: 171–184.
Robertson, Alexander F. 2010. "Conviviality in Catalonia." *Gastronomica: The Journal of Food and Culture* 10(1): 70–78.
Roigé, Xavier. 2016. "Museos, identidades territoriales y evolución de las políticas culturales en España. De la expansión a la crisis económica." In *Treinta años de políticas culturales en España. Participación cultural, gobernanza territorial e industrias culturales*. Edited by Joaquim Rius-Ulldemolins, Rubio Arostegui and Juan Arturo, 265–284. Valencia: Universitat de València.
Roigé, Xavier. 2014. "Més enllà de la UNESCO. Gestionar i museïtzar el patrimoni immaterial." *Revista d'etnologia de Catalunya* 39: 23–40.
Roigé, Xavier, Camila del Mármol and Mireia Guil. 2019. "Los usos del patrimonio inmaterial en la promoción del turismo. El caso del Pirineo catalán." *PASOS Revista de Turismo y Patrimonio Cultural* 17(6): 1113–1126.
Roigé, Xavier and Joan Frigolé (eds). 2010. *Constructing Cultural and Natural Heritage. Parks, Museums and Rural Heritage*. Girona: ICRPC Llibres (4).
Roma, Francesc. 2004. *Del Paradís a la Nació. La muntanya a Catalunya*. Valls: Cossetania.
Rondissoni, Josep. 1927. *Classes de cuina: curs 1927–1928*. Barcelona: Institut de Cultura i Biblioteca Popular de la dona.
Ros i Fontana, Ignasi. 1997. *Aquelles muntanyes se n'han anat al cel. La memòria col·lectiva a la vall de Castellbò (Alt Urgell)*. Tremp: Garsineu Edicions.
Rubert de Ventós, Xavier. 2000. *De la identidad a la independencia*. Barcelona: Anagrama.
Sahlins, Marshall. 2000. *Culture in Practice: Selected Essays*. New York: Zone Books.

Sahlins, Marshall. 1994. "Goodbye to tristes tropes: Ethnography in the context of modern world history." In *Assesing Cultural Anthropology*. Edited by Robert Borofsky, 349–360. New York: McGraw-Hill Inc.

Sánces-Biosca, Vicente. 2007. "Las culturas del tardofranquismo." *Ayer* 68(4): 89–110.

Sánchez-Carretero, Cristina. 2013. "Hacia una antropología del conflicto aplicada al patrimonio." In *Geopolíticas patrimoniales. De culturas, naturalezas e inmaterialidades*. Edited by Beatriz Santamarina, 195–210. Alzira: Germania.

Sánchez Cervelló, Josep (ed.). 2010. *Història de les Terres de l'Ebre*. Barcelona: Aeditors.

Sanjaume-Calvet, Marc and Elvira Riera-Gil. 2022. "Languages, secessionism and party competition in Catalonia: A case of de-ethnicising outbidding?." *Party Politics* 28(1): 85–104.

Santamarina Campos, Beatriz and Camila del Mármol. 2020. "'Para algo que era nuestro … ahora es de toda la humanidad': el patrimonio mundial como expresión de conflictos." *Chungara: Revista de Antropología Chilena* 52(1): 161–173.

Santamarina Campos, Beatriz and Albert Moncusí Ferré. 2015. "El mercado de la autenticidad. Las nuevas ficciones patrimoniales." *Revista de Occidente* (410–411): 93–112.

Santino, Jack. 2009. "The ritualesque: Festival, politics, and popular culture." *Western Folklore* 68(1): 9–26.

Scruton, Roger. 2014. *How to Be a Conservative*. London: Bloomsbury.

Scovazzi, Tullio. 2011. "Cavalli, pesciolini, bambini e saracini: Brevi riflessioni su controversi patrimoni culturali intangibili." *Rivista Giuridica dell'Ambiente* 26: 841–858.

Serrano, Ivan. 2013. "Just a matter of identity? Support for independence in Catalonia." *Regional & federal studies* 23(5): 523–545.

SIEF. 2019. Abstract of the panel "Performing transformation, claiming transition: public gatherings and rituals in Catalonia from the 1970s to the present." Convened by Dorothy Noyes, Mariann Vaczi and Alessandro Testa for the 2019 Conference of the SIEF.

Smith, Anthony D. 2013. *Nationalism*. 2nd ed. Cambridge: Polity Press.

Smith, Anthony D. 2009. *Ethno-Symbolism and Nationalism: A Cultural Approach*. London and New York: Routledge.

Smith, Anthony D. 2001. *Nationalism: Theory, Ideology, History*. Cambridge: Polity Press.

Sobral, José Manuel. 2014. "The country, the nation, and the region in representations of Portuguese food and cuisine." In *Food Between the Country and the City: Ethnographies of a Changing Global Foodscape*. Edited by Nuno Domingos, José Manuel Sobral and Harry G. West, 145–160. London and New York: Bloomsbury.

Solsona Turisme. 2018: "Solsona: a *giant* experience." http://solsonaturisme.com/wp-content/uploads/2018/08/Solsona-EN-FR.pdf (accessed December 2018).

Song, H. Rosi and Anna Riera. 2019. *A Taste of Barcelona: The History of Catalan Cooking and Eating.* Maryland and London: Rowman & Littlefield Publishers.
Sonnevend, Julia. 2016. *Stories Without borders: The Berlin Wall and the Making of a Global Iconic Event.* Oxford: Oxford University Press.
Sonnevend, Julia. 2012. "Iconic rituals: Towards a social theory of encountering images." In *Iconic Power.* Edited by Jeffrey Alexander, Dominik Bartmanski and Bernhard Giesen, 219–232. New York: Palgrave Macmillan.
Soula, René. 2005. *Les Cathares: Entre légende et histoire. La mémoire de l'albigéisme du XIX siècle à nos jours.* Toulouse: Institut d'Études Occitanes.
Steinkrüger, Patrick. 1995. "Okzitanien. Eine europäische Region." *Ethnos-Nation* 3 H: 67–77.
Stowkowski, Wiktor. 2009. "UNESCO's doctrine of human diversity: A secular soteriology?" *Anthropology Today* 25(3): 7–11.
Strubell, Miquel. 2011. "The Catalan language." In *A Companion to Catalan Culture.* Edited by D. Keown, 117–142. Suffolk: Tamesis – Boydell & Brewer.
Suari, Carlos. 2020. "El baile tradicional asturiano como práctica étnica performativa en la primera cuarentena global." *Perifèria, revista de recerca i formació en antropologia* 25(1): 170–183.
Testa, Alessandro. 2021. "The anthropology of cultural heritage in Europe: A brief genealogy from the desk (1970–2020) and empirical observations from the field (2010–2020)." *Traditiones* 50(1): 15–28.
Testa, Alessandro. 2020a. *Rituality and Social (Dis)Order: The Historical Anthropology of Popular Carnival in Europe.* London and New York: Routledge.
Testa, Alessandro. 2020b. "Intertwining processes of reconfiguring tradition: Three European case studies." In *Re-enchantment, Ritualization, Heritage-making: Processes Reconfiguring Tradition in Europe.* Edited by Cyril Isnart and Alessandro Testa. Special issue of *Ethnologia Europaea* 50(1): 20–38.
Testa, Alessandro. 2019. "Events that wánt to become heritage: Vernacularization of ICH and the politics of culture and identity in European public rituals." In *Heritage and Festivals in Europe: Performing Identities.* Edited by Ullrich Kockel, Cristina Clopot, Baiba Tjarve and Máiréad Nic Craith, 79–94. London and New York: Routledge.
Testa, Alessandro. 2017a: "From post-transition to pseudo-transition: What is going on in Catalonia? Reflections from and beyond fieldwork." In *Europäische Ethnologie Wien, Jahresbericht 2017,* 49–55. Vienna: Univeristät Wien.
Testa, Alessandro. 2017b. "'Fertility' and the carnival 1: Symbolic effectiveness, emic beliefs, and the re-enchantment of Europe." *Folklore* 128(1): 16–36.
Testa, Alessandro. 2017c. "'Fertility' and the carnival 2: Popular Frazerism and the reconfiguration of tradition in Europe today." *Folklore* 128(2): 111–32.
Testa, Alessandro. 2014a. "Rethinking the festival: Power and politics." *Method & Theory in the Study of Religion* 26(1): 44–73.
Testa, Alessandro. 2014b. "L'homme-cerf, l'ethnologue et le maire. Les politiques du folklore dans un contexte rural italien." In *Folklores et politique. Approches comparées et réflexions critiques (Europes – Amériques).* Edited by Staniaslaw

Fiszer, Didier Francfort, Antoine Nivière and Jean-Sébastien Noël, 99–120. Paris: Le Manuscrit.
Tibi, Bassam. 2001. *Europa ohne Identität? Leitkultur oder Wertebeliebigkeit*. München: Siedler.
Tkac, John A. 2014. "The role of bullfighting and FC Barcelona in the emancipation of Catalonia from Spain." *Revista de humanidades* 23: 137–156.
Trnka, Susanna, Christine Dureau and Julie Park (eds). 2013. *Senses and Citizenships: Embodying Political Life*. London and New York: Routledge.
Trouillot, Michel-Rolph. 1995. *Silencing the Past: Power and the Production of History*. Boston, MA: Beacon Press.
Turisme Solsonès. 2019. "Pinós." http://turismesolsones.com/punt/pinos/ (accessed November 2019).
Turner, Victor. 1977. "Liminality and communitas." In *The Ritual Process: Structure and Anti-Structure*, 94–130. Chicago, IL: Aldine (1st ed. 1969).
UNESCO. 2020. *Intangible Cultural Heritage in Emergencies Responding to the COVID-19 Pandemic: Addressing Questions of ICH and Resilience in Times of Crisis: Report*. Venice: UNESCO.
UNESCO. 2003. *The Convention for the Safeguarding of the Intangible Cultural Heritage*. Paris: UNESCO. https://ich.unesco.org/en/convention (accessed 23 July 2021).
UNESCO. 1995. *Our Creative Diversity: Report of the World Commission on Culture and Development*. Paris: UNESCO. https://ich.unesco.org/en/convention (accessed 25 July 2021).
Vaccaro, Ismael and Oriol Beltran (eds). 2010. *Social and Ecological History of the Pyrenees: State, Market, and Landscape*. Walknut Creek, CA: Left Coast Press.
Vaczi, Mariann. 2023. *Catalonia's Human Towers: Castells, Cultural Politics, and the Struggle toward the Heights*. Bloomington: Indiana University Press.
Vaczi, Mariann. 2016. "Catalonia's human towers: Nationalism, associational culture, and the politics of performance." *American Ethnologist* 43(2): 353–368.
Vaczi, Mariann and Cameron J. Watson. 2021. "Corporeal performance in contemporary ethnonationalist movements: The changing body politic of Basque and Catalan secessionism." *Social Anthropology/Anthropologie sociale* 29(3): 602–618.
Valldepérez, Santi. 2004. *Natros!: gent i identitat de les Terres de l'Ebre*. Barcelona: Pòrtic.
Ventura Subirats, Jordi. 1960. *El catarismo en Cataluña*. Barcelona: Boletín de la Real Academia de Buenas Letras de Barcelona, XXVIII.
Vergés-Gifra, Joan and Macià Serra. 2022. "Is there an ethnicity bias in Catalan secessionism? Discourses and political actions." *Nations and Nationalism* 28(2): 612–627.
Vilaseca, Noemí and Marc Trilla. 2011. *El Carnaval de Solsona*. Solsona: Associació de Festes del Carnaval de Solsona.
Vilaseca, Noemí and Marc Trilla. 2007. *Solsona, la Festa Major*. Solsona: Ajuntament de Solsona i Lunwerg Editors.

Villarroya, Anna. 2012. "Cultural policies and national identity in Catalonia." *International Journal of Cultural Policy* 18(1): 31–45.
Vovelle, Michel. 1985. "El desvío por la historia en el redescubrimiento de la fiesta." In *Ideologías y mentalidades*. Edited by Michel Vovelle, 187–203. Barcelona: Ariel.
Waldren, Jacqueline. 1996. *Insiders and Outsiders. Paradise and Reality in Mallorca*. Oxford: Berghan Books.
Waterton, Emma and Steve Watson. 2013. "Framing theory: Towards a critical imagination in heritage studies." *International Journal of Heritage Studies* 19(6): 546–561.
Weig, Doerte. 2015. "Sardana and castellers: Moving bodies and cultural politics in Catalonia." *Social Anthropology* 23(4): 435–449.
Wittlin, Curt. 1994. "Folklore and politics in Catalonia. Traditional popular activities as symbolic expressions of nationalism." *Catalan Review* 7(1): 103–122.
Woolard, Kathryn. 2016. *Singular and Plural: Ideologies of Linguistic Authority in 21st Century Catalonia*. Oxford: Oxford University Press.
Wright, Susan. 1998. "The politicization of 'Culture'." *Anthropology Today* 14(1): 7–15.
Xifra, Jordi and Krishnamurthy Sriramesh. 2019. "Public relations and the concept of 'nations within nations'." In *The Global Public Relations Handbook: Theory, Research, and Practice*. Edited by Krishnamurthy Sriramesh and Dejan Vercic, 246–257. London and New York: Routledge.
Yotova, Maria. 2014. "Reflecting authenticity: 'Grandmother's yoghurt' between Bulgaria and Japan." In *Food Between the Country and the City: Ethnographies of a Changing Global Foodscape*. Edited by Nuno Domingos, José Manuel Sobral and Harry G. West, 175–190. London and New York: Bloomsbury.
Žižek, Slavoj. 1993. *Tarrying with the Negative: Kant, Hegel, and the Critique of Ideology*. Durham, NC: Duke University Press.

Index

Afro-Brazilian traditions   120
Agulló, Ferran   133–134, 144
Aldavert, Adriana and Sara (Marta Sàlvia)   133
allegory   14, 19, 32–33, 151
Alta Ribagorça   118
Amades, Joan   59 n.6
America (Central, North, and South)   20, 57, 129, 135, 138
Andalusia   150
Anderson, Benedict   67, 74, 81, 128, 139
Andorra   39, 57, 118
Appadurai, Arjun   80, 82, 109, 131
Aquelarre   119–123
Arab people *see* Maghreb, Morocco
Aragon   94, 130
architecture   151
    symbolism of   20, 32–33
Aribau, Carles   132
Ariño, Antonio   111, 113
Arrieta, Iñaki   113
arrossada   147
Asia   130
Assemblea Nacional Catalana (ANC)   22, 25 *see also associacionisme*; Òmnium Cultural
Associació de Festes del Carnaval de Solsona   42, 56, 58
associacionisme (associational culture)   10, 13, 22, 39 n.9, 42, 56, 60, 69, 74, 103–104, 153
authenticity   9, 12, 17, 36, 56, 84, 106
Ayora-Diaz, Steffan   129

Bakhtin, Mikhail   63

Barça *see* FC Barcelona
Barcelona   20, 22, 25, 29, 32–33, 36, 39, 58, 63, 65 n.10, 96, 98, 127, 130, 133, 142–144, 150
    conflict between Madrid and   11
    dominance of   38, 91, 94, 98
    independence rallies in   24–27
    transformations of   11
Barthes, Roland   20, 31–32
Basque Country   8, 25–26, 31
Bawidamann, Loïc   125
Bel, Germà   6
Bell, Catherine   110
Bellas, Lluís   11, 153
Beneditti, Mario   101
Benjamin, Walter   14, 20, 26, 33
Berga   25, 37–39, 41, 49, 52–53, 56, 65 n.9, 66, 120, 122, 130, 150
Billig, Michael   128, 141, 145, 152
Bindi, Letizia   109, 113
blasphemy   68, 70–71
Blok, Anton   66–67
body, social   42, 45, 47, 62, 65, 75, 155
    mythical meaning of   29–32
    politics of   13–14, 27–29, 155
    See also performance
Boissevain, Jeremy   93, 110, 112
bons homes (*bones dones*)   78, 84, 86–87
botelló   121, 155
Bourdieu, Pierre   27, 62–63
bous (*correbous*)   12, 15, 93–107, 151, 153
    bou capllaçat, ensogat, amb corda   95, 103
    bou embolat   95
    bous a la mar   95
    bous a la plaça   95
    bous al carrer   95

bous (*correbous*) (*continued*)
  la corrida 95
  revival of 93–108
  See also bull sports
Brandes, Stanley 6, 27, 33, 45, 96, 122
Brazil 120, 129, 140
Brubaker, Rogers 68
Brulotte, Ronda 130
Brumann, Christoph 105, 106
Buck-Morss, Susan 14, 20, 33
Bulgaria 130
Bullen, Margaret 104 n.8
bull sports 12, 14–15, 93–107, 151
  decreasing popularity of 96–97, 99
  heritagization of 104–105
  as *la fiesta nacional* 96
  legislation of 97–98, 103
  revival of 151
  See also bous (*correbous*)

Caillois, Roger 28
Camus, Albert 29–30
Carbonell Camós, Eliseu 75 n.22
Cardona 37
Caribbean 129
Carlism 37 n.5
del Carme Nicolau, Maria 134
carnival 15–16, 38–76, 115, 119–121, 148–149, 152, 154
castells (*castellers*, human towers) 12, 13, 41, 115
  boom of 22
  Castellers de Barcelona 20
  colla castellera 11, 22
  colla gegantera see comparsa (*comparses*)
  Concurs championship 22, 24
  enxaneta 19, 20, 26, 29
  gentrification of 22–23
  integrative purpose of 22
  as nation building 20, 28–29
  origins of 21–22
  politics of 19–34
  as Sisyphean striving 29–30

catalanisme (Catalan national consciousness) 1–4, 8–12, 14–15, 27–29; 37 n.5 and n.6, 38–39, 45–48, 51–54, 65, 66 n.11, 71, 74, 130, 132–134
  and high culture 4 n.1
Catalanitat (Catalanness) 48, 51–54, 74–76
  hegemonic 15, 98, 100–101
  imaginary 94
  the other "Catalanness" 99–102
  radical 101–102
  and violence 15, 99, 102
Catalonia, administration 35
  autonomy of 4
  Catalan Republic 2, 25, 81
  Catalunya profunda 35–36, 48, 52, 74
  Catalunya Vella 35, 94, 151
  Generalitat of 39, 98
  historical regions of 35, 25, 140
  identities of 4, 61, 66, 113, 134, 139–140, 145
  language of 4, 36 n.3, 60, 65 n.10, 66 n.13, 132, 138, 145
  regional elections of 3
  south vs. north of 101–102
  territorial question of 4, 67
  Statute of Autonomy of 3, 5–7, 53
Cathars 13, 77–91, 151
  Cathar Trail 84, 86, 91
  as heretics 82
  and the Pyrenees 82–84
  as symbolic resource of history 81–82
Catholicism 10, 71–72, 78, 119, 152 *see also nacionalcatolicismo*
Cercamón (novel) 82–83
Cervera 119–123
centralism, Spanish 4, 7, 8, 15, 24, 47, 82
  Catalan 102
citizenship 13, 159 *see also associacionisme*

INDEX

civil society 3, 22, 24–28, 42, 56, 74, 80, 89 *see also* Assemblea Nacional Catalana; *associacionisme*, Òmnium Cultural
Civil War 5, 8, 27–28, 38, 81, 84, 95, 114, 134, 141
Clifford, James 33
Coleridge, Samuel Taylor 33
Coll de Nargó 116–117
colla / colles see comparsa (*comparses*) and *castells, colla castellera*
comarca / comarques 15, 35, 118
commensality / conviviality 14, 16, 58, 62, 68–73, 85, 130, 137, 144, 148
communitas 45–46, 60 n.6, 63
comparsa (*comparses*) 11, 16, 40, 42–43, 50, 54–74, 150
Constitutionalism, Spanish 4; *see also* centralism
Conversi, Daniele 8, 52
convivència (the art and politics of "living together") 50, 74, 152, 154
Cooper, Frederick 68
corruption 4, 45, 47, 150
Costa Solé, Roger 39 n.9
Covid–19 pandemic 4, 16–17, 33–34, 38, 53 n.16, 90–91, 98, 109–126, 148, 153, 155
  and cultural creativity 153
  and cultural resilience 153
Crameri, Kathryn 8, 24, 39, 52 n.14, 89, 131, 141,
Csordas, Thomas 62
Cuadras-Morató, Xavier 6
Cuixart, Jordi 144–145
culture, and diversity 69 n.16, 100, 138
  cultural homogeneity or homogenization 36, 67, 69 n.16, 76, 101, 128, 137–138
  cultural plurality 69 n.16, 100–101
  and identity 12–17, 47, 66, 74, 113, 123–125, 128, 138

multiculturalism 69 n.16, 73, 76, 91
  politics of 9, 12–17, 39, 42, 113, 122, 125, 141
  See also popular culture
Cunill de Bosch, Josep 132
cuynera catalana (Catalan cuisine) 127–146, 149, 152, 154
Czech Republic 73 n.21, 117 n.6

Dalmau, Antoni 134
Davies, Karen 111, 125
decentralization 6–7
Delanty, Gerard 68
Delgado, Manuel 15, 27, 36 n.4, 66 n.13, 99, 111, 113, 119–122, 124, 151, 153
democracy 9, 19
  of the Cathars 78, 86
  "democratic deficit" 9
Desfor Edles, Laura 7
DeSoucey, Michaela 70 n.17, 129
devil-like figures 28, 40, 94, 119–120
diables 40, 94 *see also* devil-like figures
Diada (Catalan National Day) 3, 12, 13, 22, 24–27, 41, 141
Di Giovine, Michael 130
digitalization / digitization (of culture) 16, 26, 49, 110–112, 115–116, 125
Domene, José 122
Domènech, Ignasi 133
donkey, importance and symbolism of 40, 47, 50, 151
Dostoevsky, Fyodor 101
Douglas, Mary 61
Dowling, Andrew 3, 4, 5, 6, 7, 8, 10, 11, 36, 37 n.6, 38, 45 n.4, 50, 52 n.14, 76 n.24, 80
drunkenness *see* intoxication; excess
Durkheim, Émile 75

Ebro region 12, 15, 93, 94, 96, 101–102, 151

economy   5–6, 7, 111, 150
  crisis of the   5–6, 23, 80
  local   36 n.2, 41
Elias, Norbert   27
Erickson, Brad   13, 27, 151
escudella   148
España de las Autonomías   5
Esquerra Republicana de Catalunya (Republican Left of Catalonia)   47, 98
essentialism   31–32, 67 n.14, 75, 94, 98
estelada (Catalan independentist flag)   11–12, 26, 49, 51, 60, 111, 141–143, 152
Estrada Bonell, Ferran   75 n.22
ethnicity   9
Europe, history of   41, 47, 70–71, 137, 150
European Union   38, 138, 140
excess   40, 41 n.11, 70–72, 99, 111–122, 124 *see also* intoxication
excursionisme (hiking)   60, 140, 149

Fabre, Daniel   111
Fajans, Jane   129, 140, 145
family, the centrality and importance of   59–60, 68, 74–75, 115
FC Barcelona ("Barça")   26, 28–29, 81, 137
federalism   6–7
fet diferencial   65–66, 148 *see also* identity, nationalism, nationhood
Ferguson, Priscilla   129, 131
Fernandez, James   150
fer pinya (make a base), the symbolic meanings of   13, 19, 21, 26, 28–29, 56 *see also castells* (*castellers*, human towers)
feminism   10–13, 78, 104 n.8, 120
festes (festivals)   10–11, 16, 36–76, 77–91, 109–126, 135, 138–140
  with animals   97, 104–105
  during Covid-19 pandemic *see* Covid-19 pandemic
  and excess *see* excess
  festes majors   38, 71
  Festival Càtar del Pirineu Català   83
  fiesta nacional   14–15, 71, 117
  Fiesta de Interés Nacional   39, 117–118
  with fire   40–41, 114, 147; 117–119, 119–121, 123
  heritagization of   75 n.22, 103–104, 108–113, 115–120
  Josa de Cadí   13, 77–91, 150
  lasciviousness in   70, 72 *see also* excess
  Raiers   116–117, 122
  San Félix   123
  Sant Jordi   141–142
  of transition   73, 74 n.21
Fira del Gran Boc   121
Folch Monclús, Rafel   39 n.9
folklore *see* popular culture
Fournier, Laurent Sébastien   110
Fraga, Manuel   10
France   25, 78, 82–85, 129, 131
Franco dictatorship   1, 3, 6, 10, 13, 27–28, 38–39, 71, 74, 94, 119, 134, 152, 153 *see also* Transition
French Revolution   2
Frigolé, Joan   79, 80, 84, 106, 113,

Gabriel, Anna   89
García Canclini, Néstor   111
Garth, Hannah   129
gastronomy *see* identity, and food; gastronationalism; *cuynera catalana* (Catalan cuisine)
Gaudí, Anthony   32
Geertz, Clifford   154
gegants (giants)   73, 74 n.21, 40–44, 49, 57, 71–73, 94, 115
Girona   49, 94, 96
globalization   11, 26, 29, 33–34, 91, 105, 110, 113, 124
González, Antoni   99
González Fernández   96

Gonzalez, Roberto 111
gralla 94
Grisostolo, Francesco 96
Grosby, Steven 66 n.13
groupness *see* togetherness
Guibernau, Montserrat 9, 128
Guil, Mireia 16, 118, 153
Guiu, Claire 75 n.22, 113
Gutiérrez, Ramón 124
Guttman, Allen 24

habitus 27, 62
Hargreaves, John 131, 137
Harris, Max 119
Herb, Henrik 61
Herder, Johann Gottfried von 2 *see also* Romanticism
heritage (cultural), heritagization 2, 9, 17, 39 n.9, 75 n.22, 90, 110, 113, 115–122, 130
  exclusion from 104–106
  and identity 15, 75 n.22, 130
  ideological intentions of 104–106, 122
  legislation of 102–106
  making of 9, 23–24, 39, 75 n.22, 80
  as popular resistance 102–106
  regimes 10, 24
  top-down control of 104–107, 140, 154
  See also UNESCO
Herzfeld, Michael 28, 30, 64, 82
hierarchy / hierarchies 41 n.11, 57, 59, 63, 71
history 13, 62, 77–91, 128, 131–133, 144
  and construction of national identity 67 n.14, 74, 81, 113, 128, 131–133, 144–145
  and "invented past" 84, 138
  romanticizing 82–83, 138
  symbolic resources of 81, 131
  See also Cathars

Hlinsko v Čechách 73 n.21
hymns and anthems 36 n.2, 40, 42–46
Hodges, Matt 85,
Hutchinson, John 67 n.14, 76 n.24

Ichijo, Atsuko 129–130, 140
iconicity 13, 20, 26, 28, 30, 50, 57, 94, 133, 151
identity
  commodification of 90
  contestations of 16
  in Ebro region 98
  and food 14, 70, 127–145
  historical construction of 39, 66, 67 n.14, 75, 78–79, 113, 118, 140
  and history 62, 82–84, 127–146
  and language 3, 60, 63–68, 100, 132, 134, 138, 145
  national 2–3, 6, 12, 39, 51–54, 64–68, 70, 74, 82–84, 100
  nested 61, 74
  politics of 46–54, 77–91, 123–125, 141
Imber-Black, Evan 115–116, 124
inclusion / inclusiveness 9, 12, 16, 22–23, 28–29, 57–58, 60, 63–68, 68–76, 111, 138, 150
independentisme (pro-independence politics) 1, 3, 4 n.1, 6, 11–12, 13, 24–27, 39, 45 n.12, 46–47, 49, 77–78, 79–81, 127–128, 141–144, 152
  and the economic crisis 4 n.1, 6
  imaginaries of 80–81
  reasons for 4–9, 80
India 131
integration *see* inclusion / inclusiveness
intoxication 40, 60, 62–64, 70–73, 121, 150
Iran 131
Isil 118
Islam 69–70, 72–73
Isnart, Cyril 51, 110

Johannes, Venetia 14, 41, 51, 65, 70, 143, 149, 152
Jordà, Sebastià 118

Kaplan, David 61
Kammerer, Nina 10, 11, 39, 40–42, 49, 52–53, 59 n.5, 60, 74, 79, 113
Keating, Michael 128
Keown, Dominic 8–10, 38, 52 n.14, 131
Khalvashi, Tamta 79, 90,
King, Michelle 130
Kundera, Milan 30

language, and identity 3, 4, 8–10, 60, 64–68, 132, 134, 137, 145
  linguistic normalization 9
  maintenance 9, 14, 36 n.3, 134
  policy of transition 73, 74 n.21
  39, 100–101, 134
Lanternari, Vittorio 41
La Pobla de Segur 116–117
Leitkultur 69 n.16, 72
Leoussi, Athena 66 n.13
Les 118
Lithuania 130
llaçets grogs (yellow ribbons) 73, 74 n.21
26, 49–51, 77, 127, 143–144, 152
Lladonosa i Giró, Josep 134
Lleida 25, 49
Lliga Catalana 133
Llobera, Josep 8–10, 36, 38, 52 n.14, 60, 66 n.11, 76 n.24, 128, 131, 134, 138
locality, social construction of 43, 52–54, 63, 67, 75, 113, 118–119, 140, 145
Long, Lucy 129–130
Luis, José 96

MacClancy, Jeremy 10, 14, 85, 129
Madrid 5, 11, 47, 132
Majumdar, Margaret 8

Maghreb 58, 68
Malinowski, Bronisław 41
Manning, Erin 27
Mansilla, José 109, 112
Maquieira D'Angelo, Virginia 104 n.8
Marlovits, John 111
Mármol, Camila, del 11, 13, 52, 75 n.22
Martí i Pérez, Josep 33
Martín López, Sarai 15, 151, 153
Martínez Algueró, Romina 15, 151, 153
Marx, Karl 32
Masopust 73 n.21
Mauss, Marcel 41
medievalism 52, 82–83, 132, 150
Mediterranean 16, 94, 116, 133, 151
Meskell, Lynn 105
Mexico 105, 129
Middle Ages 14, 37, 40, 52, 77–78, 82, 87
  cooking in the 131–132, 135
Mieres 130
migration 47, 57–58, 66 n.11, 69–73
modernisation 4, 99, 149
Monarchism 4, 8
Morocco, 58, 69, 72–73
Mueller, Sean 7
museums / musealization 24, 75 n.22, 109 n.1, 112–115 *see also* heritage
Muslims *see* Islam
myth and myth-making 14, 29–33, 67, 82–83
  of history 8, 78, 131

narcissism of minor differences 66–68
nationalism 1–2, 16, 45, 47, 64, 66 n.11, 66 n.12, 65–76, 128–129, 133, 140-144, 148–149
  "affective" 90, 75, 128
  banal (or "everyday") 128, 152
  Basque 9, 31

INDEX

bottom-up   24–27, 64–65, 67, 76, 89
Catalan *see catalanisme*
civic   9, 65–76, 99
ethnicist   8–9
and ethnosymbolism   66 n.12, 68 n.15, 76 n.24 *see also* Grosby, Steven; Hutchinson, John; Leoussi, Athena; and Smith, Anthony
"gastronationalism" *see* identity, and food; and DeSoucey, Michaela; and Johannes, Venetia
imagined communities   67 n.14, 128, 139 *see also* Anderson, Benedict
and liberation/emancipation movements   2, 8
nacionalcatolicismo   10, 38, 71
narratives of   149, 154
nation building   51–54, 66 n.11, 65–76, 79–81
national imaginaries   52, 67, 79–80, 132
social class of   27, 31, 61, 85, 99
Spanish   24, 66, 141
and state-region conflict   11
symbolism of   24–27, 46, 135
top-down   4, 67, 89, 140
See also Catalanisme; Constitutionalism; *independentisme*; Monarchism
nationality   5–6, 8, 16, 58, 74
nationhood   5–6, 8, 16, 74, 65–66, 132, 148, 154 *see also* nationalism and its sub-entries; nationality
Nietzsche, Friedrich   30
Noguera Pallaresa   116
Nola, Robert, de   131
Noyes, Dorothy   10–11, 22, 28, 31, 37–38, 40–42, 45, 52, 56, 60 n.7, 61, 63–64, 66–68, 72–73, 75 n.22, 113, 122, 130, 149–155

Occitanism   82–83
Olesa   114
Olympic Games   11, 154
Òmnium Cultural   19, 22, 143–144 *see also* Assemblea Nacional Catalana (ANC); *associacionisme*
Orozco, Aura Patricia   122
othering   73, 84

pacto fiscal (economic agreement)   5
pactisme   7, 41, 69, 74
Països Catalans   25, 66 n.13, 99, 144
País Valencià   101
Pallars Sobirà   118
Palmer, Catherine   128
Parellada, Ada   127
parochialism   42
Patum   28, 38–39, 41, 45, 49, 51, 56, 75 n.22, 104, 120, 122, 152, 154
performance   13–14, 42, 56–57, 67–68, 109, 113, 128, 138
of politics   85–86, 124–125
the politics of   19–34, 90
Pinós   35–34
plaça   10, 21, 34, 77 *see also* public sociality
Plan Hidrológico Nacional (National Hydrological Plan)   98–99 *see also* Ebro region
political rallies   19–21, 78
"Catalans Want to Vote" rally   19–20
politics, and the body   27–29, 129
independentist   3–4, 6
of the past   77–91
political prisoners   49, 52, 77–91
spectacularization of   24–27, 50
of streets   10, 93
See also political rallies
popular culture   2–3, 9–12, 33–34, 40–54, 67, 113, 132, 147
commercialization of   24, 154, 155
and community conflict   49–50, 66–76, 154

popular culture (*continued*)
  as embodied practice   61, 148
  under Franco   37–39, 60, 71, 94, 113, 134
  gentrification of   13
  history of   79–80
  homogenization of   152
  inclusion and exclusion in   66–76, 150
  institutionalization of   103, 113, 148
  local governance of   42, 154
  nationalization of   149, 99
  political instrumentalization of   46–51, 122, 125, 149, 155
  politics of   47–48, 51–54, 113, 125, 141
  revival of   51–52, 93–94, 113
  and solidarity   153
  vitality of   147, 149, 151, 153
popular religion / devotion   38, 71–72, 134, 138
pork   70, 72, 150
Portugal   105, 130–131
Prats, Llorenç   107
presos polítics (political prisoners)   43–44, 49, 51, 78, 89, 127, 143–144, 150, 152 *see also llaçets grogs* (yellow ribbons)
Primo de Rivera's dictatorship   141
procés (independence process) 13, 14, 49, 79, 81, 90
province / provincial   37–38
public sociality   16, 33–34, 93
Puigdemont, Carles   3, 8, 29
Pujol, Jordi   3, 65
Pyrenees   12–13, 52, 77–91, 116–119, 150
  and national narratives   52, 83

Racionero, Lluís   82–83
Rajoy, Mariano   74, 81 n.8
Ranta, Ronald   129, 140
rauxa (madness)   31, 151 *see also seny*

referendum (on the independence of Catalonia)   3, 16, 19, 25–26, 28, 37, 49, 50, 74, 81, 86, 96, 141, 143, 150, 152, 154
religion   10, 82, 119–121, 138–139 *see also* Catholicism; Islam; popular religion
Renaixença   14, 87, 94, 101, 132, 149
Resina, Joan   6
respecte (respect)   45, 73
Reus   123, 151
Riart, Oriol   118
Riera, Anna   130–131
Ripoll   116
rite of passage   59, 64
ritual / rituality   2, 16–17, 20, 40–55, 59, 62, 73–76, 109–112, 115, 117–118
  continuity   13, 40, 70–73, 112, 115, 124
  refusal of   63, 70, 73, 76, 150
  ritualesque / ritualoid   40, 42, 46
rivalry
  between *comparses*   63
  between localities   41
  See also parochialism
Robertson, Alexander   70, 130
Rodon, Toni   6
Roigé, Xavier   11, 16, 52 n.16, 75 n.22, 79, 110, 113, 153
Romanticism   2
Rubert de Ventós, Xavier   2
rurality   12, 14, 36, 38, 43, 60, 76, 91, 137

Sahlins, Marshall   63, 82
Santino, Jack   46
sardana (dance)   27, 29, 33
seny (common sense, good sense, measure)   15, 27, 30–32, 45, 73, 89, 99, 128, 137, 139, 141, 149, 151
  see also Barthes, Roland
senyera (Catalan national flag)   11–12, 49, 51, 141–143

Sitges 150
sleep deprivation / fatigue *see* excess
Smith, Anthony 1, 8, 32, 68 n.15, 76 n.24
Spain, the Constitutional Court of 3, 5, 7, 53, 78
   Constitution of 6–8, 49, 141
   National Day of 141
   War of Succession 37 n.5, 132
social distancing 16, 109–113, 115
solidarity 5–7, 20, 22, 25, 77, 84, 110, 114–115, 152
   principle of the Spanish Constitution 6–7
Solsona 12, 35–76
Solsonès 15, 35–38
Song, Rosi 130–131
sovereignty 4, 6–7, 93
   and popular culture 10, 93
sport 21–22, 81
   soccer / football 27–28
   See also FC Barcelona; Olympic Games
Stowkowski, Wiktor 105
Strubell, Miquel 66 n.13
Suari, Carlos 124
Subirats, Ventura 82
symbolism 3, 46, 50, 67–68, 75, 94, 124, 130, 135, 143
   of architecture 20
   of belonging 56, 60, 67
   of festival 45, 48, 70, 87
   of food 14, 36, 70, 127, 130
   of national identity 16, 20, 50, 66–68, 94, 100, 107, 127–128, 134
   of past 13, 81, 83, 96
   political 24–26, 28, 38, 43, 46, 49–50, 51, 67–68, 77, 78, 86
   symbolic capital 56, 59, 73, 75, 118–119
   symbolic centrality 36, 41, 46–54, 74–75, 102, 130
   symbolic geography 14, 35–37, 52, 101, 151

symbolic grievances of Catalanisme 7, 143
"symbolic reevaluation" 85
syncretism 72

Tarragona 22, 25, 94, 100, 150–151
Testa, Alessandro 37 n.7, 41 n.11, 48, 70–72, 75 n.22, 76, 110, 120–125, 149–150, 152, 154
Tibi, Bassam 69 n.16
togetherness 13, 19, 30, 42, 54–56, 59–60, 68–69, 73–75, 106, 119–120, 128
Torra, Quim 78
tourism 39, 77–91, 110–111, 118, 150
   and festivals 41, 58, 63, 75 n.22, 84, 116–118
tradition 2, 42, 73, 97, 110–111, 113–115, 124–125
   invented / invention of 42, 73, 90, 116, 147, 149, 155
   legislation of 102
   reconfiguration of 90, 110, 124
   resilience of 109–126, 148
   traditionality / traditional knowledge 14, 36, 42, 73, 113–115, 148
transgression *see* excess
Transition (from the Franco dictatorship to democracy) 1, 6, 15–16, 22, 36 n.3, 47, 50, 52 n.14, 71, 73 n.21, 74, 80, 89, 93, 116
   post–, 9–12, 13, 47, 73 n.21, 74, 134, 150, 152, 154
Turner, Victor 45, 63
Turull, Jordi 77–79, 85, 87, 89, 90

UNESCO 11, 24, 75 n.22, 97, 104–105, 111–113, 117–118, 122, 132, 154 *see also* heritage
utopia 63, 67, 80

Vaczi, Mariann 13, 15–16, 45, 56, 150–151, 153

Val d'Aran   118–119
Val de Boí   114, 119
Valls   115
Vic   115, 130–131, 141
Vilafranca del Penedès   123
Vilanova del Camí   115
Vilanova i la Geltrú   23, 151
Vilaseca, Noemí   38, 46, 59 n.6
Vovelle, Michel   93

witches   119–120
Wittlin, Curt   51

women, in popular culture   13, 22–23, 137
Woolard, Kathryn   9
workers' movement   153
Wright, Susan   105

youth   10, 40, 58, 69, 73, 83, 119, 121, 124, 151

Žižek, Slavoj   32

Printed in the USA
CPSIA information can be obtained
at www.ICGtesting.com
LVHW011836041124
795688LV00004B/560